Iron Man
McGinnity

Iron Man McGinnity

A Baseball Biography

DON DOXSIE

McFarland & Company, Inc., Publishers
Jefferson, North Carolina, and London

LIBRARY OF CONGRESS CATALOGUING-IN-PUBLICATION DATA

Doxsie, Don.
　　Iron Man McGinnity : a baseball biography / Don Doxsie.
　　　　p.　　cm.
　　Includes bibliographical references and index.

　　ISBN 978-0-7864-4203-4
　　softcover : 50# alkaline paper ∞

　　1. McGinnity, Joe, 1871–1929.　2. Baseball players—
United States—Biograpy.　I. Title.
GV865.S87D69　　2009
796.357092—dc22　　　　　　　　　　　　　　　　2009012373
[B]

British Library cataloguing data are available

©2009 Don Doxsie. All rights reserved

*No part of this book may be reproduced or transmitted in any form
or by any means, electronic or mechanical, including photocopying
or recording, or by any information storage and retrieval system,
without permission in writing from the publisher.*

Cover photograph: Joe McGinnity in 1904 (National Baseball Hall
of Fame Library, Cooperstown, New York)

Manufactured in the United States of America

McFarland & Company, Inc., Publishers
　Box 611, Jefferson, North Carolina 28640
　　www.mcfarlandpub.com

*In memory of
William Thomas Markward (1893–1973).*

*He probably saw Joe McGinnity pitch ...
and he imbued his grandson with a passion
for baseball the way it was meant to be played.*

Acknowledgments

In order to write a book about someone whose greatest heroics were performed more than a century earlier and who died three-quarters of a century earlier, an author requires an immense amount of help.

I will forever be indebted to Charles W. Brown for his valuable insights and extensive research, and for his frequent e-mails, which always seemed to prod and push this project toward its completion. Frank Williamson of Wilburton, Oklahoma, deserves considerable credit for his drive to learn more about Joe McGinnity and his passion for collecting McGinnity artifacts.

Also deserving of recognition are Julia Hancock of the Krebs (Oklahoma) Heritage Museum; Clyde Wooldridge of McAlester, Oklahoma; Carol J. Greene of the Decatur Staley Club; Don Wentler of Rock Island, Illinois; Marc H. Blau of the Shannaman Sports Museum in Tacoma, Washington; Gabriel Schechter, Jon Blomquist and John Horne of the Baseball Hall of Fame in Cooperstown, New York; Ed Rothberg of Boynton Beach, Florida; Jim Eakland of Great Falls, Montana; employees of the Butte-Silver Bow Archives; and the wonderful ladies at the Pittsburg County (Oklahoma) Historical Society. Father Joseph McGinnity of Chicago, who endeavored for years to prove that he was a descendant of his namesake, contributed greatly to my earliest research. Sadly, he passed away in 2008, before the book was published.

Employees of public libraries in Kansas City, Missouri; St. Louis, Missouri; McAlester, Oklahoma; Van Buren, Arkansas; Springfield, Illinois; Decatur, Illinois; Dubuque, Iowa; Rockford, Illinois; and Davenport, Iowa, were of considerable assistance, as were people at the Abraham Lincoln Presidential Library in Springfield and the Founders Library at Northern Illinois University.

Obviously, too, this book could not have come to fruition without Gale, Ryne and Emily Doxsie, who dared to believe that Dad could actually do this. They were extremely understanding when he dashed off to spend a day in Decatur or Springfield, and when he spent so many evenings hunched over the computer in the den. Their love and support made this possible.

Table of Contents

Acknowledgments vii
Preface 1
Prologue 3

1. A Coal Miner's Son 5
2. Decatur 9
3. Indian Territory 13
4. A New Profession 18
5. Kansas City 25
6. The Nickel Rocket 32
7. Robbie and Mac 42
8. Brooklyn 49
9. A Whole New League 57
10. Back to the NL 63
11. Arm of Iron 69
12. Total Domination 74
13. A World Series 82
14. Comeuppance 91
15. Signs of Decline 95
16. One Final, Wild Season 101
17. Newark 111
18. Tacoma 120
19. Montana 133
20. Northwest Encore 147
21. Working for Staley 151
22. Back to the Minors 161

23. A New Challenge.............................. 166
24. The Final Years 176
25. A Faded Legend............................... 185

Appendix A. Statistics 189
Appendix B. Records Held 190
Chapter Notes....................................... 191
Bibliography.. 203
Index 207

Preface

This project began simply enough as a gesture to recognize the great sports legacy of a two-state region. It led to a two-decade obsession and a profile of a forgotten hero.

As sports editor of the *Quad-City Times* in Davenport, Iowa, in 1987, I proposed to my superiors that we initiate a Quad-City Sports Hall of Fame to honor those who had contributed greatly to the sports scene along the Iowa-Illinois border. The Hall of Fame soon became a reality and in the second year of its existence, one of the inductees was an old pitcher named Joe McGinnity. As the baseball historian on staff, it was left to me to research and profile a man that few modern-day sportswriters knew much about.

The more I learned, the more fascinated I became. Part of the fascination was that so little had been written about a man who averaged 24.6 wins per season in a fairly brief but luminous major league career. McGinnity had very few living descendants and during his life he kept his private affairs carefully under wraps. He was suspicious and distrustful of most newspapermen and reluctant to cooperate with their efforts to analyze or canonize.

Long after my McGinnity profile appeared in print, I continued to do sporadic research on the man, generally just tossing what I found into a file cabinet. On the 100th anniversary of his amazing three doubleheader sweeps in August 1903, I wrote a retrospective that caught the eye of a Chicagoan named Charles Brown.

Brown was a distant descendant of McGinnity's and he had done extensive research of his family tree. He contacted me and upon learning that I had occasionally contemplated writing a book about McGinnity, he invited me to ceremonies in McAlester, Oklahoma, in May of 2006, at which Brown and other relatives planned to dedicate a new headstone at McGinnity's gravesite.

The fuse was lit. Suddenly, all those years of casual research had a purpose. I went to Oklahoma, did some research in Kansas City on the way, did a little more in Arkansas and Springfield, Illinois, on the way home, and began pulling all my information together, supplementing it with Charles Brown's exhaustive family data.

Over the next several months, there were frequent trips to libraries throughout Iowa and Illinois to fill in the gaps. I skimmed through old newspapers on microfilm until my eyes hurt. Within six months, I had the basic nucleus of a book that was further tweaked and expanded in the months that followed.

The fascination continues. McGinnity's story is unique. Despite not playing professional baseball for four years while he was in his 20s and not making it to the major leagues until he was 28, he ended up winning more games in the minor and major leagues combined than any pitcher except Cy Young. He was unbelievably durable and cagey, and he pitched until the age of 54. And yet, until now, he was one of the members of the Baseball Hall of Fame who never had been profiled in a full-length book.

I suspect he would acknowledge the irony in the fact that in spite of his disdain and distrust of the media, his story finally is being told by a lifelong newspaperman.

Prologue

We can only imagine that as he warmed up for a Mississippi Valley League game on May 11, 1925, Ottumwa pitcher John Welch might have glanced over across the way at the hurler who was loosening his arm for Dubuque.

Welch was a gifted 18-year-old kid almost straight off the sandlots, but this other guy looked old enough to be his grandfather. He was almost completely gray, had tanned features creased by decades of hard work, and he was using some sort of crazy, underarm, submarine motion in which his knuckles nearly grazed the dirt before he released the ball. His pitches weren't moving fast enough to outrun a Model T.

Welch might have wondered if this was some sort of joke. Or maybe there was an old-timers game preceding the regular game that he hadn't heard about. This couldn't really be his pitching opponent, could it?

Little more than an hour or so later, after "Iron Man" Joe McGinnity had scattered 13 hits and beaten him, 7–3, Welch probably was convinced and perhaps a little embarrassed. McGinnity was, in fact, old enough to be his grandfather. He was 54.

The old man's conquest of a pitcher a third his age grabbed a few national headlines and was the final major achievement in a thoroughly unique and amazing career that stretched from the Gay '90s to the eve of the Great Depression.

McGinnity spent 10 years in the major leagues and averaged more wins per season than any pitcher in history, emerging victorious 246 times. (He won 218 of those before John Welch was born.) The only other pitchers to average more than 20 wins per season were Cy Young and Christy Mathewson. McGinnity's total of 481 victories in the minor and major leagues combined is second only to Young's 511.

McGinnity set modern-day National League records for games started (48) and innings pitched (434) in 1903. In August of that year, he worked more than 100 innings, pitching and winning both ends of a doubleheader three times during the month.

Hall of Fame manager Hughie Jennings once said he was the best fielding pitcher he ever saw.[1] John McGraw, who was McGinnity's manager in all but one of his major league seasons, called him "the hardest working pitcher I ever had on my ballclub."[2] The legendary Connie Mack described him as "a magician."[3]

"It was difficult for a batter to get his measure," Mack wrote in his autobiography. "Sometimes his fingers would almost scrape the ground as he hurled the ball. He knew all the tricks for putting a batter on the spot."[4]

Before he bounced around the country in a playing career that spanned more than three decades, McGinnity had bounced his way around the middle of the country as an itinerant coal miner. He also ran a saloon, worked in an iron foundry (the source of the nickname), worked for a corn starch company, ran a company that made foundation blocks, worked in an orthodontist's office, helped coach the pitchers at two different colleges, worked as a coach and scout in the major leagues, and owned and managed several minor league teams.

He also pitched and won games far into his 50s, not because he couldn't do other things but because that is what he loved to do most.

McGinnity was a mass of contradictions. He was one of the largest men in the major leagues at the dawn of the 20th century—5-foot-11 and 206 pounds—but he was hardly a power pitcher. In his prime years, he relied almost exclusively on a baffling, rising curve ball that was so dear to him that he gave it a name.

He was a jovial, easy-going man off the field who had a raging Irish temper that occasionally got him into trouble on it.

He ran saloons in the 1890s but in a robust, rollicking age in which ballplayers often were a tavern's best customers, he frequently just munched on an apple while his teammates guzzled down beer.[5]

As a child growing up in the coalfields of Illinois, he received almost no formal schooling, but he was one of the most cerebral players of his time, charting and chronicling the strengths and weaknesses of opposing batters long before it became the norm.[6]

Although he was inducted into the Baseball Hall of Fame in 1946, he is not a modern-day icon, someone who is frequently mentioned as one of the all-time greats, someone deemed to be worthy of being remembered and revered by ensuing generations of fans.

But that's exactly what he was.

1. A Coal Miner's Son

The legend of Joe McGinnity is fraught with misconceptions and misrepresentations. Many baseball historians attributed his nickname to his durability on the mound when it actually originated from his work in his father-in-law's iron foundry. Others have the iron foundry part right, but say he worked there in his youth when the business wasn't even started until McGinnity was 26 years old. Several accounts of his life don't even have the iron foundry located in the correct state.

Probably the most widely disbursed untruth about McGinnity surrounds his birth. For a century or more, nearly every book and every record listed him as being born in Rock Island, Illinois, on March 19, 1871. In truth, his birth took place on March 20, 1871, and it happened in a farmhouse in Cornwall Township, Henry County, Illinois, just south of the modern-day town of Atkinson.[1]

Peter and Hannah McGinnity were married in Rock Island, a bustling Mississippi River metropolis that was enjoying a post–Civil War boom, but their third child was born 30 miles to the east in a thriving coal-mining community.

Peter McGinnity was born in Dublin, Ireland, in 1823 and lived the first 39 years of his life in that country. During the American Civil War, he emigrated to the United States and drifted westward. In 1862, he found work in the coal mines of western Illinois and found lodging as a boarder with the family of John and Rebecca Denning. Peter was a hard worker, both in the mines and on the farm that the Dennings maintained, and he became an accepted member of the family.[2]

The Dennings were growing a pretty sizeable brood of their own. John, a Methodist minister in addition to working the mines and the farm, had come to the U.S. from Scotland in 1850. He and his first wife, Jane, temporarily moved the family from Scotland to Liverpool, England, and he came across the ocean to get established. In August of 1852, he brought the rest of the family across to join him, including an 8-year-old daughter named Hannah. (Their last name had been Dinning back in Scotland, but a clerk wrote it incorrectly on their naturalization papers and the name was Denning from then on.)[3]

By 1856, John and Jane Denning had settled with five young children in Clay County, Indiana, just east of Terre Haute. Shortly thereafter, though, Jane and a newborn son died of the milk fever, leaving John to care for the four remaining children. A young lady named Rebecca Ann Little was enlisted to help him and their relationship soon grew into something more. John took Rebecca for his second wife, the couple continued to add to the size of the family and they continued to move westward, settling in Henry County, Illinois, in 1862. They hadn't been there very long when they befriended Peter McGinnity.[4]

John Denning had ambitions of moving even further west. He heard about the rich land of the Oregon territory and in the spring of 1864, he and Rebecca were on the move again, leaving their Henry County homestead in the hands of 41-year-old Peter McGinnity and their 20-year-old daughter, Hannah.

What they may not have realized was that Hannah was falling in love with their Irish boarder. As John and Rebecca and the rest of the family headed west, the relationship between Peter McGinnity and Hannah blossomed and in the spring of 1865, Hannah became pregnant.[5] She and Peter married in August 1865, just three months before the birth of a son, William Patrick McGinnity.

Meanwhile, John and Rebecca were on their way back to Illinois. They had gotten as far as Virginia City, Montana, where a gold rush was in progress. Along the way, a younger daughter, Elizabeth, had married an Italian immigrant named Bruno Ferrero, who changed his name to Brown Ferrell. Rebecca also had given birth to one child on the trip west, then lost another baby in Montana in the summer of 1865. At her urging, the family returned to Illinois, leaving Elizabeth and Brown Ferrell behind.

John Denning didn't care that his oldest daughter had gotten married while he was gone. He was less happy that she had given birth on November 26 to a child that was clearly conceived out of wedlock.

John and Rebecca continued to move around. They helped open new mines in Lafayette County, Missouri, and eventually moved to Streator, Illinois, in 1870. There they established a coal mine of their own—John Denning Coal Co.—and also helped found the Primitive Methodist Church.[6]

Peter McGinnity also opened a little coal mine of his own in Henry County, just down the road from the Spring Creek mine in which he had worked.[7] According to a published history of the county, he had persistent problems with the mine flooding with water until he realized that a woodchuck was playing havoc with his drainage system. He trapped the woodchuck and never had a problem again.[8]

He and Hannah McGinnity continued to add to their family. A son, Peter, arrived in the fall of 1869 and in March 1871, Joseph Jerome McGinnity came into the world. Three more children were born in Henry County before the couple began to get the urge to relocate.

Coal mining was a highly transient business in those days. Miners would live in one area only as long as the coal held out. When they'd quarried all the coal out of the ground in one area, it was time to move on to another location.

In the spring of 1878, Peter and Hannah were on the move to Gallatin County in southeastern Illinois, where a large community of Irish immigrants had unearthed some rich coalfields. They settled in a small, principally Irish community called Equality Point, near the mining village of Shawneetown. There, Hannah gave birth to one more child, a daughter named Hannah, on July 12, 1879.[9]

The joy of the new arrival was very short-lived.

Two days later, Peter was performing his usual duties as a muleskinner in the mines. His job was to drive a mule-drawn wagon through the mines, stopping under coal chutes. Miners would release the coal they had taken from the earth and it came flooding down into the bed of the wagon. Peter would then transport it to a station where it would be shipped to wherever it was needed. This time he missed his mark. He did not have the wagon in the proper place and when the coal was released, it fell on top of him and crushed the life out of his body.[10]

Hannah suddenly was a widow with seven children under the age of 14, the youngest one only two days old. She appealed to her father for help. Rev. John Denning became the official guardian of the children, but he was soon on his way back to Streator, leaving Hannah to survive in any way she could. The three oldest sons—William (age 13), Peter (9) and Joseph (8)—went to work in the mines in place of their father.[11] They learned the job of muleskinner and between them made enough money to keep the family fed.

Before long, the family was on the move again. In the summer of 1880, Hannah and her seven children moved to Springfield, Illinois, where William, Peter and Joseph went to work for the Springfield Coal Company's No. 2 mine. They stayed there less than six months, then moved 35 miles east to Decatur, Illinois.

In Decatur, the McGinnitys initially took up residence in the rugged Fourth Ward, along south Broadway Street (now known as Martin Luther King Drive). Hannah managed to scrape together money cleaning homes for some of the more affluent citizens of the city and her three oldest boys again found work in a mine operated by the Decatur Coal Company at East

Main and Broadway, in the southern part of what is now the city's downtown.[12]

In 1884, the family was listed as living at 857 N. Calhoun in Decatur[13] but by 1889, Hannah had moved them into a home at 1612 E. El Dorado, east of downtown. It was a neighborhood that one of her sons clearly loved. Over the course of his life, Joe McGinnity lived in five different homes in Decatur and all of them were within a block of one another in that same neighborhood.

Unlike Henry and Gallatin Counties, this was more of an urban setting. Decatur was a city of 30,000 people and as they progressed into and through their teenage years, the McGinnity brothers found themselves among a rougher, more streetwise crowd during the hours when they were not in the mine. Many of their buddies would spend their Sunday afternoons (sometimes their only day off) drinking and playing cards under the shade of a huge tree in a vacant lot east of an area known as Cassell's Hill.[14]

But it wasn't long before the third McGinnity son, Joe, found something better to do with his leisure time. In the post–Civil War era, young men all over the country were discovering a game that they played on prairies and vacant lots with a hard, woven ball and a wooden club. Joe McGinnity took to it immediately. He loved the action and the strategy and the competition. He loved the fact that the game rewarded those who grabbed every little edge they could find and those who played it with reckless abandon. He fell head over heels in love with baseball.

2. Decatur

In an interview with *Sporting Life* many years later, Joe McGinnity said his organized baseball career actually began in 1887 when he played for a Decatur semi-pro team in a game to benefit the people who lost their homes in the famous Johnstown, Pennsylvania, flood. "I was so young I had to have a written note from my mother granting permission," he said.[1]

It was a good yarn, but clearly untrue. The Johnstown flood, one of the great catastrophes of the late 19th century, took the lives of 2,209 people but it didn't occur until May 31, 1889.[2] There were several benefit games played in and around Decatur in the weeks that followed but by then, McGinnity was an established 18-year-old pitcher for the local semi-pro club. He had been a prominent player on the local baseball scene for a year or more by then.

Baseball had begun to grow in popularity in Decatur in 1885 when a couple of the town's young players took it upon themselves to build a small ballpark out on the west side of town, not far from where Millikin University now stands. The Decatur Baseball Association was founded in 1886 with its first chairman being O.B. Gorin, who also happened to be the secretary/treasurer of the Decatur Coal Company.[3] Perhaps Gorin was hoping to give his young miners something healthy to do in their leisure hours instead of going over to Cassell's Hill and drinking themselves senseless. If that was his intent, it hit home with at least one employee.

McGinnity took the game more seriously than almost anyone else in town, developing an eye for tactics and a deep-rooted love for competition. When his pals gathered to drink and carouse near Cassell's Hill, he often went to a barn across the alley and practiced throwing a ball at a knothole. Every now and then, a catcher named Cronin would join him, but when Cronin wasn't around, that knothole was the target.

As *Decatur Herald* sportswriter Earl Obenshain noted in 1929, some of Joe McGinnity's peers regarded him as a "nut."[4] But he was building up strength in that right arm, honing his control and devising new ways of making the ball move, developing skills that would alter his life and blaze a pathway out of the mines.

In those earliest days he played for the East Enders, a neighborhood team that regularly took on the West End boys who had built that modest ballfield out on their side of town. By 1888, each of the city's five wards had a baseball team and many of the leading businesses in town also sponsored teams. McGinnity began as an outfielder. Lineups in the Decatur newspapers in 1888 usually listed him as playing left field, often for a team sponsored by Fleurys, a local tailor shop.[5]

He also began playing for the Decatur Shamrocks in the semi-pro Interstate League and it was in an 1888 game between Decatur and its rivals from Springfield that McGinnity's baseball career changed course. He started the game in the outfield, but the Decatur pitcher struggled to throw strikes and McGinnity replaced him in the second inning. He won the game and was a pitcher from then on.[6]

In 1889, a new semi-pro league came to Decatur. The Illinois-Indiana League, a forerunner of what later became known as the Three-I League, was formed under the direction of a man named Harry F. Smith, who already had lined up teams in Bloomington, Champaign and Danville, Illinois, and Terre Haute and Lafayette, Indiana. Smith, who was to manage the Danville team himself, decided Decatur was the logical choice to round out the six-team aggregation.[7]

He learned, however, that the Shamrocks and their manager, J.C. Gogerty, held the lease to the little ballpark on west Main Street in Decatur. Smith convinced Gogerty to manage the new team, contingent on a show of local support sufficient to show that the team could be profitable.[8]

"They then called upon some of the business men and admirers of our national game for subscriptions to assist in placing the team on a sound financial basis," the *Decatur Review* reported. "They responded liberally, and as a number of season tickets were sold at $6 each, Manager Gogerty felt so much encouraged that he announced that he would enter a nine in the I.I. league."[9]

Each team in the league was given a $600 salary limit and Gogerty decided to bring in some outside help to supplement the players he already had on the Shamrocks. The *Review* reported that the only holdover players who were likely to make the team were "Payne, O'Brien and Donohue, and perhaps McGinnity."[10] The Shamrocks were to open with an exhibition game against the St. Louis Standards on Sunday, May 20, but the Standards missed their train so the Shamrocks took on a team of players from Sangamon and Cerro Gordo instead. They won, 27–5, with McGinnity pitching the full nine innings.[11]

Gogerty continued to bring in more new players after that, recruiting a pitcher named Conn and another named William Barnes, who the *Review* reported was "the best all-around player in southern Indiana."[12]

The team played two more exhibition games against Smith's Danville team on May 27 and 28 and split, losing the first game, 9–5, and winning the second, 16–9. McGinnity did not pitch in either game but did see action in center field.[13]

When the league season began a few days later, it quickly became apparent that Gogerty had not done a very good job of recruiting. The Shamrocks lost by astronomical scores nearly every day.

On June 3, McGinnity pitched in relief in a 15–2 loss to Terre Haute. The visitors from Indiana collected only seven hits, but the Shamrocks committed 16 errors. The *Herald* wasn't exaggerating a bit when it referred to the Decatur teams as "very ragged." "The crowd guyed the poor plays, hooted the umpire and was inclined to be noisy," the paper added.[14]

The team's management wasn't any more precise than the fielders. A June 4 home game with Danville was scheduled to start at 3:30 P.M., but didn't get under way until 4:20 because no one could find a ball to use. Assistant manager Charles Kilpatrick finally rushed downtown to buy one so the game could go on. The Shamrocks, with McGinnity batting eighth and playing right field, at least came close to winning that game, going down to a 4–3 loss.[15]

The next day's game at the west side park was cancelled because a band competition was taking place on the field. The rest of the league quickly was losing patience with such fiascoes. "The Decatur club will probably soon be fired out of the league if they don't do better, and Logansport admitted," the *Danville Press* reported. "Logansport is a fine ball city and we hope to see them in."[16]

McGinnity suffered a 24–3 loss at Champaign on June 12 and the Shamrocks lost to the same team, 15–4, the next day. At that point, they were 0–8 and even the hometown papers were beginning to take shots at them. The *Review* noted that "The boys were expected back from Champaign last night, but if they came they must have sneaked home through some dark alley, for no trace of them could be found."[17]

There were several games played for the benefit of the Johnstown survivors during that time period. A large flood benefit game between a couple of amateur teams was played in Decatur on June 13 and attracted a crowd of about 3,000. The *Review* estimated the profits at about $1,000.[18]

The Shamrocks played disaster relief games on June 8 in Bloomington and on June 17 at home, but they were pretty much a disaster themselves. That June 17 game with Danville, which resulted in a 19–1 loss, was their last.

They never did win a league game. At the end, McGinnity wasn't even seeing any action in the outfield. The Bloomington team also folded. It did much better on the field—it was in third place at the time—but its financial situation was hopeless.[19]

It was to become a recurring theme for McGinnity. At least four more times in his life, he would be part of a professional team or league that folded in the middle of the season.

He still had his job in the mine, but things weren't always so pleasant there either. On June 22, one of his co-workers, Charles Oberofskie, was crushed to death under a car carrying more than a ton of coal.[20] It was another recurring theme.

3. Indian Territory

After several years in Decatur, Hannah McGinnity began to feel that old coal miner wanderlust. It seems she and her family never stayed anywhere for a very long period of time (a trait her later-to-be-famous son perpetuated). She began to hear from her sister, Elizabeth, what a great place Montana was.

It certainly sounded better than Decatur. The average Illinois coal-mining family in that era earned less than $400 a year[1] while Brown and Elizabeth Ferrell had found gold instead of just coal in Montana. Near the end of 1889, Hannah packed up a few belongings and her seven children, most of whom were now in their teens or older, and boarded a westbound train.

It's not clear how her third-born son felt about this. He had become a ballplayer of some repute in Decatur. He even had earned a few bucks playing the game and he probably hated to leave that part of his life behind.

Joe McGinnity never made it all the way to Montana anyway. The family ran out of money part of the way there, so Joe and his brothers stopped off to work in the Osage Coal Company's No. 1 mine in the Indian Territory, which was still almost 20 years away from achieving statehood and being renamed Oklahoma. The family eventually continued on its way to Montana, but when it did so, Joe stayed behind.

In the early 1870s, a man named James J. McAlester had come to the Indian Territory and discovered deep veins of coal east of the Oklahoma town that now bears his name. He married into the Choctaw tribe to gain access to the coal and eventually set up a general store to service the miners at the corner of what is now Main and Choctaw in McAlester.[2] When the railroad came through shortly thereafter, McAlester became a boomtown. Coal miners who had been working in Illinois, Ohio and Pennsylvania began flocking to the Indian Territory.

That included young Joe McGinnity. He got there late in 1889, at the age of 18, and went to work in the mines in Krebs, a small town about five miles east of McAlester.

Among those working with him was a man named John Redpath and several of Redpath's sons. John had been born in Scotland in 1849, came to the U.S. in 1867 and had seen a sizeable portion of the country in the previous 20 years. When he first arrived, he bought a ticket to go as far west as his money would take him. He ended up in southeast Ohio and lived for a time in the town of Pomeroy, where he met and married a woman named Margaret Potts.[3]

A year later, Redpath was on his way west again. He worked for the Union Pacific Railroad in the Rocky Mountains and was present in Promontory, Utah, in 1869 when the golden spike was driven to complete the transcontinental railroad. He worked as a locomotive engineer, but eventually went back to Ohio and worked for eight years as a machinist in the coal mines at Minersville. He narrowly escaped death when a mine along the Ohio River flooded and he set off for the west again in 1884, finally settling into a job as the assistant master mechanic for the Osage Coal and Mining Company in Krebs.[4]

He and Margaret had 12 children and it didn't take long for Joe McGinnity to take notice of the oldest daughter, Mary, who was four years younger than he was. It's entirely possible she was the reason he didn't accompany the rest of his family to Montana.

John Redpath later got out of the mining business and opened the McAlester Foundry and Machine Shop in 1900. A few years later it merged with bigger operations and became Union Iron Works.[5] Its original building still stands at the corner of Ninth and Grand in McAlester.

However, in 1889, John was working the mines along with McGinnity and a few thousand others who represented a true melting pot of a growing nation. Included were immigrants from Italy, Poland, Russia, Ireland, Scotland, Wales, England, Lithuania and Czechoslovakia. By 1887, 600,000 tons of coal a year was being taken out of the ground in the area around McAlester, most of it being shipped south into Texas.[6]

In addition to working in the coal mines, Joe McGinnity also continued to dabble at baseball and was largely responsible for developing it as a favorite sport in the area. In fact, Charles Saulsberry, a sportswriter for *The Oklahoman* newspaper in Oklahoma City, referred to him a half century later as "the father of Oklahoma baseball."[7]

It became a favorite leisure time activity with the miners who were streaming in from the eastern U.S. and all over the world. In the beginning, they played it in prairies, using hay bales or tin cans for bases.

McGinnity organized and managed at least three different teams in Krebs and the surrounding communities. One of his old friends and teammates, Harry Hokey, recalled many years later that McGinnity's first big splash as a pitcher took place in the unlikely surroundings of New Year's Day 1891 in

Alderson, a town only a few miles southeast of Krebs.[8] In truth, Hokey may have had his dates mixed up. It almost certainly was 1890, not 1891.

"We had a spell of pretty weather," Hokey told *The Oklahoman* in a 1940 interview. "Somebody got the brilliant idea of playing a ball game and it was then we found out what a great pitcher this new fellow McGinnity was. I don't remember the score but Krebs won with McGinnity pitching and it's just about a cinch it was a shutout because the clubs around here couldn't score very much on Joe."[9]

The sport up to that point had been played mostly among the townspeople in the mining communities. But now the Krebs team began traveling to other towns to play. In addition to McGinnity and Hokey, the team included the four McGuire brothers—Johnny, Pat, Jim and Barney—plus Bill and Johnny Powers, Tom Fisher, Walter Stark, Jack McCully, Tommy Donohue, Scarface Mullen and many others.[10] While some of the nearby towns were lucky to scrape together nine players, Krebs usually had 20 or more from which to choose.

Because it was near a spur of the Missouri-Kansas-Texas Railroad (better known as the Katy), the Krebs team frequently went up and down the line playing teams from Muskogee, Coalgate and Lehigh in Oklahoma, and Denison and Sherman further south in Texas. They later even ventured over to Arkansas to play teams in Fort Smith and Van Buren. They didn't often ride the passenger trains. They were more likely to hop into vacant freight cars and "hobo" their way to the town in which they were scheduled to play. The brakemen on the railroads usually knew what was going on, but looked the other way.[11]

McGinnity not only organized the teams, but he did the majority of the pitching. Hokey said he once saw him pitch seven games in seven days. He was a dominant player, so much so that Hokey remembered the Krebs second team players challenging the first teamers to a game for $25 as long as McGinnity didn't pitch. The scrubs ended up beating the McGinnity-less regulars, 8–6.[12]

When Krebs played at home, it was not uncommon for more than half the town's population of 4,500 to turn out to watch. Fans flooded in from all over that part of the Indian Territory to watch McGinnity pitch.

Another old friend and teammate, Bill Collins, recalled many years later that the folks in Lehigh felt they had developed the strongest team in the territory. They came to Krebs brimming with confidence and McGinnity shut them out, 2–0, in front of a crowd of about 2,500. Lehigh demanded a rematch but the Krebs team refused to play in Lehigh, about 50 miles southwest. The teams met instead a few weeks later in Denison, Texas, with many of the Krebs and McAlester townspeople making the 100-mile trip by train. Krebs won that one, 14–0.[13]

McGinnity's services began to be in demand by teams outside the Krebs and McAlester area. He did some pitching for the Patterson Mercantile team of Muskogee [14] and also worked for a team sponsored by the Choctaw Coal Company in the neighboring town of Hartshorne,[15] which many years later produced a Hall of Fame pitcher of its own named Warren Spahn.

He received offers from teams even further away, in Arkansas and Texas, but resisted the temptation to go too far. Baseball still was just a game to be played on weekends and off days. He still thought of himself as a coal miner and in his limited perspective, it was hard to envision himself doing anything else with his life.

Coal mining obviously could be dangerous work. McGinnity understood that as well as anyone because of what had happened to his father. There also had been an accident in Krebs in 1885 that killed 12 men[16] and an explosion in 1887 that killed 18 men in the No. 2 mine at Savanna, just south of McAlester.[17] McGinnity had seen men grow old before their time from breathing the black dust of the mines day after day for years on end.

But the perils of the profession were hammered home even more firmly on January 7, 1892, in Krebs.

McGinnity was working in the Osage Company's No. 11, the largest mine in a region in which you couldn't walk more than a mile without seeing a shaft of some sort. He was performing his usual duties of muleskinner, driving a wagon through the diggings, picking up coal. His future brother-in-law, Ed Redpath, was with him, serving as his "trapper," opening and closing compartment doors to provide air circulation.[18]

It was the end of the work day, shortly after 5 P.M., and miners gradually were making their way out of the main shaft. It was estimated that 400 men went into the mine that day. They were transported 470 feet down into the earth in a steel cage that carried six men at a time and was cranked up and down by a wench.

At 5:07 P.M., the process of bringing workers back to the surface had just begun. The estimates of how many men already had come out varied greatly, ranging anywhere from 30 to 150. However many it was, McGinnity and Ed Redpath were among them. They had just stepped out of the steel cage.[19]

It was customary after a work shift to set off explosions inside the mine to loosen coal for the crew in the next shift. But this time someone accidentally set off a blast too early and it was done incorrectly. It ignited trapped methane gas and resulted in an even larger explosion that shot the 3,000-

pound steel cage 100 feet into the air and sent flames shooting out of the mine's openings.[20]

People eating dinner in the Elk House Hotel in McAlester, five miles away, reported that the building shook violently from the force of the explosion. Burned and battered men began climbing out of the mine. At least 150 men crawled out through an air shaft, but at least 100 never made it out. The exact number never was determined, but it took more than a week to dig out all the bodies.

Miners from neighboring towns immediately flocked to the site to help in the recovery effort. The few doctors in the area were sent to the scene to help care for those emerging from the mine alive. Workers hastily repaired the steel cage and spent days trying to rescue workers through both the main shaft and the air shaft.

It became a heart-wrenching scene, described by newspapers as far away as New York. Families waited around the outside of the shaft for days as blackened bodies or pieces of bodies were dragged from the wreckage. A nearby blacksmith shop was converted into a temporary morgue.[21]

One woman named Quinn lost her husband and two sons in the disaster. When informed of what happened, she reportedly fell over and died, too.[22]

A company in Dallas sent boxcars full of cheap coffins up the Katy to Krebs and most of the dead were buried in a mass grave in St. Joseph's Cemetery.

The disaster and the fact that he nearly became a victim of it made a powerful impression on Joe McGinnity. He relived that day frequently in his mind in the decades that followed.

And the next time one of the big towns offered him money to come and play baseball, he was much more inclined to listen.

4. A New Profession

There are several versions of the story of how Joe McGinnity was first noticed by a professional baseball team. The tale has taken on legendary proportions and the complete truth almost certainly will never be known.

One story is that McGinnity struck out 19 men in a game in 1892 while pitching for a semi-pro team in Van Buren, Arkansas, against its archrival, Fort Smith. A traveling salesman witnessed the achievement and returned to his home in Montgomery, Alabama, where he told John McCloskey, the manager of the local Southern League team. McCloskey is supposed to have said "Even if he fanned 19 women, I could use him. Send him down here."[1]

In another version of the story, someone sent a telegram to McCloskey telling him what they had seen.

In yet another version, McGinnity supposedly struck out 22 girls in a game and McCloskey was in attendance to see it himself. The manager's alleged quote has appeared on McGinnity's page on the Baseball Hall of Fame web site: "I saw a pitcher named McGinnity strike out 22 members of a girls team at Van Buren, Arkansas, last year. Get him for me. If he can strike out 22 girls, perhaps he can strike out two men. And I don't have any pitchers who can."[2]

The truth? Probably none of the above. There is no evidence that McGinnity ever struck out 19 or 22 batters in any game at any level. The notion that he would have been pitching against a girls team is even more far-fetched. Few women even contemplated competing in athletics in that era, certainly not against men. And McCloskey, one of the true characters of baseball, was managing in Texas in 1892. There's no reason to believe he traveled all the way over to the Arkansas-Oklahoma border to take in a girls game.

What is true is that McCloskey somehow heard about McGinnity's pitching prowess and signed him to play for Montgomery in 1893. It's entirely possible that he heard about the first game McGinnity ever pitched for Van Buren, a town about 100 miles northeast of Krebs. He struck out 16 batters in that game and it did happen against Fort Smith, on May 20, 1892.[3] We'll never know if there was a traveling salesman in the stands that day, but it's likely that's the game that first led McCloskey to sign him.

There's a good chance that if McGinnity had only pitched for the town teams around the Indian Territory, no one ever would have discovered him. But as early as 1890, he and the Krebs team began venturing over to nearby Arkansas for an occasional game. In one 1890 game, McGinnity and catcher Johnny McGuire combined to deliver a 1–0 victory over the Fort Smith semi-pro team that was widely acclaimed as "a miracle." McGinnity struck out 21 batters in that game to outduel Fort Smith's Emerson "Pink" Hawley, who fanned 24. McGuire hit a home run in the eighth inning for the only run of the game.[4] It was the first McGinnity-Hawley duel, but far from the last. It was a rivalry that ultimately would carry all the way to the major leagues.

Early in 1892, another team that McGinnity helped to organize traveled over to Arkansas again to play the highly regarded Van Buren Browns, who had won the championship of Arkansas and the Indian Territory the previous year. Manager W.L. Mace had almost his entire team back from the championship season with the only new import being a pitcher named McCormick, who had been brought in from Houston.[5]

The Browns opened their season on May 6 and 7 against the team from Hartshorne, another small coal mining community near Krebs. The *Van Buren Argus* reported on May 4 that the "Hartshorns have a better team than last season, and are in good practice. They have their old battery, McGuire and McGinty, and our boys will have to look well to their laurels."[6] Van Buren won both games, 5–2 and 6–2, but the Hartshorne gang must have made an impression because two weeks later, McGinnity and McGuire both began playing for Van Buren. The *Argus* reported that "Joe McGinty, a most promising and gentlemanly young player" had been signed by the Browns.[7]

It was in his very first game that he blew away the Maroons from just across the Arkansas River in Fort Smith, claiming a 10–2 victory in the second game of a doubleheader. Hawley was there again, registering 17 strikeouts for Fort Smith in the first game of the twin bill.[8] The scouts noticed him, too. By August, Hawley was working for the St. Louis Browns of the National League.

A week later, Van Buren swept the regular Krebs team in a doubleheader, 8–1 and 3–2.[9] There was no mention in the *Argus* of McGinnity playing for either team that day, but he was a regular for Van Buren from then on.

In mid–June, he beat Weir City, Kansas, 3–2, and even performed some offensive heroics. With the score tied at 2–2 in the ninth inning, he singled to center, stole second, raced to third when the catcher threw wildly, and trotted home when the centerfielder also threw wildly trying to get him at third.[10]

On the Fourth of July, he pitched a two-hit shutout against J.L. Hudsons, considered the best amateur team in St. Louis.[11] The following week,

McGinnity defeated the *Sporting News* team of St. Louis, 10–3, in spite of what the *Argus* described as a "bone-felon" on his left hand, and later that week he allowed only one hit in an 11–1 conquest of a Brinkley, Arkansas, team that had won 12 straight games.[12] In a hotly contested three-game showdown with the hated Maroons in late July, he pitched well in a 3–2 loss on Tuesday, then defeated the Maroons, 5–4, on Thursday.[13]

It's not known when or how John McCloskey and the Montgomery Colts contacted him about pitching in Alabama, but that's where McGinnity was headed in the spring of 1893.

He was a late arrival, however. The *Sporting News* reported on April 22 that "McCloskey has signed a pitcher by the name of McGinnity who hails from the Indian Territory. He has not arrived here yet but we are expecting him to be here every day. Mac says he is a jewel and I take it for granted that he knows what he is talking about."[14]

The Montgomery Colts, who played their home games at Patterson Field on Madison Avenue,[15] appeared to have the makings of one of the better teams in the 12-team Southern League even before their new pitcher arrived.

Catcher Red Armstrong, who was referred to at various times as "a very talkative fellow"[16] and "a ball field clown,"[17] had led the Texas League in batting the year before. Outfielder Bill Hassamaer was accomplished enough as a hitter that he would bat .322 for the Washington Senators the following season. Infielders Harry Raymond and Danny Minnehan, pitcher Frank Wilson and pitcher-outfielder Billy George were established veterans with reputations developed in other leagues in previous seasons. Later in the season, the team would acquire Art Twineham, a lefthanded catcher from Galesburg, Illinois, who was destined to finish the season with the St. Louis Browns.

McCloskey also claimed to have signed Jimmie Stafford, a slick-fielding center-fielder, although the league awarded Stafford's rights to Augusta. McCloskey screamed that he had given Stafford advance money and he announced that he would claim a forfeit victory for every game his team was scheduled to play against Augusta.[18] Even without him, all the Colts really lacked was pitching and help was on the way from the Indian Territory.

McGinnity finally arrived on April 20. He stepped off the train and was thrown into a game the same day. He held Nashville to five hits in a 10–4 victory and a star was born.[19]

"There is not very much of the youngster, but what there is every bit there," raved the *Montgomery Advertiser*. "He is one of the best pitchers ever seen in Montgomery and if he can work like he did yesterday, right after a trip, what can he do when he gets in good shape?"[20]

Sporting Life added its own plaudits: "The wonderful thing of the game was the work of McGinnity for Montgomery. McGinnity is the latest find of Manager McCloskey, and to judge of his work in the game he is a jewel of the first order. He is a wonder and pitches a lightning ball."[21]

Two days later, McGinnity won again, beating the same Nashville club by a 7–4 score as the Colts grabbed the early lead in the pennant race.[22] They won 13 of their first 16 games, but then began to drop in the standings. After his rapid start, McGinnity lost three games in five days in early May, giving up 31 runs in the process.

The *Sporting News* in that era did a thorough job of covering minor league baseball through a network of correspondents who used such pseudonyms as Red-Bird, Ivanhoe and Rowne About. It was not uncommon for these once-a-week writers to engage in back-and-forth banter about the teams they chronicled and as Montgomery fell in the standings, its correspondent, Red-Bird, engaged in some less-than-friendly exchanges with Ivanhoe, who covered the Mobile club.

In the May 20 *Sporting News*, Ivanhoe wrote: "There was considerable talk about the Montgomery team being drunk when here. By request, I investigated this report fully and found no truth whatsoever in it. The hotel at which they stopped told me they were as gentlemanly a set of people as he ever had at his hotel. But they are certainly great kickers and must expect to win games on kicking as they play very little ball."[23]

By "kicking," he was referring to the manner in which the Colts verbally assaulted umpires in an attempt to get games called their way. McCloskey, who managed 47 different teams during his career, already had a reputation for baiting umpires at that point. The *Sporting News* reported that his constant complaining while serving as the manager of a team in Houston in 1892 was "outrageous" and "disgusted everyone."[24] McCloskey was kicked out of one game in April of 1893 for calling an umpire "a big old stiff" and in May he was fined $35 by umpire Norman Baker for his incessant whining.[25]

McGinnity was to have more than his share of run-ins with umpires as the years passed—he undoubtedly learned something about umpire abuse from McCloskey—but as a 22-year-old rookie, he apparently just stood back and watched. "He is a favorite here and is well liked by everybody," Red-Bird reported, "not only on account of his playing but he is such a gentlemanly and well-behaved young fellow."[26]

Not everyone on the Montgomery team was so well-behaved, though. McCloskey had trouble with Minnehan and George, and finally suspended the pair for "indifferent playing." He eventually released both of them and they signed with Mobile (much to the delight of Ivanhoe). Red-Bird bid them good riddance in the *Sporting News*: "The release of George and Minnehan has put new life in the team and perfect harmony now prevails."[27]

McGinnity recovered from his May slump to pitch a four-hit shutout at home against Augusta in early June. He even rapped out two hits himself. He then lost eight straight games although he wasn't getting much support, either at the plate or in the field. In a June 21 game with Savannah, the Colts committed 10 errors behind him.[28]

Red-Bird didn't lose faith in him. In a June 20 dispatch, he wrote: "Joe McGinnity has been one of the greatest finds this season as far as pitchers are concerned. His pitching and stick work have been remarkably fine and if we only had a couple more like him and (Frank) Wilson we would certainly be in the race to stay."[29]

Red-Bird and others did not have as much faith in McCloskey and the rest of the team's management. As the Colts sank in the standings, the *Montgomery Advertiser* began inserting sketches of hearses and tombstones into stories about the Colts. A meeting of the team's stockholders was called in late June and Red-Bird reported that "an effort will be made to remove the present board of directors and a general shaking up of the team will take place.... It is said that Manager McCloskey's head is in danger."[30]

The Colts finished ninth in the standings in the first half of the season, which ended July 7, but things began to turn around somewhat in the second half. Raymond took over as the team captain and the Colts got a boost from a gifted 20-year-old outfielder from Iowa named Fred Clarke, who was destined to become player-manager of the Pittsburgh Pirates and a rival of McGinnity's in the decades to come.

Then came some stunning news. On July 14, it was reported that the New York Giants of the National League had signed five Southern League players, one of whom was Joe McGinnity. The others were Augusta catcher Parke Wilson and three other pitchers—Savannah's Charlie Petty, Charleston's Tom Colclough and Augusta's Les German.[31] It seemed odd that the Giants would be signing four new hurlers since most teams in that era only employed three or four pitchers, and the Giants already had a future Hall of Famer in hard-throwing Amos Rusie.

It's not entirely clear why, but only three of the players—Petty, German and Wilson—ended up playing for the Giants that season. Colclough finished the season with Pittsburgh of the NL.

McGinnity didn't go to the NL at all. He seemingly was only placed on the Giants' "reserve list," which meant they had the rights to him for the following season.

The news that McGinnity might be taken away by New York at any moment did not sit well in Montgomery, as reflected in a diatribe by Red-Bird in the July 22 *Sporting News*: "There is but one thing to dampen our enthusiasm—pitcher Joe McGinnity has been taken away from us and given to New York. Of course, Montgomery got a neat sum for him but that hardly soothes our wounded feelings. The pitiful tale is being put up here that the local club has no say in this—that New York can take the pitcher whether Montgomery objects or not.... This is the most absurd idea ever heard—according to them we are just allowed to play on sufferance and New York can come here at any time and take any of the Colts they want. New York put McGinnity on her reserve list and by paying $500 takes him at the beginning of next season but anyone with the least suspicion of common sense can see how absurd it is to say that New York can take him now without the consent of Montgomery."[32]

The article went on to say that the people of Montgomery were happy for McGinnity, but they didn't view themselves as a developmental team for the big city clubs and there would be "a loud howl when Joe leaves here."[33]

He didn't leave. He never even missed a start with Montgomery. He eventually would end up with the Giants, but that would be nine long years later.

There was a reason that Augusta, Charleston, Savannah and others began selling off some of their best players in July. The Southern League was in trouble. The entire country was thrown into a depression by the Panic of 1893 and it took its toll on minor league baseball teams, most of which were operated on a shoestring.

On June 21, the floundering Birmingham franchise was taken over by the league.[34] It later was replaced by a team in Pensacola, Florida, a move that ultimately made the league's situation worse. In July, Charles Hart resigned as the president of the league and was replaced by J.B. Nicklin of Chattanooga.[35] There were reports that Nashville owner Ted Sullivan was in such desperate straits that he deserted his team in Montgomery, leaving the players there without any means to get home. Sullivan vehemently denied the report.[36]

On August 5, the *Sporting News* reported that the league's collapse was imminent: "The Southern League will not last two weeks more as the best players are being sold to Northern clubs.... Three or four clubs are only watching for someone to throw up the sponge and then there will be a general stampede."[37]

The Montgomery franchise suffered from "poor patronage" and "hard luck," according to the *Sporting News*,[38] but it kept plugging along. So did most of the western teams in the league, but the eastern clubs were crumbling. There was talk that those teams might fold and leave the western contingent of Montgomery, Mobile, Macon, Memphis and New Orleans to finish out the season and split whatever minuscule profits there might be.

The league owners met on August 11 and decided to call off the rest of the season.[39] By then, the Charleston and Nashville franchises already had fallen by the wayside. The end was largely the product of financial duress, but it didn't help that there was a yellow fever scare in Pensacola and worries that the dreaded disease might be spread throughout the south by traveling ballplayers. It was generally agreed that the league might be able to come back for the 1894 season, but that it would be better off with only eight teams instead of 12.

McGinnity stayed in the league to the very end. The hoped-for call from New York never came. "While nearly all the Southern Leaguers have been 'called,' Mr. McGinty seems to have been overlooked," the *Sporting News* reported on August 12.[40]

It may have been because he didn't finish the season especially well. He lost each of his last five starts although he again was the victim of some tough luck. His teammates only scored nine runs on his behalf in those five games. He finished with a 10–19 record and went home to the Indian Territory.

Three months later, on November 29, he and Mary Redpath stood before Father M.B. Murphy in the Catholic church in McAlester and were united in holy wedlock.[41] Her seemingly boundless love, devotion and patience would be one of the few constants in his life over the next 33 years.

5. Kansas City

As the spring of 1894 approached, life probably never looked better to Joe McGinnity. He was a newlywed, Mary already was expecting the couple's first child and despite a less-than-stellar record at Montgomery, he was going to get a chance to continue playing the sport he loved for a living. The New York Giants didn't call, but he found another opportunity in a high caliber professional league much closer to home.

Jimmie Manning, the manager of the Savannah Electrics of the Southern League, had been impressed with McGinnity's potential when he pitched against his club and when Manning became the owner and manager of the Kansas City Blues in the newly revamped Western League, he signed the big man from Krebs to a contract.

Kansas City, only about 300 miles north of Krebs, had been a major league town a few years earlier. It had a team in the old Union Association in 1884, a team in the National League in 1886 and a franchise in the American Association (then considered a major league) in 1888 and '89. All those teams had been nicknamed the Cowboys and none of them lasted very long.

The Western League had gone bankrupt, but it was reorganized under the leadership of a Cincinnati newspaperman named Ban Johnson in a meeting on November 20, 1893,[1] in Detroit. It actually was the forerunner of yet another major league. Six years later, after raising the caliber of play to a higher level under the guidance of the autocratic Johnson, the Western League was to become the American League. The Blues would become the Washington Senators, who still exist today as the Minnesota Twins.

But in 1894, the Western League was a small-time operation, a scrap heap for has-beens, cast-offs and yet-to-bes.

Manning had bounced around the minor leagues himself after five years in the majors, capped by a season with the Kansas City Cowboys in 1889. Now he assembled a team that included several former major leaguers and several players he knew about from his days managing in the Southern League.

Kansas City, a bustling cattle and railroad town that was only beginning to be impacted by the Panic of 1893, was one of the western outposts in a league that included Detroit, Grand Rapids, Indianapolis, Minneapolis, Milwaukee, Toledo and Sioux City. The new league was progressive in its thinking. Among other things, it instituted a league-wide policy of admitting women free of charge to all games except those on Sundays and holidays.[2]

McGinnity and catcher Tim Donahue were the first players to report to the Blues' preseason camp. It was an ironic twist in that Donahue was the true iron man of that 1894 Blues team. He worked in an iron foundry in the off-season—an occupation McGinnity hadn't yet taken up—and he caught 137 straight games that season. He also may have played a major role in McGinnity's premature departure from the club.

McGinnity came up from Krebs on the morning of March 20,[3] and all three Kansas City newspapers of that era—the *Star*, the *Times* and the *Journal*—seemed to be impressed with the mere sight of him even though he may not have yet reached his full growth. They listed him as being 5-foot-10½ and 168 pounds, which still made him among the biggest players on the team.

The *Journal* made a prophetic observation: "McGinnity is a stalwart youth who looks as though he could pitch a full game every day and not get tired." Later in the same article, it added: "He is looked upon as one of the most promising young players in the country, and if he only comes up to his record of last year he will be a tower of strength to the Kansas City team.... He has good speed and a fine drop ball and in addition is an excellent batter."[4]

The *Star* liked the looks of both McGinnity and Donahue: "They are both big, strapping young fellows, and as both have been at work all winter are in good shape and will soon be in playing condition should the weather be favorable."[5]

Unfortunately, the weather was not very good at all. The Blues were supposed to practice for a few days and then take on a top amateur team, the Kansas City (Kansas) Reds, in a March 25 exhibition game. But the weather was unseasonably cold. It even snowed a few days and the game kept getting pushed back. The Reds had hoped to have Kid Nichols, who spent the winter in Kansas City, pitch for them in the game. Nichols, a future Hall of Famer, already had won 126 games in his first four years with the Boston Beaneaters and would have virtually assured the Reds of victory. However, the postponements forced him to leave for Boston before the exhibition was played.

Meanwhile, Manning and his players worked out indoors.

"Manning's men are getting into excellent shape in spite of the summer blizzard which has interfered in a manner with their preliminary practice," the *Star* reported.[6]

The exhibition game wasn't played until March 31. The Blues won, 17–0, and the Journal said it just as easily could have been 47–0 "if they had cared to exert themselves."[7] They took off immediately afterward for St. Louis, where they were scheduled to play a three-game series with a major-league team, the St. Louis Browns (later known as the Cardinals) of the National League. McGinnity had a few old friends on the Browns, including his catcher from the previous season, Art Twineham, and Pink Hawley, against whom he had pitched back in Van Buren.

The Blues defeated the Browns, 9–7, on April 1 with "Lucky Pete" Daniels pitching the entire game. The Blues did not commit an error and rightfielder George Ulrich hit a three-run home run in the second inning.[8]

The next day McGinnity lost to the Browns, 5–1, but he left an impression. The Blues did almost nothing against Browns ace Ted Breitenstein, who was destined to win 27 games that season. They managed just four singles against him and scored their only run on a dropped fly ball with two outs in the ninth, but the Browns didn't do much more against McGinnity, failing to score in the last five innings.[9]

The Blues continued to be impressive, losing the third game of the series by a 1–0 score and the *St. Louis Republic* reported that "Manning has a team that Toledo or any other Western league club will find hard to beat, while they are capable of giving a league club a warm argument for victory."[10]

McGinnity again pitched well against the Browns in a home game on April 10, but several errors by shortstop Peck Sharp and some erratic baserunning led to a 7–2 loss.[11]

He was less than impressive, but was the winning pitcher in a 7–6 victory over Minneapolis on April 16. This time, he had a 5–1 lead before giving up six straight hits and allowing four runs in the sixth inning. Bill Klusman and George Darby homered in the top of the 10th inning, but Minneapolis tore into McGinnity again in the bottom of the 10th. Centerfielder Sam Nichol threw a man out at the plate to end the game and preserve the win.[12]

In spite of some shaky moments, Manning felt he had a team that could win the league title. The Blues were loaded with talent and experience by Western League standards. In fact, the only player on the original 11-man roster who never would play a single game in the majors either before or after 1894 was Sharp, the shortstop.

Manning, who played second base as well as managing the team, had played five years in the majors with Boston, Detroit and Kansas City. He had batted only .215, but stole 58 bases in 1889. Originally from Fall River, Massachusetts, he still was only 32 years old in 1894.

Klusman had played second base for one season in the NL and one in the American Association, but would play first base for the Blues and bat cleanup. A local merchant, Ben Spitz, offered a free umbrella to any Blues player who hit a home run during the season and Klusman won enough of them that his teammates dubbed him "Rainy Weather Bill."

Nichol, born in County Antrim, Ireland, also had some experience in both the NL and American Association although his career average was only .128 in 22 games. But after bouncing from Wheeling, West Virginia, to Davenport, Iowa, to Jamestown, New York, to Toledo, he had batted .359 for Manning's Savannah team in the Southern League in 1892. He was flanked in the outfield by Ulrich, a Philadelphian who played 21 games over three NL seasons with three different teams, and 27-year-old Tommy Hernon, another Massachusetts native who would go 1-for-16 in a brief appearance with the Chicago White Stockings (now Cubs) three years later.

Ulrich also was the emergency catcher if anything ever happened to Donahue, but that didn't happen much. The Taunton, Massachusetts, native had caught 76 straight games the previous season with Dover of the New England League and he almost never missed a game with the Blues. He had played briefly in the American Association in 1891 and in 1895 he would begin a six-year stretch with the White Stockings, playing nearly as many games in the majors as McGinnity.

The third baseman was a Kentuckian, Billy Niles, who would play 11 games with the Pittsburgh Pirates the following year.

The other two pitchers on the team, Pete Daniels and George "Deacon" Darby, were both lefthanders. Darby, the only player on the team from Kansas City, had pitched four games for Cincinnati in the NL the previous year and spent most of that season with Atlanta of the Southern League, winning 22 games. Daniels, another Ireland-born player, was known as either "Lucky Pete" or the "Smiling Mickey Welch of the Western League." He had pitched four games for the Pirates four years earlier and would appear in 10 more for St. Louis four years later. Like so many of the players on the team, he had played in the Southern League the previous year, at Mobile.

It was a promising collection of talent and the Blues opened impressively, with a 12–3 victory over Milwaukee in front of a crowd of 2,500 at Exposition Park, a modest wooden bandbox along Prospect Avenue in the southeast part of Kansas City. The players gathered and dressed at the Centropolis Hotel, then rode to the ballpark in horse-drawn carriages as a band played.[13]

Most newspapers in that era didn't use many photographs, but the *Journal* published an artist's drawing of McGinnity coaching third base in that first game.[14] He made his regular-season debut the next day and it was a near disaster. The Blues staked him to a quick 6–0 lead, but in the third inning he walked two batters and hit three others. "McGinnity had plenty of speed but was as wild as a Kansas cyclone," the *Times* reported.[15]

With the score 6–6 and the bases loaded, Manning replaced him with Darby. Minneapolis ended up getting 10 runs in the inning, but they were the only runs they got all day. The Blues rallied to win, 13–10, with McGinnity playing the last six innings in right field.[16]

The next day he again finished up in right field. This time, he pitched six good innings while his teammates gave him a 13–0 lead. But another wild streak and a couple of errors prompted his departure and Daniels finally took over in the ninth to preserve a 14–9 victory.[17]

The *Times*, which never did figure out how to spell his last name, reported that "It begins to look as though our McGinity is lacking in heart and courage."[18] The *Journal* had a different view: "McGinnity showed that with a little more work he will be one of Kansas City's winning pitchers." It explained that McGinnity had worked on his control all morning and was simply tired out by the ninth inning.[19]

But it became a continuing trend. He would pitch well for while, get a lead, then put together a string of walks and hit batsmen, lose his composure, make a few wild throws on fielding plays and give up large chunks of runs.

On May 6, his wildness led to a 16–14 loss to Sioux City. On May 9, he lost to Milwaukee, 7–6. Manning had to keep putting the kid out there, actually using him more frequently than he originally intended. Darby contracted blood poisoning from a cut on his finger and had to be hospitalized on a road trip to Sioux City. Then he hurt his arm and was out for two more weeks after that. On May 13, McGinnity was hit especially hard in a 20–6 loss to Minneapolis and the local newspapers really started ragging him.

"McGinnity pitched for Manning's colts and was an easy mark for the Minneapolitans, who hit him every time that he was steady enough to get a ball over the plate," the *Star* wrote. "He gave five bases on balls, hit two batsmen and doubles, triples and home runs were the order of the day. He had neither speed nor control and the Millers swelled their batting averages at his expense. McGinnity has not yet shown any kind of pitching form and unless he gets down to pitching shortly, Manager Manning will have to look around for a successor to the Indian Territory wonder."[20]

A few days later, the *Star* reported that Manning was shopping around for new pitching talent: "He is disappointed with McGinnity's work and it is likely he will be released if he does not show a decided improvement in his work."[21]

The *Times* reported on May 20 that Manning was about to release

McGinnity and swing a trade with Toledo for a pitcher named Killeen until McGinnity begged him for another opportunity: "Yesterday morning McGinity pleaded for just one more chance and at 2 o'clock in the afternoon Manning told the man that he could get into his uniform and prepare to pitch. Half an hour before the calling of the game McGinity sought a secluded corner of the grounds and began the task of warming up. Manning watched him and saw that he had both speed and control. When the gong ran for the opening of the game Manning simply said 'Go in, Mac, and if you pitch half as well as you have done in practice we will surely win.'"[22]

McGinnity did pitch well although the Blues still lost to Toledo, 6–5. The *Journal* said he had "excellent control and was very steady at critical moments of the game."[23] He had earned a temporary reprieve.

He finally won a game against Grand Rapids on May 21 although it was hardly a masterpiece. The final score was 14–10. On May 23, he was impressive in beating Grand Rapids 11–3. Three days later, he gave up 16 hits but managed to beat Indianapolis, 15–12. He was on the mound again just two days later as the Blues pounded out 26 hits—five apiece by Manning and Klusman—and clobbered last-place Detroit, 27–4.

The winning streak ended in 6–5 loss to the hapless Wolverines on June 1 and McGinnity's season began to sour again. He gave up 14 hits, including four triples and four doubles, in a 10–4 loss to Grand Rapids on June 12.[24] On June 17, he beat Milwaukee, 8–4, in the first game of a doubleheader in front of a crowd that the *Star* pegged at 8,000 fans.[25]

"McGinnity surprised his most ardent admirers and regained the respect of his critics by pitching one of the best games seen here this season," the *Star* reported.[26]

Again, it was a very brief reprieve from criticism. Three days later, on June 20, he gave up 11 runs in the sixth inning of a 21–6 loss to Minneapolis. The Millers hit three home runs in the sixth inning alone. In the fourth, left fielder Joe Visner hit a homer off McGinnity that the *Times* said was the longest homer ever hit at Exposition Park.[27] Manning had to bring Sharp in from shortstop to pitch the last three innings.

The headline in the *Star* was "McGinnity will not do" and the story was the most scathing critique yet: "The grand fireworks display advertised for Exposition ballpark July Fourth came off ahead of time, Pitcher McGinnity of the Blues being treated to a cannonading by the Minneapolis team yesterday that he will not forget in many a day. He pitched a superb game on Sunday against Milwaukee, but it was completely overshadowed by his poor showing of yesterday. He was erratic and nervous and when the Millers commenced to touch him up, he weakened and went all to pieces, and the Blues got their worst beating of the season.... It clearly demonstrated that as a pitcher, McGinnity is a rank failure and too much of a handicap to be retained as an occasional good game will not do for a team that has pennant winning aspirations. Captain Manning has realized that for some time and has been trying to sign a good pitcher or two from the Southern league."[28]

McGinnity got just one more opportunity. On June 23, in a 19–11 loss to Sioux City, he relieved newcomer Hal Mauck for the last two innings, hit a batter, threw a wild pitch and gave up two runs in the ninth. When the game was over, he asked Manning to release him.[29] His season was over.

In later years, a story circulated which, if true, might help explain McGinnity's total ineffectiveness in some games. John J. Toohill, sports editor of the *Illinois State Register* in Springfield wrote a story at the time of McGinnity's death in which he quoted veteran umpire Joseph Warren as saying that Donahue tipped off batters as to which pitches McGinnity was throwing in at least five games during the 1894 season. It seems that one night after a game, Donahue and some teammates were shooting craps while McGinnity lay on the floor nearby reading a baseball magazine. A dispute arose in the craps game and Donahue called on McGinnity to settle it. Joe politely said he had not been watching, which infuriated Donahue and allegedly prompted him to sabotage the young pitcher in future games.[30]

McGinnity never knew anything about it until about 30 years later, according to Warren. That might explain why he was hit so hard in a few games although it couldn't explain his streaks of wildness. Donahue did develop a reputation both for gambling and for battling with teammates during his major league career. Unfortunately, he never got a chance to either confirm or deny the tale. He died of Addison's disease in 1902, just a month after playing his final game in the majors.

McGinnity's departure didn't do much to change the plight of the Blues. Manning replaced him with one of his old Savannah stalwarts, "Still Bill" Hill, who picked up where McGinnity left off, losing by what looked like football scores. He lost to Minneapolis, 19–14, in his debut on June 26[31] and on June 28 was knocked out in the fourth inning of a 26–15 loss to the Millers.[32]

The Blues, who had been running second in the league behind Sioux City for much of the spring, toppled into fourth place but then, bolstered by a few new players, they won 12 straight games in late August to move into a tie for first with Sioux City. Then, they faltered again and finished third.

By then, McGinnity was long gone, headed back to Krebs and even more heartache than what he'd experienced on the mound with the Blues.

6. The Nickel Rocket

The Panic of 1893 was beginning to take its toll everywhere in the United States, creating the worst economic crisis the country experienced prior to the Great Depression of the 1930s. By some estimates, unemployment nationwide reached 18 percent in 1894 and it stayed in double digits for five straight years.[1] It was especially hard on communities that depended on agriculture or mining for their livelihoods. When 50,000 employees of the Pullman railroad company went on strike in the spring of 1894, it had a crushing trickle-down effect on the coal mining industry.

The operators of coal mines were forced to cut wages. The mines in Krebs that McGinnity had worked for a few years implemented a 20-percent wage cut, but in such nearby communities as Alderson and Hartshorne, the reductions were even larger.[2] Many of those workers also staged strikes and at one point in June, federal troops were called in to evict the Hartshorne miners and transport them out of the territory to Fort Smith, Arkansas.[3]

This is what Joe McGinnity returned to after being released by Kansas City in late June. If all that wasn't enough, there was anguish in McGinnity's personal life. Mary was pregnant but in mid-summer, a daughter named Rebecca was stillborn. Joe and Mary buried her in Oak Hill Cemetery on the outskirts of McAlester.

Suddenly, the Indian Territory was not a happy place for the young couple, and they decided to see if they could find a better life back in Illinois.

They moved to Decatur, where Joe still had plenty of family. In fact, they moved in with his younger brothers, George and John, in the same small house at 1612 E. El Dorado Street. Mary found work as a domestic for the family of William and Minnie Scruggs, who owned one of most popular stores in Decatur. Linn and Scruggs Dry Goods and Carpet Company advertised that it carried "elegant dress goods and ladies' muslin underwear at low prices."[4] Joe found some work in the local mines but also continued to dabble in baseball.

He was mentioned in newspaper reports pitching for the George W. Jones team of Decatur as early as July 10[5]—less than three weeks after his release in Kansas City—although he did much of his work in 1894 for a team sponsored by J.D. Moore's Dental Parlor, which often paid him as much as $5 a game.[6]

On August 28, he struck out 13 batters in a 10–1 victory over a town team from nearby Sullivan.[7] On September 2, J.D. Moore played an exhibition game against the same Toledo team McGinnity had faced in the Western League, and he was knocked out in the third inning of a 15–4 loss.[8] A week later, the *Decatur Daily Republican* called him "invincible" and credited him with giving the opposing team "lessons in baserunning" in an 11–5 victory over Bloomington.[9] McGinnity even got to face a major league team when the Washington National League club passed through town on September 26. The pros pretty much toyed with the J.D. Moore crew in a 23–4 rout. The *Decatur Review* described the game as "a farce from start to end."[10]

Although the McGinnitys lived in Decatur, the strongest semi-pro team in the area was in Springfield, 35 miles away, and that team quickly latched onto Joe. He made his debut with Springfield on September 9, 1894, on the day after his impressive performance against Bloomington. The team had a pitcher named Ryan who had been struggling with his control, allowing three runs to score on wild pitches the previous week in an 11–10 loss to Belleville,[11] so the Springfield team was more than happy to find a pitcher with some actual minor league experience.

They called him "McGinty," as almost everyone did at that time, and he made an immediate impression, defeating Hillsboro, 2–1, in a Sunday afternoon pitcher's duel with a hurler named McDermott in front of about 1,000 fans at Springfield's Sportsman's Park. He struck out 11 batters in the game. When Hillsboro got runners to first and third with nobody out in the seventh, he fanned the next three hitters. Hillsboro finally grabbed a 1–0 lead with the help of a couple of errors in the eighth inning, but with two outs in the ninth, McGinnity reached base when the shortstop fumbled his grounder. The next batter, Gabe Ford, did the same. McGinnity then stole third and when he got tangled up with the third baseman, Ford raced to second. Leftfielder Sam Gibson then singled both of them in.[12]

The custom in those days was for the home team to bat first, so McGinnity still had to retire Hillsboro in the bottom of the ninth. When he did so, the fans celebrated wildly. The *Springfield Journal* described the scene in detail: "Men converted cushions into boomerangs and women fluttered bits of lace and everyone screamed and yelled and screamed again. The Sabbath was fractured in several places and the splintered pieces were kicked and cuffed when the visitors were retired without a run, leaving the score 2 to 1 in Springfield's favor."[13]

It was the start of a run of three-plus years in which McGinnity pitched for the Springfield semi-pro team owned by Mike Wright and managed by his younger brother, Pat, who also played second base. The team included such colorful characters as catcher Fatty Feeney, shortstop Watty Walsh and another pitcher, Joe Figueira,[14] who went on to become a prominent local politician.

In 1895, the Springfield team began playing in a new league, the Southern Illinois Amateur League. Games at Sportsman's Park in that era were gala community events with the local Watch Factory Band coming out and playing between innings. But the action on the field was every bit as intense as what McGinnity had seen in the minor leagues as Springfield tried to get the best of teams from Jacksonville, Decatur, Peoria, Joliet, Beardstown, Belleville and Murphysboro.

Every now and then, a major league team would pass through town to play the locals, too. The St. Louis Browns and Chicago White Stockings stopped frequently and on at least one occasion, the famously cocky Baltimore Orioles, under Ned Hanlon, stopped off for an exhibition game.

McGinnity had pitched a game in the morning in Chatham, Illinois, south of Springfield, but he got back to town in time to face the Orioles. He apparently didn't look like much to the visiting big leaguers. He wore a faded shirt and, according to the *Illinois State Register*, he had a hole in his shoe. His toe was just about to poke through. The Orioles looked at his ragged appearance, watched the speed (or lack thereof) of his pitches and began to snicker and crack jokes.[15]

But when the game started, the Orioles had trouble doing much against McGinnity. Hanlon began to get mad and started hounding his men to put the busher in his place.

"Well, suppose you take a crack at him," one of the players told Hanlon after striking out. "I've been trying to get a hit ever since the game opened, and I can't connect. He's got something."[16]

McGinnity couldn't have realized it, but he was pitching that day against players who would someday become his teammates, including two who would become lifelong friends.

Years later, Pat Wright remembered the competitive fire that McGinnity brought to every game, whether it was against a big-league club like the Orioles or a band of bush-leaguers from Beardstown. "He was a hard player," Wright said. "He was a hard loser. He will fight to the last. He always did. He will not give up."[17]

Not long after moving back to Illinois, Joe and Mary conceived another child and this time the birth was successful. On June 5, 1895, Marguerite McGinnity was born in Decatur.[18]

Joe and his little family moved to Springfield about two months later, buying a house at 724 W. Washington Street. He went into business with a man named Fitzgerald, opening a saloon in downtown Springfield just across the alley from a similar Sixth Street establishment owned by Freddie Yager.[19] He still apparently also did some work in a coal mine at the north end of town.

McGinnity generally just pitched for the Springfield team on weekends after working all week in the mines or in the saloon although when he died many years later, umpire Joseph Warren told the *Journal* that he recalled McGinnity pitching as many as eight games a week at times.

"He would go to a picnic somewhere and hurl a game in the morning and then take the mound for nine or more innings in another game in the afternoon," Warren remembered. "He received from $3 to $10 for most games he pitched but he loved the game so well that he would go out and play for $1 rather than not play at all."[20]

In 1898, though, McGinnity began playing for a little more than that.

If Tim Donahue did, in fact, sabotage the young pitcher from the Indian Territory in Kansas City in 1894, he might have enjoyed a chuckle or two at the way he had ruined the kid's baseball aspirations. In truth, Donahue may have done Joe McGinnity the favor of a lifetime.

Had McGinnity enjoyed a bit more success in Kansas City, he might have stuck around for a few years, perhaps made it to the major leagues, possibly had a modest amount of success there. Instead, he was forced to work that much harder on every aspect of his game and develop a whole new way of pitching, leading to a career of legendary proportions.

During his few months in Kansas City, McGinnity had seen a veteran named Billy "Bunker" Rhines pitch for the Grand Rapids club. Rhines, a slender right-hander, had won 28 games as a rookie with the Cincinnati Reds in 1890 and 17 more in 1891, but his career had waned after that, so much so that he was back in the minor leagues in 1894. He threw with a peculiar, underarm motion that made the ball rise and swerve, and he had great success with it against Western League batters, earning back his job with Cincinnati the following year. McGinnity never had seen anything like it and when he was let go by the Blues, he went to work on copying Rhines' delivery and adding it to his arsenal.[21]

We'll probably never know why McGinnity chose to call his rising curve ball "Old Sal." Through all his years in baseball, no reporter appears to have ever asked the question. He may have called it that because the pitch invariably sailed as it approached the plate. We do know that during his Springfield semi-pro years, McGinnity polished and practiced the underarm motion until it became a devastating weapon.

McGinnity gripped the ball the same way any pitcher did when throwing a curve ball, but he swept his arm downward and released the ball somewhere around the knee. Sometimes as he let go of the ball, his right knee was nearly touching the ground. The underarm motion allowed him to throw one breaking pitch after another with less snap of his wrist than pitchers who threw an overhand curve, reducing the wear and tear on his arm.

"Old Sal" did not break abruptly as many modern off-speed pitches do. It was more of a sweeping curve. Some players referred to it as a "nickel rocket" because of the way it seemed to take off and rise. He not only could make it rise, but he also could make it veer right or left. Batters frequently popped it up or slapped weak dribblers to the infield trying to get on top of the pitch.

As baseball historian Robert Smith marveled many years later, "the damn pitch never came straight at you. It started near Joe's shoes, for his fingers almost scraped the ground as he completed the pitch. And it appeared to be approaching crossways and upward, looking big enough to be broken in two, but always just escaping the full weight of the bat."[22]

McGinnity attempted to explain it himself many years later in an interview with the *Decatur Review*: "You know, if you take a flat rock and throw it underhand, it will sail and curve. Well, a baseball will do the same thing if thrown just right. I have tried to teach that to lots of pitchers, but it's hard to make them get that 'just right.' If you put it up there too speedy, it's no good. If you throw it up just right, it drops across just right. The batter thinks he can hit it a mile but he can't. If he hits it, it just pops up in the air."[23]

As the years passed, McGinnity began to use the pitch more and more, only occasionally reverting to a more normal overhand or sidearm delivery. John McGraw once explained to a reporter that McGinnity sometimes would pitch the first game of a doubleheader with a normal overhand motion, then go to the under-arm delivery in the second game to save his arm. "It was as different as if two pitchers had been working," McGraw added. "With his overhand delivery he had a fine drop ball and he used to pitch it when he got in a hole. He could control that drop better than he could a fast one."[24]

But there was no question that McGinnity's best weapon, the one that eventually made him a star was "Old Sal."

He used it so frequently that Hall of Fame catcher Roger Bresnahan, who played with McGinnity in eight of his 10 major league seasons, frequently said he never even bothered to give Iron Man signs.[25] It's ironic that Donahue may have punctuated McGinnity's career by telling batters what pitches were coming. When McGinnity finally did reach the major leagues, batters very often knew exactly what was coming, but they usually were helpless to do much about it.

McGinnity also experimented with the use of the spitball,[26] a tactic that was legal in baseball until 1920. And he eventually also developed a drop pitch that he could throw with his submarine motion, but all hitters ever seemed to talk about was the way his nickel rocket seemed to leap over the top of their bats. McGraw said the pitch had "a peculiar hop on it."[27]

Pitching wasn't the only thing McGinnity worked on during his exile from organized pro leagues. He also eliminated the fielding deficiencies that plagued him in Kansas City. Many years later, Hughie Jennings, who played with and against McGinnity, called him the best fielding pitcher he ever saw. Batters who tried to conquer "Old Sal" by dropping bunts were only playing into his hands. He swallowed up everything that fell in front of him and turned them into outs.

"I have never seen a pitcher with more confidence in himself than McGinnity had," Jennings said. "He was so cocksure of his fielding ability that he would take any sort of chance, throwing to any base under any circumstance, and this fielding ability lifted him out of many tight spots."[28]

Frank Redpath, McGinnity's brother-in-law and later his business partner, said many years later that he felt Iron Man revolutionized the way the pitching position was fielded by frequently throwing to second or third base to cut down baserunners. "He was the first pitcher to take any such chances and it helped him plenty," he said.[29]

Despite all these improvements, McGinnity needed a connection to get a second chance at pro ball. He got it when Pat Wright was hired to run the Peoria team in the Western Association for 1898. Wright had been the second baseman and manager in Springfield, and he was going to play first base and manage the team in Peoria. He took McGinnity with him.

Wright began gushing about how good a team he was going to have six weeks before the 1898 season even began. He told the *Peoria Herald* on March 18 that he didn't think there was a better collection of talent anywhere outside the National League. "Manager Pat firmly believes that Peoria never had a better lot of players and that they will play winning ball from the first," the *Herald* reported.[30]

However, before the season even began, there was uncertainty. A war between the United States and Spain was about to break out in Cuba in April of 1898, and there were concerns that there wouldn't be a baseball season for anyone anywhere.

"There have been rumors on the street for the past few days that the Western Base Ball Association may disband, either before the beginning of the base ball season on the 29th or after playing a few association games," the *Herald* reported. "The *Herald* has not been able to trace this to any authentic source, although there is a disposition among the managers of the big eastern leagues to regard the war with Spain, which now seems so probable, as a 'deadener' on the baseball season."[31]

The Peoria team had other problems. Because of heavy spring rains, its field at Lake View Park, just a few blocks from where most of the players lived at the Northern Hotel, was underwater. But by April 29, the ballpark at the corner of Abingdon and Adams was in playable shape. It was moist and muddy, but usable.

Peoria started badly, going down to a 7–4 loss to Cedar Rapids with "Old Man" Roach doing the pitching, but things began to turn around in the second game when McGinnity beat Cedar Rapids, 2–1. He not only pitched well, but went 2-for-4 at the plate and drove in the first run of the game in the seventh inning. "McGinnity is the coming pitcher of the Peorias. You can put that down in your scrap book," the *Herald* predicted.[32]

As the season progressed, the prediction came true. It also became apparent that Peoria was the class of the league. It wrestled with rival Quincy for first place for a while, then took control, much to the delight of the *Herald*.

Some members of the Western Association weren't even sure they wanted Quincy in the league because the fans there were so raucous. Visiting players were verbally abused—or worse—every time they played there and it created hard feelings all over the league, especially in Peoria.

When Peoria strung together several victories over Quincy in mid–June, most of them by shutouts, it took control of the pennant race. When McGinnity blanked Quincy, 4–0, with seven strikeouts on June 18, the *Herald* chortled "Well, well. Another shutout for the Quincys."[33]

After a 12–2 win the next day, the paper took several shots at Quincy manager Pete Lohman: "The Quincys should not be discouraged. There are other clubs in the league that his lulus can beat." And: "The Americans are landing in Cuba and the Peoria batters are landing on the Quincy pitchers." And: "It will be some time before the Quincys will forget their visit to Peoria."[34]

While Peoria was beginning to dominate the league, McGinnity did just about everything for the team. In the first game of that Quincy series, the umpires failed to appear as scheduled so he took on that role for a day. Even the Quincy players and fans thought he treated them fairly.[35]

A few days later, on June 20, he started in center field, hitting third in the batting order, and finished the game at shortstop. He played shortstop again in the next two games, both victories over Ottumwa. The regular shortstop, a player named Crotty, had been struggling in the field and McGinnity filled in until a replacement could be found.

"Is there any place in the team where McGinnity cannot play ball?" the *Herald* asked. The paper said it seemed the only thing he couldn't do was play poker. His teammates always got the best of him there.[36]

But they hadn't seen his finest moment yet. On June 26, last-place St. Joseph came to Lake View Park for a Sunday afternoon game and McGinnity squared off with a promising youngster named McDonald. The game attracted only 261 paid admissions, but it would be talked about all over the country by thousands.

Peoria finally won the contest, 8–4, in 21 innings with both pitchers going the distance. For 16 straight innings, from the fifth through the 20th, neither team touched home plate.

The *Herald*'s headlines called it a "Battle Royal" and a "World's Record" and probably set some sort of record of its own. The opening sentence of its game story was 124 words long: "There have been many interesting games of base ball played on the Peoria diamond, from way back in the times when this city was raising up ball players who have achieved national reputations down to the present season, which has not been devoid of interest, consisting in such ball playing as shutting out the team that had been at the head of the association for two successive games, but never in the history of the national game, here or elsewhere, within any of the leagues or associations, has there been such a game played as was given on the diamond yesterday, in the great game that will become historical of twenty one innings, nineteen of these being played without the Peorias making a run."[37]

McGinnity actually was not as dominant as McDonald. The kid from St. Joseph struck out 14 batters, but McGinnity matched him goose egg for goose egg in an incredible display of stamina and concentration.

Peoria scored three runs in the first inning to get an early lead, but St. Joseph countered with a run in the third and two in the fourth. Then the pitchers took over. Over the next 11 innings, neither team even got a baserunner as far as third base and very few as far as second. Peoria got a man to third with two outs in the 16th, but McDonald fanned Davy Seisler to end the inning.

Finally, in the top of the 21st inning—the home team batted first—McDonald faltered. Peoria strung together five straight hits, including a two-run triple by second baseman Harry Truby, and poured across five runs. McGinnity tired a bit, too, but limited St. Joseph to a single run in the bottom of the inning and Peoria won the game.

It was believed to be the second longest game in baseball history to that point. Tacoma and Seattle had played a 22-inning marathon in the Pacific Northwestern League in 1891.[38]

Even though it went 21 innings, the game was completed in 2 hours, 50 minutes.

"No one who witnessed yesterday's ball game was heard to complain that he did not get the worth of his money," according to the *Herald*.[39]

Catcher Tom Quinn injured his hand in the eighth inning of the marathon game, which meant Jerry Connors had to move in from center field to catcher. So, a day after throwing 21 innings, McGinnity was back in center field in a game against St. Joseph.

The day after that, on June 28, the Western Association folded. The season was over. Two of the eight teams—Cedar Rapids and Burlington—had gone under earlier in the month and all the teams were struggling to make ends meet. An especially rainy spring had made for dozens of postponed games, and the specter of the Spanish-American War was still there, too. Some other leagues around the country also were calling it quits. Although the economic depression prompted by the Panic of 1893 was just about over, the war was a distraction for people. Fans weren't turning out in great numbers.

The *Herald* lamented the end of the great season with a lengthy poem that included one entire stanza about the team's star pitcher:

> McGinnity, too; we bow our knees,
> Played all positions and with ease—
> Who played the dickens with the nerves
> Of visitors with drops and curves.[40]

Wright lamented that attendance was not very good in spite of the fact that his team had lost only five times at home. "The present team is the best base ball team Peoria ever had and it is the best team I ever played with," he said.[41]

There was one more game to be played. A large group of Springfield fans had arranged to travel 75 miles up to Peoria for a June 29 game specifically to see McGinnity pitch. The team decided to go ahead and play a game against a group of former Western Association players to entertain the folks from Springfield and raise money to help pay off the players in full.

McGinnity didn't disappoint his friends from Springfield. He pitched a shutout, singled in two runs in the fourth inning and won, 8-0.

There was much speculation as to where the Peoria players would end up. Connors claimed to have four offers from teams in the Western League. Quinn was likely to go to Norfolk in the Atlantic League. Third baseman Jimmy Burke, outfielder Archie Cole and Truby were likely to get offers, too.[42]

The *Herald* reported that McGinnity was "almost sure" of getting into the Eastern League, probably with Syracuse,[43] but it never happened.

He went back to Springfield and within two weeks was back on the semi-pro scene, striking out nine batters and allowing only four hits in leading Taylorville to a 12–1 victory over Clinton.[44]

He undoubtedly was disheartened that his big opportunity to show what he could do had been abbreviated. If only he could have played the full season with Peoria, he would have won at least 20 games, probably 25. Someone somewhere surely would have taken notice.

He needn't have worried. Someone *had* noticed.

7. Robbie and Mac

Among those in attendance on that Sunday afternoon in Lake View Park, when McGinnity battled for 21 innings, was George Pinckney. A former member of the Brooklyn National League team, he now lived in Peoria and had gone out to the game just to see what the local fans were buzzing about. He liked what he saw.

He contacted his old team and recommended that owner Charles Ebbets take a look at this McGinnity guy.[1] The umpire who worked the 21-inning game, Bob Carruthers, also reportedly contacted Ebbets about McGinnity.[2]

The Brooklyn and Baltimore teams of the NL were run by the same group of people, and neither really was in desperate need of pitchers in midseason 1898, but they apparently filed the name away for future reference. When the spring of 1899 rolled around, they offered Joe McGinnity a chance to play major league baseball for $150 a month. It was only $25 more per month than he'd made in Peoria, but it was the major leagues.

In that era, multiple ownership was fairly common in the NL. A syndicate of investors owned both the Cleveland and St. Louis franchises and in 1899, they loaded all their best players—including the great Cy Young—onto the St. Louis roster and stripped the Cleveland team bare. The Spiders went 20–134 that season and had six losing streaks of 11 games or more.

Baltimore and Brooklyn had a similar situation. They were operated by a group of owners that not only included Ebbets but also Ned Hanlon and Harry Von Der Horst. Hanlon was the driving force behind the operation, so much so that Von Der Horst occasionally wore a button that said "Ask Hanlon."[3] Hanlon may have had the most unusual situation of anyone in baseball history. He was president of the Baltimore team and the manager of Brooklyn at the same time. He and Von Der Horst also planned to pile most of their best players onto the Brooklyn team, but they met some resistance. Two of the best players refused to go. They insisted upon staying with Baltimore.

Those two—a diminutive third baseman named John McGraw and a burly catcher named Wilbert Robinson—were destined to become lifelong friends of Joe McGinnity's. The trio represented a unique dynamic. Robinson was even stronger than McGinnity but was an easy-going, jovial sort. He had a calming, nurturing effect on the people around him. McGraw was extremely vocal and tightly wound. He was combative and always seemed to know exactly what to do to irk umpires, opponents, sometimes even his friends. He oozed intensity.

Before McGinnity came along, Robbie and Mac had a long-running, highly successful good cop–bad cop act. Robinson would warm to the umpires before a game, complimenting them, befriending them, while McGraw was waiting to rip them apart. A 19th century player and umpire named Arlie Latham described it very well in an item in *Sporting Life*: "Robbie and McGraw are working both ends against the middle. Robbie sleeps in a salve factory and McGraw eats gunpowder for breakfast and washes it down with warm blood."[4]

McGinnity was sort of a hybrid of the two. He was much more introverted than either of his pals, but he also could be as jovial as Robinson or as intense as McGraw.

"McGinnity was the strong-armed member of the trio," Ed Burkholder wrote in a 1954 retrospective in *Sport Magazine*. "He would wade into a group of brawling players and his strength would send them in all directions. There were times in those riotous days when it seemed that an umpire needed a punch in the nose, something McGinnity would take care of with great glee. He was a close second to McGraw when it came to needling players. When he was on the mound, an enemy baserunner was in a constant state of nerves, and his bantering with the batter in the box contributed much to his success."[5]

The three men had one thing in common—a fiery, insatiable competitive spirit on the playing field. It's not enough to say they disliked losing. They were repulsed by the concept. They barely even acknowledged it as a possibility.

McGraw and Robinson already had been in the major leagues for eight years or more when McGinnity arrived as a rookie in 1899. The two of them co-owned an establishment not far from downtown Baltimore called the Diamond Café that was heavily frequented by fans. It was quite a place, a forerunner of the modern-day sports bar. The dining room and bar had an electric scoreboard with a ticker service that provided the results of baseball games and horse races all over the country. For Orioles games it provided play-by-play updates. The establishment, housed in an old saloon at 519 N. Howard Street, also had a gymnasium, a pool hall, a bowling alley, a reading room and meeting rooms. McGraw and Robinson had sunk more than $10,000 into renovating the three-story building and were making much, much more money from it than they were from baseball.⁶ They knew if they began playing for Brooklyn, their business back in Baltimore would wither away. That's why they refused to switch teams.

Hanlon and Von Der Horst finally gave in. McGraw, at the age of 25, became the player-manager of the stripped-down Orioles.

McGinnity actually came into the organization expecting to play for Brooklyn, but Ned Hanlon took one look at the funny motion and the speed of the pitches, and decided that he didn't want McGinnity on the team he was managing. He allocated him to Baltimore instead.

Wilbert Robinson, however, immediately recognized the genius of "Old Sal." To his dying day, McGinnity said he owed his career to Robinson. After warming up McGinnity for the first time in spring training, Robinson told McGraw "That boy's got something on the ball. He's going to fool you fellows with that curve ball of his."⁷

According to one story, Robinson challenged McGraw to a game. He would take McGinnity and the Yannigans—the scrubs who warmed the bench or figured to not even make the team at all—and McGraw could take the starters. A reporter visiting the team's practice that day supposedly served as the umpire. By the seventh inning, Robinson's team had a 7–0 lead and McGraw, frustrated and embarrassed, chased off the reporter and called an end to the game. He was convinced. He had a new star pitcher.

According to Burkholder's latter-day tale, however, McGraw felt he had to take great measures to keep Hanlon from knowing what he had given up. The Orioles and Hanlon's Brooklyn Superbas—a new nickname derived from a famed vaudeville act—were to play an exhibition game against one another on April 7 in Augusta, Georgia, and McGraw put McGinnity out there to start the game. Throughout the contest, they went through an act for the benefit of Hanlon and the Superbas. McGinnity would give up a couple of hits, McGraw would stomp to the mound and chew him out, threaten to send him back to Peoria, wink slyly, then go back to his position at third base.⁸

After the game, Hanlon called McGinnity a "freak" and told McGraw how glad he was that he had let him go.⁹ In the years that followed, he frequently would regret that he had.

In the Baltimore Orioles, McGinnity was joining a franchise with a rich tradition for toughness, roughness and gamesmanship. Through the 1890s, the Orioles had popularized many of the small-ball tactics that became commonplace over the ensuing century, including the sacrifice bunt and the hit-and-run. They even devised a revolutionary bit of daring they called the squeeze play.

For much of the mid–1890s, the team had six future Hall of Famers in

When McGinnity joined the Baltimore Orioles in 1899, he was introduced to two men who would be both mentors and close friends for the remainder of his life. McGinnity is in the back row, second from the left. John McGraw is in the center of the middle row, seated higher than everyone else. To McGraw's left, with the mustache, is Wilbert Robinson (Charles W. Brown, Jr., collection).

the everyday lineup. All of them ran the bases with reckless abandon and all of them could hit the ball almost anywhere they wanted, especially 5-foot-4 rightfielder Wee Willie Keeler, whose enduring motto was "hit 'em where they ain't."

Moreover, the Orioles were a profane, lawless, incorrigible bunch that would grab any edge they could. There were hundreds of instances of them "inadvertently" stomping on the foot of an umpire or an opposing player with their spikes. If they thought the umpire wasn't looking, they were liable to trip a baserunner or grab his baggy pants or belt as he raced past.[10] McGraw was especially adept at this. A reporter once described McGraw as "a rough, unruly man who is constantly playing dirty ball. He has the vilest tongue of any ballplayer.... He adopts every low and contemptible method that his erratic brain can conceive to win a play by a dirty trick."[11] His tactics undoubtedly had a major role in the National League eventually employing two umpires instead of just one. That way, one umpire could watch the flight of the ball while the other one watched McGraw.

The old Orioles epitomized him. They took no prisoners, took nothing whatsoever from any team that crossed their path. Hanlon became the manager in 1892 and with Robinson as the catcher, McGraw at third base, Keeler in right field, sleek, athletic Joe Kelley in left field and rambunctious Hughie Jennings (another ex–coal miner) at shortstop, they terrorized the National League for half a decade. They won the NL pennant three straight years, in 1894, '95 and '96. They were second in '97 and '98, but in '97 they routed first-place Boston in the Temple Cup series that followed the regular season. They were revered by their fans, but feared and despised by almost everyone else.

But now in 1899, the team was being broken up. Hanlon was moving over to manage Brooklyn, and he was taking Kelley, Keeler and Jennings with him.

McGraw was determined that the Oriole tradition would go on without them and he knew this big pitcher from Illinois, with the weird motion and a competitive streak to match his own, would help him get there.

McGinnity made his major league debut in the third game of the season, on April 18, against the New York Giants. The *New York Tribune* noted that the Orioles appeared "over-trained and nervous" in the game, but they still won, 8–4. The victory wasn't quite as easy as that score would indicate. McGinnity allowed single runs in the first, third, sixth and seventh innings before he and his teammates busted out for all eight of their runs in the eighth. Shortstop George Magoon, Robinson and McGinnity opened the inning with singles and Giants starter Bill Carrick caved in from there, forcing in two runs with bases-loaded walks and giving up a few more hits until eight runners had crossed the plate. McGinnity, destined to bat a solid (for a pitcher) .194 in his major league career, had a pair of hits in his debut.[12]

In that season, the Orioles played their home games at Union Park (also known as Baltimore Baseball and Exhibition Grounds), a wooden structure at the corner of Barclay and 25th Streets, a little bit southeast of Johns Hopkins University. It was only 300 feet down the left-field line, but the fences were 16 feet high, and a small creek called Brady Run bubbled just beyond right-field, sometimes oozing under the fence and creating a swamp.[13]

It was just one more little edge that they had, and McGraw's teams always tried to grab every edge they could. The '99 Orioles reflected his personality as well as any team he ever managed. They stole 364 bases and hit only 17 home runs. McGraw, who batted .391, stole 73 bases himself and 20-year-old outfielder Jimmy Sheckard swiped 77. Even McGinnity stole four. He also evolved into the ace pitcher very quickly, throwing $366\frac{1}{3}$ innings and going 28–16.

Despite the fact that they were comprised largely of players the Brooklyn club didn't want, the Orioles were very competitive. They were only 11–13 on May 14, but then won 20 of their next 27 games. They were playing the sort of belligerent, take-no-prisoners baseball that McGraw loved and expected from all his teams. Even Wilbert Robinson, who hadn't been kicked out of a game in 13 major league seasons, was ejected from an April 20 game for reviling the umpires.[14]

In a mid–July game with Cincinnati, McGraw went hard into second base and jabbed shortstop Tommy Corcoran with both feet. He also hurled a few threats at Corcoran—"McGraw's vile talk could be heard all over the stands," according to the *Cincinnati Post*—and Corcoran responded by grabbing McGraw's collar and throwing a punch. The Orioles' Billy Keister tried to hold Corcoran back, but he wasn't subdued until McGinnity tackled him and pinned him to the ground with what was described as "a vise-like grip."[15]

On August 18, the Orioles engaged in a near brawl with the Chicago Orphans (later to be known as the Cubs) that was precipitated by Chicago's Tim Donahue, McGinnity's untrustworthy catcher from his Kansas City days, but further fueled by the confrontational Orioles. In the first inning of the first game of a doubleheader, Donahue felt Baltimore's Steve Brodie stepped across the plate and interfered with his ability to make a throw. While Donahue engaged in an argument with umpire Al Mannassau, Brodie stood nearby ridiculing the Chicago catcher. Donahue picked up a handful of dirt and threw it in Brodie's face, and both benches quickly emptied.[16]

Donahue was kicked out of the game and had to be shielded by police from the Baltimore crowd as he walked out of the ballpark. That set the tone for the rest of the day. McGraw and his players heaped insults on the Orphans throughout the entire doubleheader and the Orioles' fans joined in, growing more and more abusive as the day wore on.[17]

"The exhibition was simply disgraceful," the *Chicago Tribune* reported. "Foul language reached the stands every minute and went unreproved, and a howling mob threatened every minute to break into the field." After Chicago managed to win the first game, 13–12, the *Tribune* reported that a squadron of 50 policemen had to be called in to protect the visitors in the second game. Mannassau finally had enough and called the second game after the sixth inning, not because of darkness but because he feared what sort of violence might transpire if the contest continued.[18]

A day later, the *Tribune* referred to the doubleheader as "a sad commentary on the degeneracy of the national game. For five hours on Friday the Baltimore park reeking with profanity and obscenity which would drive almost any self-respecting crowd from a field, never to return. McGraw in his wild effort to win and place his team above the Brooklyn club is resorting to the worst species of abuse and ruffianism ever witnessed on a ball field."[19]

The Orioles continued to win consistently and by mid-August, they were 20 games over .500, but then the National League announced that it would reduce the number of teams for the following season. It had decided 12 teams were just too many. It was going to cut to eight clubs, and Baltimore was one of the four that would be put out of business. The news punctured the spirit of the team and ended any illusions it had of winning the pennant. The ballclub's mood was further dampened two weeks later by the news that McGraw's 22-year-old bride, Minnie, had died of a burst appendix.[20]

Hanlon's Brooklyn club finished first with the Orioles limping home fourth with an 86-62-4 record.

On the final day of the season, October 14, Brooklyn and Baltimore were scheduled to meet one another one last time, but Brooklyn ended up winning by forfeit due to an incident that epitomized the stubbornness of McGraw and his team.

Sheckard attempted to steal second base in the second inning and was called out by umpire John Hunt. Sheckard put up a fuss in the best Oriole tradition and was kicked out of the game. But he refused to leave. Hunt asked catcher Aleck Smith to help him convince Sheckard to vacate the premises. He refused. Hunt then appealed to McGraw to say something to Sheckard. *He* refused.[21]

The umpire finally turned to the opposing bench where Hanlon was serving as manager of the Brooklyn team. He asked him to act in his other role as president of the Baltimore club and do something. Hanlon told Hunt he would support him in whatever decision he made. Hunt threw up his hands and awarded the victory to Brooklyn on a forfeit.[22]

When a team forfeited a game in that era, it was forced to pay $500 to the opposing team, but since both clubs were owned by the same syndicate, that wasn't much of an issue.

The two clubs then decided to play a make-up game from an earlier postponement, just so they wouldn't need to issue refunds to the spectators. They played the requisite five innings, the Superbas won, 8–3, and the season was over.

8. Brooklyn

After the 1899 season, Joe McGinnity went back to McAlester to live, but there would be no more coal mines for him. For the first time, he began working in the iron foundry that his father-in-law, John Redpath, had opened two years earlier. He, Mary and Marguerite lived with the Redpaths at 901 E. Wyandotte in McAlester, but Joe also bought a vacant lot at the corner of Seventh and Seneca Streets.

He had begun to build himself a new career in baseball. Now he had an idea to begin building a house that was every bit as special. It would take many years to complete it, but when it finally was finished, in 1907, it would be one of the showplaces of McAlester and the surrounding area.

The house, with 10 oversized rooms on the main two floors, was made mostly of stone taken from a nearby quarry owned by the McAlester Hydraulic Stone Company. Several cement pillars around the outside also were custom-made in McAlester. The house was two full stories with an attic and just off the attic, in the northwest corner of the house was a hexagon-shaped cupola that provided a majestic view. The ceilings were 12 feet high, the name "McGinnity" was stenciled into many of the moldings around the doors and windows, and some claimed the hardwood parquet floors on the first level were made by the Hillerich company, which made Louisville Slugger baseball bats. The house included three fireplaces, 87 custom-made diamond-shaped windows, several chandeliers and a ceiling fan.[1]

When McGinnity reported for the 1900 season, it was with a new team—the Brooklyn Superbas (later to be known as the Dodgers)—and he immediately earned a nickname that would stick with him forever. Baseball lore has it that Brooklyn reporter Abe Yager asked him what he had been doing in the off-season and McGinnity delivered a legendary response. "I work in my father-in-law's iron foundry back home," he is supposed to have said. "I'm an iron man."[2] It wasn't long before it became one of the best-known nicknames in the game.

McGinnity was with a new team because his old one no longer existed. The National League had 12 teams in 1899, but the owners voted to eliminate the syndicates and condense the league to eight teams for the 1900 season. Baltimore was one of the four teams that were eliminated, along with Washington, Louisville and that awful Cleveland club.

The players on those teams were split up and Hanlon, who had passed on McGinnity a year earlier, made sure he had him on his club this time. He also hoped to get his pals, McGraw and Robinson, but those plans hit a snag.

McGraw saw the league consolidation coming and announced that he would like to establish a Baltimore team in the new American League. He went so far as to attempt to take over the Baltimore ballpark in February, but he was met there by Hanlon, who was determined to stop him.[3] When the National League consolidation was formally ratified by the owners in March, both McGraw and Robinson refused to play for Brooklyn.

They eventually were traded along with infielder Billy Keister to a St. Louis team that was only beginning to be known as the Cardinals. McGraw and Robinson also refused to report to St. Louis. They finally gave in on May 8 although McGraw only reported after negotiating a special contract for himself. He would receive $100 per game,[4] an extraordinary sum for that era.

Don't let the gentle features and boyish good looks fool you. In 1900, McGinnity set a major league record that's not likely to ever be broken, hitting 41 batters with pitches in one season (Baseball Hall of Fame Library).

Robinson would receive a slightly smaller salary—reportedly about $5,500 for the season—and it was stipulated that both men would be free agents at the end of the season, entitled to go to any team of their choosing.[5]

McGraw played 98 games with St. Louis and Robinson played 60, and they did then become part of a new Baltimore Orioles team in the American League the following year.

In the meantime, McGinnity went to Brooklyn and prospered under Hanlon. He went 29–9 that season, pitched 347 innings and plunked 41 batters, setting a major league record that's not likely to ever be broken. Throughout his career, he never was afraid to give batters a close shave. Even though he played only 10 years in the majors, he remains fourth on the all-time list in hit batsmen with 184.

Thanks to McGraw and Robinson and some cunning new teammates such as Jennings and Keeler, he was beginning to learn all the tricks of the game. And it was very much a game of trickery and guile back then. A player had to use his head and grab every edge he could. The ball was dead, the fences were very long, and there were few hitters hitting the ball over them.

The Superbas played in Washington Park, which had been built only two years earlier. It ran alongside the Bay Ridge Railroad tracks in the Red Hook section of Brooklyn, where a Consolidated Edison plant now stands. Like so many of the parks then in use, it had unusual dimensions. It was only 295 feet down the right-field line but it was a 500-foot poke to centerfield. It was impossible for anyone to hit a ball over the fence. But because the fence was up on poles, it occasionally was possible to hit a ball *under* it.[6]

Hitters used much bigger, heavier bats then, as much as 50 percent heavier than modern bats, and they did much more bunting and running. Pitchers were allowed to do anything they wanted to the ball—nick it, smudge it, wet it. The spitball wasn't outlawed until 1920, and anything a hurler wanted to do to deface a ball was legal.

Dozens of balls were not used in the course of a game, as is the case now. The only time a new ball was put into play was when the old one was hit into the stands on a foul ball and even then, the ushers sometimes tried to get the ball back from the customer who grabbed it. When a new ball was put into play, it wasn't long before it was scuffed and muddied. It was not uncommon for a pitcher to intentionally fumble the ball or miss it completely when the umpire flipped him a new one. An infielder would then pick it up and throw it around to the other infielders a few times before getting it to the pitcher. There was hardly a player then who didn't chew tobacco or licorice during the game and they frequently spit into their gloves. Sometimes the ball was dark brown before a pitcher even threw it for the first time, making it difficult to see.[7] Most games were played at 3 or 4 P.M. to allow people to get there after work and the concept of installing lights was still 30 years away.

In short, pitchers had all sorts of advantages.

McGinnity found one more edge in his use of the quick pitch, a tactic that is now illegal but then was widely used to deceive unsuspecting batters. McGinnity was considered the unmatched master of the ploy. The catcher would give him a signal, throw the ball back to him and McGinnity would immediately deliver it back to the plate without any sort of windup. If the batter wasn't paying close attention, he was liable to find the ball was already back in the catcher's glove with an extra strike added to the count.[8]

McGinnity started quickly in 1900. On April 21, he beat the New York Giants and his old Fort Smith adversary, Pink Hawley, 5–2, and he strung together an 11-game winning streak that lasted until Chicago beat him on July 1.

On July 17, he pitched against the Giants in a game in which a tall, handsome, 19-year-old rookie straight out of Bucknell College made his major league debut. The Superbas had battled back to tie the score at 5–5 and had two runners on in the fifth inning when Giants manager George Davis brought in a kid named Christy Mathewson, who already had won 20 games that season for Norfolk. Mathewson didn't have quite the same success against the Superbas. He hit three batters and ended up allowing six runs in a 13–7 loss that was charged to starting pitcher Ed Doheny.

McGinnity pitched 32 complete games that season and had three games in which he pitched more than just nine innings, all against Boston. On May 1, he won, 3–2, in 10 innings; on June 18, he won, 6–3, in 11; and on October 1, he lost, 4–3, in 11.

The Superbas held onto first place for most of the season and the rest of the league never had a chance down the stretch. In a bizarre bit of scheduling, they played 35 of 37 games at home from August 27 through October 1, including 26 in a row. The only two road games they played in that stretch were just across town in the Polo Grounds.

McGinnity crossed paths with his old buddies, McGraw and Robinson, during that extended homestand. In a September 19 game at Washington Park, Robinson became uncharacteristically enraged at John Gaffney, the same umpire who had kicked him out of a game the year before. He threw a ball at Gaffney's legs and hit him in the chest before being ejected again. When McGraw stubbornly refused to put a new catcher into the game, the contest was awarded to Brooklyn on a forfeit.[9]

As the season progressed, it became clear that McGinnity was the undisputed ace of the Brooklyn staff. Hanlon began to lose confidence in his other pitchers—Kitty Kitson, Brickyard Kennedy, Jack Dunn and Harry Howell—and in September Hanlon began trotting out McGinnity almost every day. During one 11-day stretch from September 5–15, he appeared in eight games, throwing 40 innings. During another eight-game stretch against Pittsburgh late in the season, McGinnity was used six times.

In the midst of one of those stretches, he came on in relief to finish both games of an historic doubleheader against Cincinnati on September 12. The Reds committed 17 errors that day, which is still a major league record.

Brooklyn ended up winning the pennant by 4½ games over Pittsburgh, but Pirates owner Barney Dreyfuss just couldn't imagine that he didn't have the better team. The *Pittsburgh Chronicle-Telegraph* didn't believe it either and proposed a best-of-five playoff series between the Superbas and the Pirates to decide the issue. The newspaper even commissioned a special trophy for the series—an 18-pound silver punch bowl, reportedly made at a cost of $500.[10] The winning team would receive the bowl and the players on both teams would receive a share of the gate receipts. The Superbas gladly accepted the challenge.

Pittsburgh had a formidable team that included Honus Wagner, arguably the best shortstop to ever play the game. Player-manager Fred Clarke, McGinnity's old teammate from back in Montgomery, was one of the premier outfielders of the era, and he had five excellent pitchers in Deacon Phillippe, Sam Leever, Jess Tannehill and a pair of future Hall of Famers—fireballing Rube Waddell and crafty Jack Chesbro, who four years later would set a major league record with 41 wins. A majority of those players had been with Louisville the previous year, but they transferred to Pittsburgh when the league cut back from 12 teams to eight.

McGinnity undoubtedly had great respect for many of the Pittsburgh players, but there is evidence that he didn't have a very high regard for Wagner, almost certainly the best player in the National League at that time. There should have been a natural kinship between the two men. Both were the sons of immigrant parents (McGinnity's from Ireland, Wagner's from Germany). Both grew up working in the coal mines. Both sometimes were underestimated by opponents based on their appearances. And both of them played the game with the same tough, no-holds-barred approach, earning the grudging respect of their peers.

But there is some question about how much they respected one another. Many years later, in 1919, McGinnity told a *Decatur Review* reporter he thought Pirates third baseman Tommy Leach was a better clutch hitter than the legendary Flying Dutchman.[11]

"Honus Wagner led the National League in batting, but I believe figures will show he didn't hit over .200 against me," McGinnity said. "One day we were playing Pittsburgh and we were one run ahead. I was pitching and there was a Pirate on second and third with one out and Leach at bat. Wagner was next up and he was sitting on his bat, out at one side, roasting me. I considered Leach a harder hitter in a pinch than Wagner, so I passed Leach purposely. Then Honus walked up, kidding me and asking me to just give him a chance at the ball once. I said 'Get up there and I'll make you hit one right back at me.' And sure enough, he did. He hit the first ball right into my hands and we doubled up on them, retired the side and won the game. From that day on, it seemed I had it on Wagner when he came to bat."[12]

Those sorts of acrimonious feelings gave an added edge to the post-season series that began on October 15 at Pittsburgh's Exposition Park. In fact, all the games were scheduled to be played in Pittsburgh and the Pirates were brimming with confidence. Behind home plate, they had whitewashed on the grass "Champions of the World." Down one of the foul lines was a large sign that said "The Cup Will Stay in Pittsburg Sure." There were billboards and signs on trolley cars all over town imploring the Pirates to put Brooklyn in its place.[13]

The series opened on a Monday and the trophy presentation was scheduled for Saturday night at the Alvin Theatre, at which time Pittsburgh mayor William Diehl hopefully would hand the trophy to Clarke, Wagner and friends.[14]

The Brooklyn players were just as confident and they arrived in town with a chip on their shoulders. They felt their clinching of the regular-season championship had not been greeted with the proper amount of fanfare, perhaps because so much emphasis was being placed on this post-season series. "It was the tamest ending I ever saw," Joe Kelley told the *Chicago Daily News*.[15]

McGinnity started the opening game and was in control the whole way. The Superbas scored three runs off Waddell in the third inning and built a 5–0 lead. The *Chicago Tribune* reported that McGinnity "had his opponents completely at his mercy up to the ninth inning, allowing only three dinky hits up to that time."[16]

McGinnity was on base in the eighth inning when he was trapped in a rundown between third and home. Waddell ran him down, tagged him out as he lay on the ground and then drove his knee into the side of McGinnity's head. Iron Man lay motionless on the ground for several minutes, but finally got to his feet and came back out to pitch the ninth. The Pirates scored a pair of runs on a hit batsman, a walk and two hits, but McGinnity gathered himself and got Bones Ely to ground out to shortstop to end the game, preserving a 5–2 win.

The loss seemed to deflate the Pittsburgh fans. Only about 1,800 of them turned out in cooler, blustery conditions for Game 2. But the Pirates remained confident. Clarke told the *Chicago Daily News* before the game that the series was far from over.

"Every time Brooklyn has visited Exposition Park this year it has won at the start, but Pittsburg had made a strong finish each time, and I expect to see it do so in this series," he said. "I don't know why it is, but it seems to take us a game or two to strike our stride in bouts with the champions, but when we do get started we are hard to drop. Remember the last pennant series the champs played here? At the start we looked like dubs, but we wound up by giving McGinnity his medicine and I want to confess right here that any team has to play ball every minute to get ahead of that man."[17]

The Pirates also had problems with Kitty Kitson. They scored only two runs off him in Game 2 and committed six errors (four of them by third baseman Jimmy Williams) in a 4–2 loss.

Players from other teams around the league, including John McGraw, came to Pittsburgh to catch a glimpse of the series, and the *Chicago Daily News* reported openly on wagers being placed on the games by players and family members. Joe Kelley's brother-in-law, John Mahon, won $400 as result of the Superbas' victory in Game 2. Chicago Orphans pitcher Nixey Callahan won $200 betting on Brooklyn. Chicago catcher Tim Donahue, McGinnity's unscrupulous teammate from back at Kansas City, was notorious for his gambling ways and he also won money. However, he was unable to collect because the neutral party assigned to hold the cash apparently ran off with it.[18]

If any of those players bet on a Brooklyn sweep, they were disappointed. The Pirates bounced back, just as Clarke predicted they would, and hammered Harry Howell and the Superbas, 10–0, in Game 3. According to some reports, McGinnity lost $100 betting on that game.[19]

However, he was pitching Game 4 himself. Jesse Tannehill was scheduled to oppose him, but he was replaced at the last minute by Sam Leever, the tough-luck loser in Game 2. After the Superbas scored three runs with the help of a Leever error in the fourth inning to open a 4–0 lead, Clarke switched to Waddell. It made little difference.

McGinnity with the giant silver cup presented to him by teammates following a 1900 post-season conquest of Pittsburgh (Charles W. Brown, Jr., collection).

"After that, the locals seemed to lose their snap and while they played hard to win, it was conceded by the spectators that the home team was outclassed," the *Chicago Tribune* reported.[20]

McGinnity scattered eight hits, gave up just a single run in the sixth inning, and Brooklyn had a 6–1 victory and another title. For his efforts, McGinnity not only received his share of the gate receipts, which ranged anywhere from $100 to $400, according to published reports, but he also was given a $100 bonus by the Superbas[21] and he received one very special souvenir from his grateful teammates.

They had planned to draw straws to see which of them received possession of the big silver punch bowl, but they decided that one player deserved it more than anyone else. They had it engraved "Presented to J.J. McGinnity by the following players" and then had their names listed. They then gave it to him.[22]

McGinnity kept the cup for 20 years and brought it out to display on special occasions. It was perhaps his proudest possession. In the 1920s, he gave it to the Fellowship Club of the A.E. Staley Company of Decatur,[23] which donated it to the Baseball Hall of Fame in 1965.

9. A Whole New League

Legend has it that John McGraw and Wilbert Robinson were so eager to get out of St. Louis that they caught the first train back to Baltimore after the final game of the 1900 season. As the train rumbled over the Mississippi River, they peeled off their Cardinal jerseys and tossed them into the water.[1]

McGraw knew exactly what he wanted to do now and since he was a free agent, he was completely free to do it.

Ban Johnson already had been working to convert the old Western League into the new American League, adding franchises along the East Coast and launching it as a second major entity—equal to the 25-year-old National League—for the 1901 season. He wanted to place a team in Baltimore and he knew he had an eager accomplice in McGraw. The two men did not especially like one another and they would become bitter enemies in the years to come but for now, they had a common goal—a new Baltimore Orioles franchise.

McGraw was given stock in the team, was named the manager, brought Robinson along as his first lieutenant and began stockpiling talent. One of the first things he did was recruit a crafty starting pitcher with a rubber arm and a kindred spirit.

After the glorious ending of the previous season, Brooklyn offered McGinnity a salary of $5,000 for 1901 and Ned Hanlon was shocked by Iron Man's reaction. McGinnity turned it down and gave indications that he may be done playing professional baseball. Although he'd had a great season, he didn't enjoy it as much as he had the previous season with McGraw and Robinson. The iron foundry was doing well. Maybe he'd spend the rest of his life back in McAlester doing that.

"I had fully made up my mind to retire from base ball and devote myself to my business, which had been flourishing right along," he explained in an interview a few years later. "But then came the declaration of war between the National and American Leagues, the sudden inflation of salaries and temptations that no man with an eye to finances could resist."[2]

He heard from McGraw in February and agreed to meet him in St. Louis. McGraw told him exactly what he had in mind. He and Robinson were jumping to the new American League and they wanted him to come along. McGinnity signed a contract right there in Union Station in St. Louis, bending over, placing the paper on his knee and scribbling his name. But it wasn't for some hugely inflated salary. In fact, he signed for $2,800 a season, little more than half what Hanlon offered him.[3] He was leaving the only established major league and a team on which he had become a major hero to enter an uncertain new league for much less money. Such was the pull of McGraw.

As famed sportswriter Heywood Broun wrote more than 20 years later, McGraw's leadership qualities were such that he could "take kids out of the coal mines and out of the wheat fields and make them walk and talk and chatter and play ball with the look of eagles."[4] Whatever it was about McGraw that made him successful, Joe McGinnity was drawn to it. He would never again play for another manager at the major league level.

He undoubtedly also was eager to get back onto the same team with Robinson, with whom he felt more at ease than with any other catcher he'd ever thrown to.

"He knew how to get the best out of a pitcher and could keep a hurler from blowing up no matter how trying the situation," McGinnity said many years later. "Besides that, he was familiar with many twirling tricks which I never knew existed before he spilled them to me."[5]

The 1901 season not only reunited McGinnity with McGraw and Robinson but for the first time he became a teammate of another fiery competitor who would become a close friend and ally behind the plate. McGinnity also would never again play for a major league team that did not include Roger Bresnahan.

Bresnahan was not yet a full-time catcher, but he was destined to revolutionize the position. He was a pitcher and outfielder then. At 5-foot-9 and more than 200 pounds, he was fast enough to be used as a leadoff man and skilled enough to play almost any position.

At one point in 1901, Bresnahan was warming up on the sidelines, and one of the Orioles' reserve catchers was having a hard time handling his pitches. He complained to McGraw that he needed to find some better catchers. McGraw, who had earned the nickname "Muggsy" because of his feistiness, snarled right back at Bresnahan and told him if he thought he could do better, he should get down and try.[6] Bresnahan was in the starting lineup behind the plate that day, caught a complete game victory by McGinnity and the rest was history. He became one of the greatest catchers in the history of the game. In the coming years, he would invent shinguards and develop other innovations to better protect catchers from stray pitches.

McGraw also signed a solid infielder named Billy "Wagon Tongue" Keister, who had been with him in Baltimore and St. Louis, and a multi-talented, but wildly rambunctious, young outfielder named Mike Donlin. New York Giants outfielder Cy Seymour and Pittsburgh second baseman Jimmy Williams also were persuaded to jump to the new league. McGraw even stole pitchers Harry Howell and Jerry Nops off Hanlon's Brooklyn squad.

He also tried to make use of the superior infield skills of a player named Charley Grant who was working as a bellhop at the Eastland Hotel in Hot Springs, Arkansas, where the Orioles were going through spring training. Grant was black and forbidden from playing in the major leagues by baseball's "gentleman's agreement," but McGraw planned to call him Chief Tokahoma and pass him off as a native American. When he learned Grant had played in Chicago for a Negro League team the year before and might be recognized by someone there, he abandoned the idea.[7]

McGinnity also convinced McGraw to give a chance to one of his baseball-playing pals from back in the Indian Territory. Amzie Beal Snodgrass, known to almost everyone as "Chappie," was blazing fast, speedier than almost anyone anywhere in baseball.[8] Unfortunately, his other skills weren't quite up to major league standards. He played just three games in the outfield for the Orioles in 1901, managing one single in 10 at-bats.

Baltimore had built a new wooden stadium for 1901—Oriole Park—just three or four blocks north of the old one, and it christened it on April 26 against the Boston Americans. McGinnity struck out nine batters, Donlin ripped a pair of triples, and the Orioles claimed a 10–6 win. Three days later, McGinnity also was the starting pitcher in the first American League game played in Washington D.C., going down to a 5–2 loss to a Senators team managed by his old boss from the Kansas City days, Jimmie Manning.

It was a zany debut season for the new league. Things happened that didn't happen in any other league anywhere anytime. In a game in Philadelphia in July, McGraw was running toward first base to try to beat out a slow roller when a collie bolted out of the Athletics' dugout and chased him down the baseline, nipping at his heels. The dog belonged to first baseman Harry Davis and when it saw McGraw running toward his master, he interpreted it as a threat.[9]

A few weeks earlier, the Orioles had strung together 11 straight wins, but were denied an opportunity to make it 12 when the visiting Boston Americans showed up in the wrong town for a game. They were supposed to be playing the Orioles in Baltimore but traveled to Philadelphia instead. McGraw quite rightfully insisted his team should be awarded a victory by forfeit, but Ban Johnson refused.[10]

However, Johnson did allow a forfeit to stand *against* the Orioles as a result of a May 31 game in Detroit. Baltimore had a 5–4 lead in the ninth inning when Detroit's Ducky Holmes hit a deep drive into the right centerfield gap. He tried to stretch it into an inside-the-park home run, and umpire Jack Sheridan called him safe, ruling that Robinson tagged Holmes after he touched the plate. In the ensuing argument, McGraw and Howell were kicked out of the game. Donlin picked up a bat and flung it in Sheridan's direction. The umpire called for the game to resume, the Orioles refused and he declared Detroit the winner.[11]

McGraw and Johnson already were having trouble getting along. In midseason, Johnson accused McGraw of trying to conspire with two other teams in the new league to jump back to the old NL. He referred to McGraw as a "Benedict Arnold." McGraw called Johnson a liar.[12]

In order to attract players into his new league, Johnson had announced a rule that no player ever would be suspended for more than 10 days. However, Johnson also was a big believer in discipline. He felt that was what was missing in the raucous old National League. He felt players and managers (and even owners) showed too little respect for umpires in the NL and he was determined that things would be different in his AL.

Needless to say, that caused friction between him and McGraw, who constantly baited umpires and unabashedly encouraged his players to do the same. Johnson quickly found he wasn't going to be able to adhere to his 10-day maximum on suspensions with the Orioles or any other team.

When Baltimore first baseman Burt Hart punched out umpire John Haskell in an August 5 game, Hart was suspended indefinitely and never played another game in the major leagues. When Chicago shortstop Frank Shugart also assaulted Haskell little more than two weeks later, he too was banished for life.[13]

Despite all the turmoil, the Orioles managed to mount a late-season run. They closed to within 3½ games of the first-place White Sox with a 4–3 victory over Detroit on August 19. But the next day McGraw tore cartilage in his knee and was done for the season. And the day after that, McGinnity was involved in an altercation that very nearly put him in the same situation as Hart and Shugart.

During the earliest days of his career, McGinnity was frequently described as a "gentleman" in newspaper articles, but a few months with John McCloskey and a few years with McGraw and the renegade remnants of the old Orioles undoubtedly influenced him. By 1901, he shared their disdain for umpires and saw that it was possible to intimidate them. And like McCloskey and McGraw, he occasionally took it too far.

On August 21, 1901, Baltimore was again playing Detroit at Oriole Park and diminutive, British-born Tommy Connolly was serving as the umpire. The Orioles already disliked the 5-foot-7, 135-pound Connolly for calls he had made against them in previous weeks and when he called Jack Dunn out on a close play at first base in the fourth inning, McGinnity's Irish temper came uncorked. He stalked over from the first-base coaching box, stomped on Connolly's feet and shot streams of tobacco juice into the umpire's face.[14]

Detroit shortstop Kid Elberfield, who was even smaller than Connolly, dashed over to intervene but was tackled by Donlin, who began swinging at every opposing player he could find. Players on both sides clashed, spectators flooded onto the field and a few police officers battled to gain control of the situation. They finally managed to do so, took Elberfield into custody and began to walk him off the field.[15]

The Orioles didn't want that to happen either. Ballplayers felt then, as they do now, that any battles that take place on the field should stay on the field, without outside intervention. McGinnity and Keister both vigorously tried to keep the police from arresting Elberfield and ended up being arrested themselves. McGinnity, Keister, Elberfield and one fan that had jumped into the middle of the fracas all were hauled in front of a judge.[16]

It was their lucky day. The judge was Harry Goldman, who was a stockholder in the Orioles and in his spare time, the team secretary. He immediately released Elberfield, McGinnity and Keister. The fan was fined $20.[17]

In the midst of the chaos, Connolly had awarded the victory to Detroit on a forfeit.

But the incident wasn't over, not as far as Ban Johnson was concerned. He announced that McGinnity was permanently suspended from the league.

When the Orioles headed west for a road trip about a week later, McGinnity and McGraw, who was hobbling on crutches, stopped off in Chicago for a face-to-face meeting with Johnson. Both of them were unusually humble, and they carried with them a letter of testimony from Judge Goldman. McGinnity promised to apologize to Connolly, McGraw conceded that he sometimes overreacted, and Johnson backed off. He reduced McGinnity's suspension to 12 games.[18]

But it was too late to save the Orioles. With Wilbert Robinson filling in as manager, they were swept by first-place Chicago and went 2–12 on their road trip. They fell to 58–58 and toppled into fifth place.

McGinnity came back fresh after a dozen games on the sidelines and started 12 games in the month of September. On his first day back, September 3, he pitched both ends of a doubleheader for the first time in his major league career, shutting out the Milwaukee Brewers in the first game but losing the nightcap, 6–1. Nine days later, he did it again. He defeated Philadelphia in the first half of a twin bill, then took a tough 5–4 loss in the second game.

The Orioles finished fifth, 12½ games out of first place, but it was hardly McGinnity's fault. He went 26–20 and led the new league in games pitched (48), complete games (39), and innings pitched (382). He also set a modern-day record by allowing 412 hits.

10. Back to the NL

John McGraw and Ban Johnson never liked one another much, and their feud escalated even more in 1902. Johnson was more determined than ever to have his American League be free of the open rancor and umpire abuse that had become so prevalent in the National League. And McGraw was equally stubborn in his quest to continue showing disrespect for the men in blue.

He was ejected from the Orioles' season-opening game with Boston and was kicked out of another game less than a week later, drawing a five-game suspension from Johnson.[1] In late May, he was severely spiked by a Detroit baserunner and sidelined for several weeks although he managed to beat up the offending player before being carried off the field.[2]

During another game with Boston on June 28, McGraw and some of his players launched a wholesale attack on McGinnity's old foe, Tommy Connolly. Not only were McGraw and Joe Kelley ejected from the game, but Connolly was so beleaguered that he declared the game a forfeit in Boston's favor. This time, Johnson suspended McGraw indefinitely and accused him of intentionally trying to disrupt and discredit the AL.[3]

McGraw had been hearing rumblings that the troubled Baltimore franchise would be moved to New York for the following season with new owners and new management. He and the other Oriole stockholders would be left out in the cold. McGraw had dipped into his own pocket to help the club meet its payroll, reportedly shelling out as much as $7,000. He saw Johnson's force-out scheme coming and moved to defuse it. He started by telling the other stockholders in a meeting that he wanted to immediately be reimbursed for his $7,000 or released. They stalled, telling him to be patient.[4]

The solution to his problem appeared in the form of Andrew Freedman, the controversial owner of the New York Giants. Freedman was at war with the other National League owners. In fact, he was at war with almost everyone. He had publicly criticized his players, his managers, his fellow owners, umpires, almost everyone who had any connection to his floundering franchise. When the New York newspapers criticized *him*, their reporters were barred from the Polo Grounds.[5] His franchise needed help and he saw the volatile but ingenious McGraw as a potential savior. He invited him to New York and offered him an opportunity to take over complete management of the Giants. He even offered him control of the concessions. McGraw declined that, but he jumped at the baseball job.

He now had the escape hatch he needed, giving him leverage in his negotiations with his fellow stockholders. He returned to Baltimore and again demanded immediate payment in full of the money that was owed him. The stockholders didn't have it. They gave him his release instead.[6]

Little did they know that McGraw already had signed a contract with Freedman that would pay him $11,000 to play for and manage the Giants for the rest of the season. And little did they know that there was even more to McGraw's scheme. McGraw publicly announced "I shall not tamper with any of the Baltimore club's players."[7] But eight days later, it was announced that a man named Joseph France had plopped down $50,000 to buy 201 of the 400 shares of stock in the Orioles. France, in fact, was acting as an agent for Freedman.

Freedman, now in control of the Baltimore team, gave outright releases to most of the Orioles' best players, including McGinnity, Bresnahan, Kelley, Cy Seymour, first baseman Dan McGann and pitcher Jack Cronin.[8] Mike Donlin, another McGraw favorite, had been released at the start of the season for punching out a showgirl and her boyfriend.

McGinnity, Bresnahan, Cronin and McGann immediately signed with the Giants. They signed contracts that were hastily scrawled out longhand on stationery from the Stafford Hotel in Baltimore. McGinnity's contract, dated July 16, was brief and to the point:

> I agree to play Base Ball for the New York Base Ball club the balance season 1902 for the sum of two thousand dollars, $2,000. I also agree to sign for season 1903 for four thousand dollars, $4,000. Salary above mentioned to be paid in semi monthly installments. I further agree to live up to all club rules ... etc. Joe McGinnity.[9]

Donlin, Kelley and Seymour signed with the Cincinnati Reds and owner John T. Brush, an Indianapolis clothing store magnate who also was a minority stockholder in the Giants and who also had been part of a secret meeting with McGraw. The final piece of the puzzle fell into place in September when Brush sold the Reds for $150,000 to an ownership group headed by Max and Julius Fleischmann, who had made millions in the yeast business. Brush then bought the Giants from Freedman for $200,000, allegedly getting the remaining $50,000 from fellow National League owners who were eager to get the capricious Freedman out of the league.[10]

Ban Johnson was outraged, but he had one more little maneuver of his own. The wholesale release of talent left the Orioles, now under Robinson's management, without enough players to even field a team. They had to forfeit a July 17 game, and Johnson exercised a clause in the league's bylaws, seizing control of the franchise from the befuddled Freedman. By late August, Johnson announced that the franchise would move to New York in 1903 and become the New York Highlanders.[11] Many years later, they would be renamed the Yankees.

At the end of all the mid-season maneuvering, McGraw was in command of the Giants, and he already had begun to surround himself with his kind of players. He was an instant hero in New York. The fans and newspapers loudly applauded Freedman's ploy although it didn't take long for Freedman to become a little outraged himself.

McGraw took one look at the talent that had been assembled by Freedman, general manager Horace Fogel (a former Philadelphia sportswriter) and interim manager George "Heinie" Smith, and turned up his nose. He immediately released nine of the 23 players on the roster. Freedman screamed that those players had cost him $14,000. McGraw shrugged and sternly reminded him that he was running the team now.[12] The moves proved to be prudent. By 1904, only two of those released players were still in the major leagues.

He continued to make more changes. In one of the most colossal miscalculations in baseball history, Fogel and Smith had been trying to make a first baseman out of Christy Mathewson, who had pitched 39 consecutive scoreless innings and been a 20-game winner for a 52–85 Giants team the previous year. They had even used the former Bucknell College football and baseball star in the outfield in a few games and were considering moving him to shortstop.[13]

McGraw immediately recognized that he had in his possession a pitcher even more gifted than McGinnity. Mathewson's days as a position player were over.

It was the beginning of arguably the greatest Mutt-and-Jeff pitching tandem the sport has ever known. Mathewson and McGinnity couldn't have been more different as people or as pitchers, but they were a devastating combination. Only twice has a major-league team had two 30-game winners in one season and both times it was Mathewson and McGinnity. They did it in 1903, then repeated the feat in 1904.

Through the years, Mathewson was to be romanticized into virtual sainthood by writers such as Ring Lardner. Born and raised a Baptist, he became a Presbyterian as part of a marital agreement with his wife Jane (she had to become a Republican)[14] and he refused to pitch on Sundays during the first 16 years of his major league career, as part of a promise to his mother.[15] Among the Mathewson artifacts now on display at the Baseball Hall of Fame is his personal bible. But he most assuredly was no saint. He drank a little, smoked a lot, swore occasionally and gambled frequently.[16] He was ejected from several games during his career and during one on-field dispute in 1905, he punched out a boy who was selling lemonade in front of the Giants' bench.[17]

In his first couple of seasons with the Giants, Mathewson was viewed as a misfit. One of those nine players that McGraw immediately released was on record as calling him a "pinhead."[18] As one of the few college-educated players of the era, he did not fit in very well with the profane, drunken, often illiterate roughnecks who then populated the sport. He had been a member of a fraternity and the glee club at Bucknell, the president of the junior class, and prior to the 1903 season he was to marry a Pennsylvania socialite named Jane Stoughton. To players who had grown up as miners and farmers, he must have seemed conceited and haughty, and he kept almost all of them at arm's length. There were even reports that some teammates intentionally misplayed balls and failed to hustle when he was pitching.[19]

All of that ended the day John McGraw walked into the Giants' clubhouse. He immediately recognized the shirkers and banished them, and he befriended the 21-year-old Mathewson, empowering him and giving him the confidence he needed to become one of the all-time greats.

Mathewson, at McGraw's urging, studied McGinnity's every move. While he never tried to throw under-arm, Mathewson patterned many of the other things he did after Iron Man. McGraw and others later gave McGinnity credit for helping the youngster learn how to field the pitching position and also for helping him learn how to throw a sinker.[20] Mathewson learned how to watch hitters and remember what worked and didn't work against them. He learned how to pace himself and make sure he had something left for the tight spots.[21] Whatever rough edges he had were quickly smoothed away by his day-to-day contact with the Iron Man.

McGinnity also learned from Mathewson. For years, he had had trouble maintaining his composure in adverse situations, especially if one of his fielders made an error. Mathewson had a natural grace and aplomb that undoubtedly rubbed off on McGinnity and made him even better than he already was.[22]

The new McGraw-led Giants made their debut on July 19 with a 5–3 loss to the Phillies in front of a crowd of about 10,000. McGinnity pitched reasonably well but as sometimes happened, he had one bad inning. The Phillies got all their runs in the third.

The team performed a little better under McGraw than it had under Fogel and Smith. The Giants were 23–52, 33 games out of first place, when

McGinnity managed to win 21 games in 1902, despite splitting the season between the last-place teams in the American and National Leagues (Baseball Hall of Fame Library).

he took over. They went 25–38 after that, but still finished a whopping 53 games behind Pittsburgh. The fans saw a difference, though. Attendance soared.

McGinnity was a different pitcher in New York than he had been in the first half of the season in Baltimore although his won-loss record didn't reflect it. He went 13–10 with a 3.44 earned-run average in Baltimore, With the Giants, he was 8–8 with his ERA dipping to 2.06. His only shutout of the season came in a Giants uniform, on September 27 against his old pals from Brooklyn.

Despite the calming influence of young Mathewson, he still had moments when that old Irish fury bubbled to the surface. In an August 29 loss to the Phillies, he became enraged at the ball and strike calls of home plate umpire Arthur Irwin in the second inning. He stood near the mound and fumed for several minutes. Irwin ordered him to pitch. McGinnity refused. His teammates told him to continue to pitch. McGinnity just stood there, scowling, muttering and grinding the ball into his hip. About 10 minutes passed with nothing happening.[23]

"After a good deal of urging on the part of his clubmates, McGinnity went back into the box and finished the game," the *New York Times* reported.[24]

Despite his occasional struggles, McGinnity still won 21 games that season and made a bit of history in the process. Only 10 pitchers ever have won 20 games for a last-place team. With the Orioles finishing last in the AL and the Giants bringing up the rear in the NL, he became the only 20-game winner who ever split the season between *two* last-place teams.

It would be the last time in a long time that he would play for a loser. He and the Giants were on their way up the baseball ladder.

11. Arm of Iron

In his first four seasons in the major leagues, Joe McGinnity had won 103 games, and yet he was not necessarily regarded as one of the game's brightest stars, perhaps because he had performed for four different teams. In his fifth season, he was going to do things no one could ignore.

Christy Mathewson, with his dashing good looks, incredible intellect, advanced education and impeccable moral fiber, was a white collar hero in New York and certainly John McGraw's favorite. But many of the fans were working class stiffs, and they adored their rough-hewn "McGinty." He had flaws. He wasn't as handsome, as smooth, as educated or as even-tempered as Mathewson. He wasn't as gifted physically. But he worked at the game as no one else did. And he won. The center-field bleachers at the Polo Grounds filled with so many Irish immigrants every day that the area came to be known as Burkville,[1] and those fans most assuredly identified with the burly blue-collar hurler with the unmistakable motion and the explosive temper.

In 1903, they were going to become even more enamored with him.

In the second game of the season, McGinnity had one of the best games of his career, throwing a one-hitter against Brooklyn. It wasn't a shutout. The lone hit was a fourth-inning single by Jack Doyle that drove in Jimmy Sheckard, but the Giants won, 6–1, and it was the lowest hit total McGinnity ever allowed in a complete game. He never pitched a no-hitter in the major leagues, perhaps not at any level for any team, and that was his only one-hitter in the majors.

The Giants were a much-improved team. McGraw had made several off-season moves to get more of the sort of tough, aggressive players he loved. He convinced several more players to jump from the American League back to the National League, and three of them—second baseman Billy Gilbert, catcher John Warner and outfielder Sammy Mertes—became starters for him. And now that he was back in the National League, away from the domineering Ban Johnson, he and his players were free to badger umpires and get under the skin of opposing teams as much as they wanted.

On May 7, McGinnity was ejected in the eighth inning of an 8–4 win over the Phillies even though he wasn't playing. Umpire Augie Moran simply objected to his critique.[2]

On May 16, the Giants and Pirates engaged in a particularly contentious battle at the Polo Grounds. Pittsburgh manager Fred Clarke interfered with catcher Frank Bowerman on the basepaths, and McGinnity was decked by shortstop Honus Wagner as he attempted to advance from second to third. Meanwhile, McGinnity and Bowerman were relentless in their needling of Pirates pitcher Ed Doheny. When Doheny hit a pop-up in front of the plate, he hurled his bat at Bowerman to keep him from catching it, then bowed demonstratively to the simmering fans.[3]

Mathewson even got into the act a few weeks later, being ejected from a June 3 game with Pittsburgh for his persistent harassment of umpire James Johnstone.[4]

The ugliness between the Giants and Pirates continued to build and on June 26 at the Polo Grounds, Bowerman got back at Clarke. With the help of McGinnity and Bresnahan, the burly Bowerman enticed the Pirates manager into a vacant ticket booth before the game and pummeled him.[5]

The tension between the teams was great for business. The next day's game attracted a record crowd of 32,240. The Giants, who didn't want to turn away any paying customers, allowed 3,000 people to stand 10-deep in fair territory in front of the right-field fence.[6] The fans went home disappointed when the Pirates, led by Honus Wagner, peppered McGinnity with 15 hits in an 11-inning, 4–2 victory over the Giants. The Pirates got at least one hit in every inning and third baseman Tommy Leach doubled in Wagner and Clarke with the winning runs in the final inning.

As good as the Giants were, they still weren't quite a match for Pittsburgh. They lost 11 times in a 13-game stretch in late July, and the Pirates extended their league lead to 9½ games. That led McGraw to do some desperate things in an effort to catch up and in turn, led to McGinnity's greatest claim to fame.

When the Giants played at Boston in a doubleheader on August 1, McGinnity asked McGraw if he could pitch both games. Actually, according to many news reports, McGinnity "insisted" upon doing so.[7] He had pitched both ends of a doubleheader before. McGraw let him do it twice with Baltimore in 1901 and Iron Man gained a split both times. In his mind, there was nothing extraordinary about pitching two games in one day.

"There never was any great trick in it," he explained many years later. "I was pitching those games with my head, more than with my arm. An arm may not be able to go 18 innings in a day unaided, but it's different with the brain. A slow ball and a few good curves—that was all I had. But I guess it was enough ... I always studied my batters and it wasn't long before I knew what they could and couldn't hit. After that, it was sort of easy."[8]

He certainly made it look easy on August 1, tossing a pair of six-hitters. The Giants took advantage of the wildness of the Braves' Togie Pittinger to score four runs early in the first game. McGinnity gave up one run in the sixth, but that was all. The Giants also jumped on top early in the second game, but the Braves tied it at 2–2 in the fifth. The Giants came back to get three in the top of the sixth to claim a 5–2 victory.

McGinnity walked just one batter in each game and "his work was a revelation to the large crowd," according to the *New York Times*.[9]

But he was just getting started.

A week later, on August 8, he did it again, this time in front of a home crowd of 31,647 at the Polo Grounds. The *New York Times* said that "never since the first baseball game was played on the Polo Grounds was there a larger or more enthusiastic gathering of local rooters on hand than that which crowded every inch of vantage ground within the big inclosure yesterday."[10]

The Giants were playing their old friends from Brooklyn, still managed by Ned Hanlon, and McGinnity wasn't really planning to pitch both games this time. But during the first game, Hanlon congratulated him on his doubleheader sweep the previous week and implied that he had been lucky. McGinnity told him he could do it again. Hanlon simply laughed and dared him to do so. McGinnity wasn't about to back down from a challenge and when McGraw heard what Hanlon had said, it was guaranteed that he was going to send McGinnity back out to pitch the second game.[11]

McGinnity handled the Superbas fairly easily in the first game, winning, 6–1. He allowed the only run in the first inning, then shut them down for the last eight.

When he walked out

McGinnity was arguably the most durable pitcher in baseball history in 1903, working 434 innings and throwing 44 complete games.

to the mound for the second game, he was greeted by what the *Times* described as "a storm of applause."¹² This game was going to be much closer and much more hotly contested with McGinnity playing a role in the offense this time.

In the third inning, he stole second base with the throw sailing into center field. He tried to get up to go to third, but became entangled with a Brooklyn infielder and wasn't able to do so. Umpire Tim Hurst ruled the Superbas had interfered with him and McGinnity was awarded third base. As the Superbas vehemently argued the ruling near the mound, they left the ball lying in the grass a few feet away. As the argument raged, McGinnity stood on third rubbing his leg as though he had been injured then suddenly dashed for home and scored the first run of the game. Brooklyn pitcher Henry "Tex" Schmidt angrily grabbed the ball, threw it into the seats and was immediately ejected. Hanlon, equally angry, yanked third baseman Sammy Strang out of the game and replaced him with Dutch Jordan.¹³

The Superbas battled back to score two runs in the fourth and another in the third to take a 3–1 lead. Mertes homered in the sixth to cut the lead to 3–2. In the bottom of the ninth, the Giants strung together four straight hits off Brooklyn pitcher Oscar Jones and Gilbert finally trotted home with the winning run on an error by Jordan, setting off a wild celebration. The *Times* described a scene in which thousands of fans rushed onto the field and McGraw was triumphantly carried to the clubhouse "on the shoulders of a score of the biggest fellows in the struggling mass of humanity."¹⁴

McGinnity still wasn't done performing Iron Man heroics for the month. He tried it one more time, on August 31, in a home doubleheader against Philadelphia that drew a much smaller weekday crowd of 3,406.

Once again, the Giants helped him out by scoring early in the first game, getting one run in the first and three in the second. McGinnity gave up five hits and walked three batters, but did not allow a run until the ninth inning.

The Phillies grabbed a lead in the second game by scoring two runs in the third inning, but the Giants took over from there. Bresnahan got them started in the fourth with a play eerily similar to McGinnity's steal of home against Brooklyn a few weeks earlier. He was called safe on a steal of second and as the Phillies argued the call by the same umpire, Tim Hurst, Bresnahan sprinted for third. The catcher threw wildly trying to get him there and he trotted home with the Giants' first run.

The Giants added two runs in the fifth, one in the sixth and five in the seventh. McGinnity contributed three hits himself and Bresnahan had four.

The entire doubleheader was over in slightly more than three hours and the *Times* noted that "at the end, McGinnity showed no sign of fatigue. In fact, he seemed fresh enough to tackle the visitors for a third contest if that were necessary."[15]

In actuality, McGinnity didn't pitch that well for most of the month of August. He went 6–0 in the three doubleheaders, but was 1–5 in the other games he pitched during the month.

But his season numbers were absolutely extraordinary—31 victories and 434 innings pitched (a major league modern-era record that's not likely to ever be broken). Mathewson also won 30 games, but the Giants finished 6½ games behind the Pirates, who met the Boston Pilgrims in the first modern World Series.

12. Total Domination

In 1903, the New York Giants had shown flashes of what they could do. In 1904, they simply took over the National League. The basic formula was the same as it had been the year before—hard, aggressive, adventuresome baserunning, solid defense, guile and cunning in every aspect of the game, and tremendous pitching.

You could make a case for the 1904 Giants having the best starting pitching in the annals of the sport. The top two pitchers combined for 68 victories, easily a major league record for two men on the same team, and the No. 3 starter, Luther "Dummy" Taylor, won 21. As a team, the Giants had an earned-run average of 2.17 and won 106 games, a major league record that would only stand for two years.

McGinnity was in his prime now. He would win 35 games that season, a total that has been exceeded only four times in the modern era.

Mathewson, who won 33 games, was beginning to blossom. By some reports, he could throw as many as a dozen different pitches for strikes. He had an above-average fastball, an excellent sinker, a sharp-breaking curveball that was probably more like a modern-day slider and a superb change-up. He was most famous for his fadeaway, which was basically a screwball. He didn't use it that often, but it almost always befuddled batters when he decided to pull it out of his bag of tricks.

Taylor also had a diverse repertoire. He had a tall, slender frame and a crazy corkscrew delivery, he could get batters out with his fastball or his curve, and he had one of the best drop pitches of his day. He also was a deaf mute, one of several who played in the majors in that era. The world wasn't quite as politically correct back then so all of them had the nickname of Dummy— Dummy Hoy, Dummy Deegan, Dummy Leitner. Taylor was the best and most visible of them. He pitched for the Giants for nine years and insisted that his teammates be able to communicate with him on his level. He virtually demanded that all of them, McGraw included, learn sign language. It became a distinct advantage for them, an extra way to communicate above and beyond the signs that every team used. If Taylor was on base and McGraw wanted him to run, he simply spelled out S-T-E-A-L with his hands.[1]

Taylor also was the team clown. One day, when umpire Hank O'Day refused to call off a game in spite of a downpour, Taylor came out to coach first base wearing a pair of rubber boots and carrying a large yellow umbrella. O'Day shouted at him, but of course Taylor couldn't hear him. Instead, he signed to McGraw what he thought of O'Day, not realizing that the umpire had been raised by deaf parents. O'Day signed back to Taylor, telling him he had been ejected from the game and fined $25.[2]

With three such accomplished pitchers, McGraw invented a concept that would soon be copied by every team in baseball—a starting rotation.[3] He used McGinnity, Mathewson and Taylor in an alternating fashion to keep them fresh and in ensuing years, he made it a four-man rotation, adding either Hooks Wiltse or Red Ames to the mix.

Wiltse and Ames were both rookies and on another club they might have been stars. On the 1904 Giants, they played bit parts. Wiltse, the team's only lefthander, won his first 12 starts and finished the season 13–3. Like Iron Man, Hooks had a nickname that he earned for one thing but fit for other reasons. His moniker came from his fielding skills—one teammate claimed he had hooks for hands—but he also had a gigantic nose and threw a devastating crossfire curve.[4] Ames, used mostly as a spot starter in 1904, had an even bigger breaking curve although he sometimes struggled to control it. In 1905, he would set a major league record with 30 wild pitches.

McGraw not only had a pitching staff that was the envy of baseball but he seemingly would have his pitchers do almost anything in his drive to win ballgames. He became fascinated with the movement that the Cubs' Mordecai "Three Finger" Brown got on the ball. Brown had lost one finger and part of another in a boyhood farming accident, and McGraw wondered if a pitcher might throw a better curve ball if he was missing a finger or two. He tested his hypothesis by having his pitchers throw curves without applying pressure with their forefingers, but finally concluded that lopping off a few fingers probably wouldn't make much difference. "It's lucky for you fellows that it doesn't," he supposedly told his pitchers, "because if I thought it did, I would have a surgeon out here tomorrow."[5]

All of his pitchers did just fine with what they had in 1904, and the most effective of them all was McGinnity although he didn't necessarily have a great spring training. In a March 23 exhibition to benefit the Vulcan statue fund in Birmingham, Alabama, he barely was able to beat the local minor league club, 5–3.[6] But when the regular season opened, he went a couple of months before he lost a game. He handled Brooklyn on opening day and in his second start of the season, he pitched 15 superb innings against the Phillies before the game finally was called a 1–1 tie.

In mid–May, he put together a string of 31 consecutive scoreless innings in games with St. Louis, Cincinnati, Pittsburgh and Chicago, all on the road. He only came close to losing a few times in the early months of the season. On May 24, he spotted Brooklyn a 3–0 lead before the Giants came back to win, 5–3. And he had to go 10 innings, again against the Superbas, to get his 11th win. He gave up a run in the top of the 10th, but catcher John Warner slapped a 258-foot home run down the Polo Grounds' absurdly short right-field line in the bottom of the inning to give the Giants a 4–3 victory.

McGinnity tried for No. 14 in a row against Cincinnati on June 4, but the game again was called with the score tied at 2–2 after 11 innings. Four days later, he collected his 14th consecutive victory when he shut out Pittsburgh.

When he finally lost on June 11, it took a 12-inning one-hitter by the Cubs' Bob Wicker to do it. The game was scoreless and the Giants were hitless until Sam Mertes finally broke up Wicker's no-hitter with a one-out single in the 10th inning. In the 12th, the Cubs got Frank Chance to second base with two outs, and pesky Johnny Evers slapped "Old Sal" just beyond the infield for a run-scoring single.[7]

McGinnity attempted to describe his pitching success in an article in *Pearson's Magazine*: "I ascribe a great deal of my success to my ability to judge the players as they come to bat. The first principle of a successful pitcher is to give his opponents what they don't want. He may have all the various curves, but every player can hit at least one curve, and a few like them all. Unless a twirler studies his men and knows the curves that worry each one, he will be batted freely. With men like (Honus) Wagner and a few others, who can locate anything, he must mix them up."[8]

McGinnity was decades ahead of his time in that he went into each game with a scouting report on the batters he was facing. He probably was the first pitcher to actually keep a "book" on opposing hitters. He stored a ledger in his locker in which he wrote down observations about hitters almost every day. With the National League having only eight teams, he saw every team more than 20 times during the course of a season so having his own systemized accounting of hitter's tendencies was invaluable. McGinnity admitted in an interview with the Butte, Montana, newspaper in 1916 that it had a lot to do with making him the pitcher he was.[9]

"It saves me a deal of trouble and unnecessary work, not to mention long chances," he said in that interview. "I don't have to try 'em out, like I'd have to if I didn't have the book. When you're trying a batter out to find his weakness you have to put a lot of stuff on the ball and tax your arm. The book saves me that trouble. It's all there in black and white, gathered from personal observation and experience for the most part. I don't trust to memory. Anyone is likely to forget, and a lapse of memory with three on in a tight game many times leads to a costly mistake, and instead of feeding the batter what he doesn't want, a pitcher is apt to put it right there in his groove and—blooey, there goes the old ball game!"[10]

McGinnity noted in that same interview that he very seldom tried to strike out a batter. "Every pitcher has eight men on his club to help him out," he said. "The secret of successful pitching is to keep the batters from hitting 'em *hard*."[11]

In 1904, he was doing that as well as any pitcher ever had. Gabriel Schechter, a researcher at the Baseball Hall of Fame, found 17 9-inning games McGinnity pitched that season in which the Giants had 15 or more assists, an indication that batters were making contact against him but not solid contact. In the 15-inning tie with Philadelphia early in the season, the Giants had 27 assists, 10 of them by McGinnity himself.[12]

He was becoming an object of adulation more than ever in New York. In June, he was the subject of Dr. Jesse F. Forbes' commencement address to the graduating class of DeWitt Clinton High School. Dr. Forbes pointed to McGinnity as someone students should emulate because he had succeeded through "self-reliance and character." The *New York Times* item on Forbes' speech was inspirational if perhaps a tad inaccurate: "When questioned as to why he was a winner McGinnity had replied by saying that he did not drink, did not associate with those who did drink, and practiced in-shoots, out-shoots, curves and drops."[13]

It's true that McGinnity did not drink heavily, but he certainly didn't disassociate himself from people who imbibed. To do that, he would have had to quit baseball. And he still was more than 20 years away from doing that.

The admiration for McGinnity took other forms. The songwriting duo of William Jerome and Jean Schwartz penned a tune called "Line it out McGinnity," which really didn't make much sense since it extolled his hitting skills, calling him "the king of all the sluggers." The chorus:

> Line it out McGinnity. Whang it, bang it on the nose.
> Soak it hard McGinnity, Mac put on your batting clothes.
> Lace it and deface it, chase it, beat it black and blue,
> And we'll change the name of Broadway to McGinnity Avenue.[14]

The song never caught on in a really big way although it reportedly was performed 77 times between April and August, 1905, as part of a vaudeville show called "Lifting the Lid."

The Giants were in and out of first place in the first couple of months of the 1904 season and were playing spirited baseball.

They defeated St. Louis, 2–1, on May 6 by stealing a pair of runs in the ninth inning. McGraw was on second base as a pinch runner when Roger Bresnahan lined a single into the outfield. As McGraw rounded third on his way to scoring the tying run, first base coach Billy Gilbert was close behind him and most of the other Giants clustered along the third base line yelling and shouting. The Cardinals argued vigorously that the Giants had come onto the field in clear violation of the rules. As they screamed at the umpires, one of the Giants who had come off the bench raced toward home plate. First baseman Jake Beckley saw it in his peripheral vision and assumed it was Bresnahan trying to score. He threw the ball to an uncovered home plate and as the ball rattled around near the backstop, Bresnahan sprinted home with the winning run. Although the Giants clearly had violated the rules, National League president Harry Pulliam denied the St. Louis protest.[15]

However, Pulliam ruled against the Giants in another dispute with St. Louis in the final game of the season at the Polo Grounds. The combustible McGraw was not even present for this one, but his lieutenants were up to the task of antagonizing James Johnstone, one of their least favorite umpires. McGinnity lost the first game of a doubleheader, 8–7, and the score was tied at 1–1 in the second game when the Giants' Doc Marshall got into an argument with Johnstone. He was kicked out of the game, and an inning later both Bill Dahlen and Billy Gilbert also were ejected. The Giants stood back and appeared unwilling to resume the game so Johnstone awarded the Cardinals the victory by forfeit. Several spectators rushed forward and threatened Johnstone as he walked off the field, but two police officers came to his rescue. Pulliam was in attendance at the game and ruled that Johnstone acted correctly.[16]

The Giants moved into first place for good with McGinnity's June 8 shutout of Pittsburgh and they were drawing mammoth crowds. The June 4 tie with Cincinnati drew the largest crowd in baseball history to that point—37,223—and the Giants broke that record a week later when McGinnity lost to Wicker.

Even after McGinnity's streak ended, the Giants kept rolling. Within a week after that, on June 16, they began an 18-game winning streak that left the Cubs, Pirates and everyone else far behind.

On July 9, McGinnity won two games in one day for the fourth time in his major league career although this time both victories were in relief. He replaced Mathewson in the eighth inning of the first game of a doubleheader against the Cardinals and allowed the tying run, but the Giants won it with three runs in the ninth. He relieved Wiltse in the second game and the Giants again won it in the ninth, running McGinnity's season record to 22–2.[17]

He cooled off a little after that and had a couple of scary moments in August. In an August 18 game with Pittsburgh, he was struck in the abdomen with a line drive, toppling to the ground after throwing the runner out at first base. He stayed in the game, however, and shut out the Pirates, 6–0.[18] Less than a week later, again against the Pirates, McGinnity collided with baserunner Moose McCormick when he was covering first base and again went down in a heap. When he finally got up and went back to pitching, even the partisan fans in Pittsburgh's Exposition Park showered him with applause.[19]

He lost that game, but won 12 of his last 13 starts to finish off one of the most remarkable seasons any pitcher has ever had. His 1.61 earned-run average was the best in the league, as were his 51 games pitched, 408 innings pitched and nine shutouts. His 38 complete games were only one off the league high.

He also became one of the few pitchers ever to lead the NL in both wins (35) and saves (5) in the same season. McGraw, who was the first manager to signal pitches from the bench and the first to use starting pitchers in a rotation, also was pioneering other new ways of using his pitching staff. Saves were not kept as an official statistic at that time, but McGraw recognized the value of bringing in a fresh pitcher in the final innings to close out a game. Historians poring through box scores have credited the Giants with 14 saves as a team that season, as many as the rest of the league combined. In fact, the top three individual save totals in the league belonged to McGinnity, Ames and Wiltse.

The Giants clinched the pennant on September 22, with 16 games to go in the season, when McGinnity beat the Reds, 7–5, in the first game of a doubleheader.

The World Series had been initiated the previous year when the Pittsburgh Pirates and Boston Pilgrims met in a post-season series matching the winning teams from the National and American Leagues. The idea was popular and there was hardly anyone outside the Giants organization who didn't think it should become a regular tradition.

But McGraw and owner John T. Brush still were not on good terms with American League president Ban Johnson. And when it became apparent that the New York Highlanders (formerly the Baltimore Orioles) were likely to win the AL title, the Giants made it clear there would be no World Series in 1904.

The NL was the older, more established, league and Brush saw no reason to risk the Giants' reputation against a crosstown team in what he regarded as an inferior league. He announced in the middle of the season that the Giants would not be taking part.

McGinnity (right) won 35 games in 1904 and teammate Christy Mathewson (left) won 33. Meanwhile, manager John McGraw (center) devised new and creative ways to use the pitching power at his disposal (Baseball Hall of Fame Library).

"There is nothing in the constitution or playing rules of the National League which requires its victorious club to submit its championship honors to a contest with a victorious club in a minor league," Brush said in a statement that must have infuriated Ban Johnson.[20]

Highlanders team president Joseph Gordon issued a personal challenge in the final days of the season and this time Brush deferred to McGraw, who reiterated the team's refusal. One of McGraw's many biographers, Frank Graham, later wrote that the manager was in favor of playing the series and that he tried hard to persuade Brush to comply.[21] But McGraw issued a statement at the time saying any blame for the decision should fall on his shoulder's, not Brush's. He said he and his players worked hard to win the pennant and "will not stand to see it tossed away like a rag" even though he admitted there was money to be made from such a series.[22]

"If the National League should see fit to place post-season games on the same plane as championship games and surround them with the same protection and safeguards for square sport as championship games then, and not till then, will I ever take part in them," he added.[23]

Even after Boston came back to edge out the Highlanders for the American League pennant on the final day of the season, the Giants wouldn't budge. The impassioned pleas of Boston president John Taylor also fell on deaf ears.

Taylor and Johnson and everyone else associated with the AL were incensed by the decision, but they were not the only ones. The Giants were almost universally lambasted in the press. The *Chicago Tribune* called the decision "ridiculous" and implied that McGraw was afraid of the American League. The *New York World* said McGraw's statement "fails to show a reason of any kind, good or bad, for the stand he has taken."[24]

The players on the teams that played in the first World Series the previous year had earned more than $1,000 per man. Owner Barney Dreyfuss of the losing Pirates kicked in his own gate receipts so the Pittsburgh players actually earned more than the victorious Pilgrims.[25] With the way the Giants had been drawing crowds all year, the gate receipts were bound to be considerably higher this time. The Giants players, most of whom earned less than $3,000 a year, were not very happy that they were missing out on a windfall that could have increased their income by 30 percent or more.

The team went on a post-season barnstorming tour instead, earning a few bucks in the towns in which it played. Brush even sweetened the pot with an extra $5,000 to be split among the participants.[26]

McGraw said in his late-season statement that the players were supportive of his choice to not play a World Series, but several of them made it clear they were not. McGinnity was the most outspoken of them all, telling reporters he was "sore to the core" over the decision.[27] "It is just like taking money out of our pockets to prevent us from playing the winners," he said in another interview. "The players are willing enough, I tell you."[28]

13. A World Series

McGinnity again spent the off-season working as a molder in John Redpath's iron foundry back in McAlester although it was no longer the small-time operation it was when it began in 1897.

A man named William Busby had come to McAlester around the turn of the century, amassed a fortune selling coal and subsequently bought or opened several businesses in the town.[1] He and another man named James Degman now held the top executive positions in what was known as the Union Iron Works. John Redpath was still the treasurer and manager, and seemingly half the employees were named Redpath. John's sons, William and Frank, were foremen in the plant, and sons Thomas and John Jr. also worked there. Joe, Mary and Marguerite lived in the Redpath's big house at 901 E. Wyandotte Avenue, just a block down the street from the foundry.

A year later, McGinnity branched out into a business of his own, developing a plant that manufactured hollow building blocks.[2]

During the winter of 1904–05, he also had wanted to go on a barnstorming tour to California and was offered $2,500 to do so. John Brush refused to let his star pitcher go, however, and when the team sailed out of New York on March 2 on the steamer "City of Macon" for its spring training camp in Savannah, Georgia, McGinnity was not with them. On March 4, the *New York Times* reported that McGinnity was thinking of quitting baseball and would not report to spring training unless the Giants paid him the $2,500 he had missed out on. The *Times* item indicated he felt he had been "badly treated by the club officials."[3]

The misunderstanding must have been smoothed over in a hurry because less than two weeks later McGinnity was pitching in another exhibition game in Birmingham.

McGinnity's money demands also may have stemmed from the fact that he still was steamed over management's refusal to play the World Series, causing the players to miss out on another big payday. Brush, McGraw and the Giants took a great deal of abuse for their refusal to play the Series in 1904, and they decided that if they got into that position again, they would comply. They insisted, though, that baseball institute some very specific rules.

Even though he was one of the biggest stars in the major leagues by 1905, McGinnity still went back to work in the Union Iron Works in McAlester, Oklahoma, in the off-season (Frank Williamson collection).

They wanted the Series to be mandatory for both pennant-winning teams, they said that only players on the rosters prior to September 1 should be eligible to take part, and they suggested that the players' pool of money should be 60 percent of the gate receipts from the first four games. The winning players were to split 70 percent of the money with the other 30 percent going to the losers. Both leagues approved what became known as the "Brush Rules," and they have remained relatively unchanged for more than a century.[4]

Now, all the Giants had to do was win another pennant.

The fans certainly were ready. About 40,000 of them showed up for the season opener at the Polo Grounds. The *Times* reported that "they filled every nick and crevice that a human body could squeeze into." They began flooding into the stadium two hours before the game. When boxing champion Jim Jeffries arrived in his automobile, he had to battle his way through the crowd to locate a seat. The Giants players arrived shortly thereafter in a celebratory parade of cars.[5]

McGinnity got things moving in the right direction that day with a 10–1 victory over Boston, holding the Braves scoreless until the eighth inning.

The Giants were off and running. In mid–May, Taylor, McGinnity and Red Ames strung together three straight shutouts against the Cubs. McGinnity's five-hitter on May 15 was the first major league game ever umpired by perhaps the most famous ump ever, Bill Klem.[6]

As so often seemed to happen, McGraw's combative nature got him into trouble early in the season. However, his litany of disputes with umpires and opponents weren't necessarily the result of an uncontrollable temper. He frequently planned his tantrums. They often were calculated to gain an edge, to either throw opponents off balance, to get inside their heads, or to intimidate the umpires. It was no coincidence that a large number of his on-field fracases took place when the Giants were playing either the Pirates or Cubs, the only two teams that presented the Giants with much of a challenge in those years.

McGraw found capable partners in these endeavors in McGinnity, McGann and Bresnahan, and in 1905 even the gentlemanly Mathewson got into the act a few times. On April 22 in Philadelphia, McGann was tagged out at the plate by Phillies catcher Fred Abbott and got up swinging. McGann was thrown out of the game and in the ensuing chaos, Mathewson punched out a youthful lemonade vendor who had ventured onto the field. The Giants won the game easily, but they were lucky to get out of town alive. They were pelted with bricks and rocks as they left the stadium.[7]

Mathewson was kicked out of another game in May for taunting the Pirates bench.[8] In a May 19 game with Pittsburgh, the third game of a contentious four-game series, McGraw took the Giants-Pirates feud to a whole new level. He accused the umpires of being paid by Pittsburgh's German-born owner, Barney Dreyfuss, and he did it loudly enough for Dreyfuss, sitting in the nearby box seats, to hear. McGraw was ejected from the game again the next day, and this time he struck up a conversation with Dreyfuss as he left the premises. He asked the Pirate owner about his gambling habits, accused him of not paying off his gambling debts, asked if he wanted to bet $10,000 on the game that was in progress, and even made fun of Dreyfuss' somewhat comical accent.[9]

Dreyfuss registered a formal complaint with league president Harry Pulliam, who only two years earlier had worked for Dreyfuss as the secretary of the Pittsburgh club. McGraw was so abusive in a subsequent phone conversation with Pulliam that the league president suspended him for 15 days and fined him $150.[10]

In a June 1 meeting, the league's board of directors did the unthinkable: It sided with McGraw. That wasn't enough for McGraw and Brush, however. They took Pulliam to court and somehow got a Boston judge to rule that the league president could not fine or suspend McGraw for his actions. Pulliam, who did not always deal well with criticism and controversy (he was to commit suicide four years later), responded with his own gesture of protest: He refunded all the fines he had collected from all players and managers up to that point in the season. It cost the league close to $500.[11]

In the midst of all this chicanery, McGinnity was having another great season, and he was one Giant who was staying out of trouble.

He did have one close scrape in late May. There was a law in New York City in those days against playing games on Sunday and a small number of players—including Mathewson—refused to even play in road games on Sundays. Of course, McGinnity had been pitching on Sundays his entire baseball life. Back in his coal mining days, that sometimes was the only day he was available to pitch. Many wanted the New York law changed and it turned into a prolonged legal battle. The city's police commissioner ordered officers to continue enforcing the law until further notice. They were to stop any Sunday games they found in progress and incarcerate the offenders, if necessary.

With the Giants idle on Sunday, May 28, McGinnity got an offer to pitch in a clandestine semi-pro game at a field at 46th Street and Second Avenue, very close to where the United Nations complex now stands. When he arrived, the organizers seemingly forgot how much money they had agreed to pay him and he refused to suit up. It was another one of those lucky accidents. When the police arrived, they arrested everyone wearing a uniform. McGinnity was in street clothes. The cops never bothered him.[12]

As the Giants were cruising along in mid-season, they took a look at a 28-year-old outfielder from Minnesota named Archibald "Moonlight" Graham. He only was with the team for a brief time and he only got to play the last inning of an 11–1 victory over the Dodgers on June 29 in Brooklyn. He never got a chance to bat, but his brief appearance was immortalized many years later in the film "Field of Dreams," albeit with some factual distortions.[13]

The game in which Graham played marked the Giants' eighth straight victory. By the Fourth of July, they had a seven-game lead on the Pirates. They put together a 13-game winning streak in late July with eight of the victories coming against fifth-place Cincinnati. They clinched the pennant on October 1 when McGinnity beat the Reds, 5–4. Pittsburgh was a distant second, 10 games back.

All that was left was for the Giants to produce the most dominating pitching performance in World Series history, certainly the most extraordinary effort by one man.

It wasn't McGinnity. Mathewson was at his peak now, so good that he was starting to overshadow McGinnity. Nicknamed "Big Six" after a famous New York fire engine company, he had mastered his "fadeaway" pitch and developed incredible control. Later, in 1913, he would have a stretch in which he went 68 consecutive innings without issuing a walk. He had amazing composure and was highly intelligent. He loved to play several games of checkers at once, against different opponents, sometimes blindfolded, and his photographic memory made him deadly in poker games as well.[14] His retention and concentration made him great on the mound, too. While McGinnity was scribbling notes in his ledger each day, Mathewson committed to memory exactly how he'd pitched every hitter in previous at-bats and remembered whether or not it worked. In 1912, he would write a book called *Pitching in a Pinch* that revealed many of the secrets of his success.

He and McGinnity were a devastating duo, as the Philadelphia Athletics were about to find out. The Giants had refused to play the Series in 1904. In 1905, they made Philadelphia and its legendary manager, Connie Mack, wish they'd done so again.

But before the series began, Mack and his A's were supremely confident that they could prevail, and the *New York Times* indicated that the two teams were "on such equal footing that that it would be difficult to detect any superiority that one possessed over the other."[15]

Mack felt he had a pretty powerful pitching staff of his own, led by Rube Waddell, Eddie Plank and Chief Bender. "Waddell and Plank will mow down those National League fellows as sure as you live and as for the rest of the

The World Champion 1905 New York Giants. McGinnity is in the back row, second from the right. John McGraw is in the middle of the front row in a dark hat. Just behind him to his right is Christy Mathewson (Charles W. Brown, Jr., collection).

team I am not a bit doubtful," Mack told the *Times*. "We can bat as good as if not better than they can while in the field there is nothing to it but the Athletics."[16]

McGraw, typically cocky, felt he had the better team although he conceded that the Athletics' pitching staff was scary. "We can beat the Philadelphians in batting and furthermore we can beat them running the bases," he said. "The only question left open for argument then is the pitching. They might put it on us there but I don't believe it. While their pitchers are working on us, you will find my pitchers having some of them on the jump. I do not say that our pitchers are better as a whole than those of the Athletics, but even if they are on a par, our superiority in other parts of the game will leave us somewhat in the lead."[17]

Unfortunately, the Athletics ended up playing the series without the fireballing Waddell, who had won 27 games and struck out 287 batters before September 1. At that point, he was sidelined for the rest of the season by a freak accident that took place on a train platform in Providence, Rhode Island. The Athletics were headed for Boston and Mack allowed young Andy Coakley, who was straight out of college, to stop in Providence to visit his family. When they stopped on the return trip to pick him up, Coakley was wearing a straw hat, considered to be out of season. The eccentric and often immature Waddell had vowed to destroy every straw hat he saw and when he reached for Coakley's, the rookie held up a suit bag that was rolled around his cleats. He accidentally spiked Waddell in the chin, which only made him go after the hat more vigorously. Waddell ended up tripping and falling on his left shoulder.[18]

The next morning and for more than a month thereafter, he couldn't raise his pitching arm above his shoulder. At least, that's the story everyone was told. There also were rumors that gamblers who had bet big money on the Giants had Waddell stashed in a Manhattan hotel room and were supplying him with all the booze and prostitutes he could handle until the series was over. There were rumors that Waddell was paid as much as $17,000 to sit out the series, but Connie Mack vehemently denied those stories to his dying day.[19]

In truth, Waddell's absence likely didn't impact the series that much. The Athletics' problem wasn't pitching; it was hitting.

The *Philadelphia North American* had erected a gigantic gong just west of city hall in the heart of downtown. It was to be rung once every time a Philadelphia player hit a double in the Series, twice for triples and three times for home runs.[20]

It was a quiet week in downtown Philly. The gong sounded just five times in five games. The A's managed just 25 hits in 45 innings, five of them doubles. They never did get a triple or a home run. They never even scored an earned run.

The Series opened in Philadelphia's Columbia Park, a compact stadium in the midst of some of Philly's finest breweries.[21] The place generally smelled like a giant saloon, which probably didn't bother the players in the least. It had no dugouts and seated only 12,000 people although 17,955 crammed their way through the gates for the opening game, including entertainer George M. Cohan and heavyweight boxing champion Gentleman Jim Corbett, both down from New York to cheer on their Giants. Ropes were strung around the outer edges of the outfield so that additional fans could stand on the field and watch the game. It was determined that any ball hit into those fans would be a ground-rule double. The *Times* reported that another 10,000 ticket-seekers were turned away.[22]

McGraw was at his cocksure best. He outfitted the Giants in special black broadcloth uniforms with white hats for the Series[23] and had them ride to the opening game through the streets of Philadelphia in open carriages, led by a marching band. He had the band stand in front of the Giants' bench, playing "Tammany" and "Give My Regards to Broadway" as the teams went through pre-game warm-ups.[24] Charles Dryden of the *Chicago Tribune* noted that the Giants were uncharacteristically polite and well-behaved, exchanging warm greetings with the Philadelphia players when they arrived. Waddell, who was adept at sign language, even carried on an extended conversation with Dummy Taylor.[25]

McGraw had been talking endlessly for days about what his team would do to the A's, calling the American League champs "a bunch of white elephants." When Philadelphia team captain Lave Cross came to home plate with the lineup card for the opener, he also carried something wrapped in paper. He uncovered it and handed McGraw a small statue of a white elephant. The *Tribune* reported that McGraw "wiggled and blushed," then removed his cap and put the elephant on the top of his head.[26]

Then the pleasantries ceased and the Giants began the task of dismantling the Athletics. Donlin singled in Bresnahan in the fifth, then scored himself on Sammy Mertes' double, and that was all Mathewson needed. Philadelphia actually sounded the gong three times in that first game, but they had only one single to go with three ground-rule doubles and lost, 3–0.

The next day back in New York, McGinnity got his chance to square off against tall, slender 21-year-old Chief Bender in front of a crowd of about 30,000 at the Polo Grounds. McGinnity allowed only six hits and just three unearned runs—one in the third and two in the eighth—but it wasn't enough.

Bender, born into the Ojibwa tribe of Minnesota and just getting started on a Hall of Fame career of his own, yielded only four hits and registered 10 strikeouts in a 3–0 victory. Although all the runs scored against McGinnity were the result of errors, the *Times* was a bit harsh in its assessment of his performance, noting that "he was lacking at crucial periods and failed to live up to what was demanded of him."[27] Red Ames, who had been a 22-game winner in the regular season, came in to pitch the ninth inning. It was the only inning in the entire series in which the Giants used a pitcher other than Mathewson or McGinnity.

The third game, back in Philadelphia, was postponed a day by rain, which was bad news for the Athletics. It gave Mathewson enough time to rest so he could come back and pitch Game 3. The *Times* reported that when it was announced prior to the game that Matty would oppose young Andy Coakley, there was a noticeable sigh of dismay among the Philly fans who had braved the damp, chilly conditions. "Nearly all of the 11,000 fans wore overcoats and shivered, and there wasn't enough excitement from the Athletics' point of view to keep real baseball blood in rapid circulation."[28]

It was the only game of the series in which either team mounted a major offensive threat as the Giants scored two runs in first inning and five in the fifth. McGann, who had struck out three times against Bender in the previous game, collected three hits and drove in four runs, and Mathewson threw another four-hit shutout for a 9–0 victory.

McGinnity took the mound in Game 4 at the Polo Grounds with a chance to really put the Athletics in the hole and no one could have possibly been disappointed in his performance this time. He allowed only five little singles. The Giants only touched Eddie Plank for four hits, but they used two errors to break through in the fourth. Sammy Mertes reached base when shortstop Monte Cross fumbled his ground ball, but Plank got the next two batters with Mertes moving to second on an infield out. Billy Gilbert then hit a routine grounder to Lave Cross at third. As the ball trickled between his legs into left field, Mertes raced around to score the only run of the game.

It was a typical McGinnity game. He didn't overpower the Athletics. They had plenty of chances, getting runners to third base twice and to second base on three different occasions. "But each time the iron man tightened up like the cork in a bottle of mucilage," Charles Dryden wrote.[29]

Three of his four strikeouts came in the last two innings. With little Topsy Hartsel, one of the fastest men in baseball, standing on third with two outs in the eighth, McGinnity fanned the dangerous Ralph "Socks" Seybold on three pitches. Or, as the colorful Dryden put it, "the foxy Joe induced Ralphy to chop three chunks of phantom ice from the ancient atmosphere."[30]

The *New York Times* reported that "spectators in all portions of the field arose from their seats and gave the Iron Man a reception that he will not soon forget."[31] When McGinnity slipped a called third strike past pinch-hitter Dan Hoffman to end the game, McGraw carved a third notch in the bat he was holding in the dugout, then jumped up and began celebrating.

Most observers assumed that Red Ames would pitch for the Giants against Bender in Game 5 on Saturday afternoon. Mathewson had thrown complete game shutouts on Monday and Thursday and McGinnity had worked on Tuesday and Friday. But this was an era in which pitchers thought nothing of throwing with only a day or two of rest, and McGraw always went for the jugular. He decided to use Mathewson for the third time in six days.

The victory celebration really began even before the game at the Polo Grounds. As the Giants came onto the field, Roger Bresnahan and Jim Corbett broke out a large green Irish flag and waved it to the crowd of 24,187. The fans roared their approval for Mathewson and called for him to doff his cap in recognition of their cheers. Instead, he walked over to McGinnity and lifted his cap in honor of his efforts the day before. McGinnity returned the favor, raising Mathewson's cap.[32]

Mathewson then went out and handled the A's one more time, winning, 2–0, on a six-hitter. The Giants pushed across one run against Bender in the fifth and Mathewson scored an insurance run in the eighth, and the Giants were the champions of the world. Mathewson had thrown three complete-game shutouts, striking out 18, walking one and giving up only 14 hits. The Giants only batted .203 in the Series, but the A's were even more feeble, hitting .161.

After the final victory, many of the New York fans refused to leave the ballpark. About 10,000 of them gathered beneath the veranda of the Giants clubhouse at the Polo Grounds, calling for their heroes. The players took turns coming out to greet the crowd, and Mathewson and Bresnahan emerged holding a homemade yellow banner that read "The Giants, World's Champions, 1905."[33]

The victorious Giants earned $1,142 apiece with the Athletics getting only $382, but the Giants players apparently were not as certain of victory as their verbose little manager. Many of them—reportedly everyone except McGraw, Mathewson and Bresnahan—had cut private deals with Philadelphia players to pool their winnings and split them evenly. When Philly owner Ben Shibe kicked in his share of the pot for his players, most of the Athletics walked away with more money than the champions.[34]

Sadly, many of the Giants—McGinnity included—never would get another chance to play in a World Series.

14. Comeuppance

As the 1906 season approached, the Giants were the toast of New York, worshipped by the blue-collar set but equally popular with the Broadway crowd and other celebrities. All of the uptown adulation might have felt a bit strange and uncomfortable for an unpretentious ex-coal miner from Illinois, but some of the Giants reveled in it.

John McGraw capitalized on his heightened popularity by opening another business—a swanky billiard hall near Herald Square in the heart of the theater district.[1] Mike Donlin married a famous Broadway actress, Mabel Hite.[2]

McGraw arranged to have his players triumphantly carted to and from every game in carriages, and he changed uniforms again, altering them to reflect the bold, brash, in-your-face attitude that he wanted his players to have. The team had always had a large "NY" on the front of its jerseys in the past. McGraw had that removed and replaced with the words "World's Champions" across the front.[3] The Giants also became the first team ever to wear uniform shirts that didn't have collars, a style that quickly caught on.[4]

But the new outfits almost seemed to work as a jinx. Mathewson contracted nasal diphtheria and missed the first three weeks of the season. He had had a milder attack of the same ailment the previous spring, but this time he was confined to bed rest at the home of his brother-in-law, Dr. P.B. Cregar, in Plainfield, New Jersey.[5] Donlin, who led the league in runs scored the previous season, broke his ankle only 34 games into the season. Bresnahan missed several games after being beaned by a pitch and McGann broke his arm. The jinx even seemed to extend to family members. Mathewson's wife, Jane, slipped on some ice back home in Pennsylvania and broke her arm.

Things really began to go awry even before the season arrived. In early February, several Giants players—McGinnity was not among them—got drunk on a train ride up to Troy, New York, where they were to be honored in a ceremony. They began throwing baseballs around the train car and incited a brawl with other passengers. Donlin attacked a conductor and produced a pistol when confronted by a porter.[6]

In spite of all that, the Giants opened their home season against Brooklyn on April 20 in a highly festive atmosphere. Team officials, anticipating a huge crowd, opened the gates at noon, four hours before the start of the game. There was a concert by the Catholic Protectory Band at 2 P.M. At 3 P.M., a massive blue pennant with yellow letters proclaiming the Giants champions of the National League was hoisted to the top of the grandstand, accompanied by fireworks and the playing of the national anthem, which was not routinely played prior to baseball games until more than a decade later. The Giants players were cheered individually by a crowd of about 20,000—even Mathewson got out of his sickbed to make an appearance—and when the pennant went up, they really broke loose. As the *New York Times* reported, "The cheers that had gone before were nothing to those that now rent the ambient air, the vocal expression that relieved the oppressive feeling of exultance that each chest of each loyal rooter had hitherto striven to restrain until this proper time arrived to give it vent."⁷

The Giants won the home opener, 3–2, behind Red Ames, and in spite of all their physical infirmities, they still led the league in the first month-and-a-half of the season, thanks to an early 10-game winning streak.

Mathewson finally came back on May 5 and although he was noticeably weaker, he pitched reasonably well against the worst team in the league, Boston, and left the game after seven innings with a 4–3 lead. McGinnity relieved him, allowed three runs in the ninth, and the Giants lost.

It quickly became apparent that the Giants were now going to have to battle more than just Pittsburgh for league supremacy. The Cubs, frequently in the shadow of the Giants and Pirates over the previous few years, were now a major force, led by the Hall of Fame double-play combination of Joe Tinker, Johnny Evers and Frank Chance and a pitching staff nearly as formidable as that of the Giants.

The Cubs had grabbed first place for good by late May and they showed what sort of season it was going to be in a June 7 game at the Polo Grounds. They hammered out 11 runs in the first inning, sending 15 batters to the plate against the two Giant aces, Mathewson and McGinnity. Mathewson gave up a walk, four hits and four runs without ever retiring a batter. McGinnity replaced him and didn't do much better. He left the game with two outs in the second inning and was replaced by rookie George Ferguson, who finished up although the Cubs added three runs in the second, two in the third and one each in the fourth and fifth.

"The sixth inning was momentous," the *New York Sun* reported, making no attempt to veil its sarcasm. "It was momentous not because of what was done. Chicago did not score that inning."⁸

In the later innings, the Cubs began making outs on purpose just to get the game over with. They ended up handing the Giants a 19–0 loss, the most lopsided defeat in the history of the franchise. They also delivered a message: The Giants' dynasty was over.

The *Chicago Tribune* reported that the Giants were "hooted and jeered at by the 'loyal fans,' who for three years have hooted and jeered all visiting teams alike at the Polo Grounds, never thinking to see McGraw at the head of as dilapidated and lifeless a band as the Giants looked today."[9]

One thing didn't change: The Giants still were getting into trouble with authority figures. Two weeks after being smoked by the Cubs, they engaged in another wild affair with their friends from Pittsburgh. McGraw was kicked out of the game in the fourth inning by umpire Bob Emslie, whose partner, Hank O'Day, ejected both McGinnity and McGann in the following inning. However, Mathewson took over on the mound, and the Giants scored three runs in the late innings and won the game, 5–4.[10]

A month later, on July 24, McGinnity played a major role in another fracas that the *New York Times* called "one of the bitterest fights that ever marred a baseball game."[11]

McGinnity and veteran catcher Heinie Peitz had engaged in an ongoing verbal battle for years. The 165-pound Peitz had been around the league even longer than McGinnity, and he was well known for raucous behavior and a fondness for beer halls, so much so that he and pitcher Ted Breitenstein became known as the "Pretzel Battery" during their years with Cincinnati.[12] Peitz was finishing out his career with Pittsburgh, spending much more time coaching first base than playing, and on this particular day he began riding McGinnity from the very start of the game, spewing a constant stream of abuse. By the fourth inning, Iron Man was primed for a meltdown. McGann had just committed an error at first base and McGinnity had gone over to bark at his teammate when Peitz unleashed a few more insults.

McGinnity walked over and socked Peitz in the eye. The two men wrestled to the ground, throwing wild punches as players from both teams and police officers tried to pry them apart. The combatants finally were pulled to their feet, dripping with blood and still shouting at one another.

Charles F. Kirschler, the mayor of Allegheny, Pennsylvania (a town that has since been absorbed by Pittsburgh) watched it all from his box seat, then stood and pointed at McGinnity, shouting "Arrest that man. I will appear against him myself." McGinnity was taken away in a paddy wagon and later released on $50 bail.[13] Officials of the Pittsburgh team stepped in, however, and persuaded Kirschler to change his mind. The charges were dropped, the Giants got their bail money back and Kirschler apologized to the Pirates (not the Giants) for his intervention.[14]

A week later, McGinnity was fined $100 and suspended for 10 days by league president Harry Pulliam. Peitz was fined $50 and received a five-day suspension for provoking the incident. And in a highly unusual move, O'Day, who was working behind the plate that day, was fined $50 for not doing enough to quell the melee before it began.[15]

In McGinnity's first game back from the suspension, on August 6, McGraw got into it with the umpires during a 3–1 loss to the Cubs at the Polo Grounds and was booted by umpire James Johnstone. When Johnstone arrived to work the game the next day, the stadium attendants, acting on McGraw's orders, refused to allow him inside the gates. The umpire declared the Cubs the winner of that game by forfeit.

McGraw was not willing to accept that and announced that the game would be played anyway with each team supplying one of its players to serve as umpires. He announced that utility man Sammy Strang would be the Giants' representative. Cubs manager Frank Chance simply laughed in his face. As far as he was concerned, his team already had won the game. Pulliam upheld the ruling and the following day, Johnstone returned to work at the Polo Grounds.[16]

McGraw and Brush, never hesitant to make work for their attorneys, filed suit against the Cubs for not playing the August 7 game, seeking $8,500 in damages for the loss of gate receipts.[17] They lost the lawsuit, too.

McGinnity kept winning, though. He defeated the Pirates, 2–1, and the Cardinals, 3–1, in his next two starts. On August 24, he blanked the Pirates, 3–0, and he threw another shutout against Philadelphia on Aug. 30. In the month of September, he went 6–1 but with the Cubs winning almost every day during the final two months, the Giants never were able to gain any ground.

The Giants and Pirates stayed reasonably close for much of the season before the Cubs closed them out with a mind-boggling stretch run. From August 6 through September 16, they went 37–2. They set a major league record that still stands by going 116–36. At the finish, they were 20 games ahead of the Giants and 23 ahead of the Pirates.

McGinnity led the league in wins again with 27, one more than Cubs ace Mordecai "Three-Finger" Brown. He also led in games pitched with 45, worked more than 300 innings for the eighth year in a row, had 32 complete games, reached a career low by hitting only seven batters and gave up just one home run all season.

But there was no pennant. The World Series was an all–Chicago affair: Cubs vs. White Sox.

15. Signs of Decline

Despite the fact that McGinnity had been one of the highest paid players in baseball in 1906, earning $11,000, the Giants began to hear rumblings that he again wasn't entirely happy with the way the team had treated him. McGraw heard the rumors all the way out in Los Angeles, where he stopped a runaway team of horses and rescued his wife and another woman in January while scouting out the area as a new spring training site.[1]

It's possible McGinnity was becoming jealous of the fact that Mathewson was now regarded as the team's marquee pitcher and McGraw's unabashed favorite despite the fact that Iron Man again led the league in victories. A story in the *Police Gazette* in 1905 indicated that there were no ill feelings between the two men, noting that "McGinnity and Mathewson work together like two thoroughbreds harnessed to the same wagon. In spite of the fact that they are close rivals for popular favor, there is never the slightest sign of jealousy between them."[2]

It would not have been surprising if there had been friction between the two pitching stars although any evidence to that effect is strictly circumstantial. There is no question that they were very different people who traveled in very different circles. Mathewson was an intellectual, college-educated with an almost photographic memory and supreme powers of concentration that made him invincible in games such as bridge and chess. McGinnity was no intellectual. He had almost no formal schooling and the only game he cared much about was the one at which he made his living.

As author John Klima put it many decades later, "Mathewson was what the America of 1905 aspired to be. Iron Joe McGinnity was what the America of 1905 was."[3] McGinnity was the roughhewn everyman toiling alongside someone who had an almost regal bearing. "It seemed he was only the dirty-faced chimney sweep who kept the place pristine for the Prince," Klima added.[4]

Moreover, Mathewson had become bosom buddies with McGraw, much closer to the Giants manager than McGinnity had been. Mathewson's wife, Jane, and McGraw's second wife, Blanche, were inseparable and the couples even lived together for about three years in an apartment on Manhattan's upper west side, near Central Park. The Mathewsons only moved out then because they started a family. They named their first-born son after McGraw.[5]

There also are small hints of a possible riff in the book that Mathewson wrote several years later, in 1912. *Pitching in a Pinch* deals extensively with Mathewson's philosophies and strategies of baseball, his opinions about the sport and his observations about rivals and teammates. Despite his apparent role in helping to mold Matty, McGinnity is hardly mentioned in the book.

Mathewson wrote that he felt pitchers should conserve their energy through the course of a game and save something for those crucial late-game moments when they needed to make a big pitch. By the accounts of many (including McGraw), this is a lesson he learned from McGinnity, but Iron Man received no credit for it in the book. A later chapter briefly mentioned McGinnity and implied that base-stealers were always able to get a good jump on him because of his pitching motion.[6]

And in a chapter entitled "Big League Pitchers and Their Peculiarities," Mathewson wrote of his admiration for such contemporaries as Stanley Coveleski, Cy Young and the Giants' old rival, Mordecai "Three-Finger" Brown. He called Brown "a finished pitcher in all departments of the game" and raved about his penchant for scooping up bunts and throwing out baserunners at third base. He did credit McGinnity with "inventing" that type of play, but he made it clear he viewed Brown as the master of its execution.[7]

At the end of the chapter, Mathewson wrote about the importance of a pitcher controlling his emotions and having good mechanics. "If a pitcher expects to be a successful Big Leaguer, he must guard against eccentricities of temperament and mechanical motion," he wrote. It almost sounds like a jab at an old mentor who occasionally failed to control his anger and whose pitching delivery was anything but orthodox.[8]

Whether or not there was some sort of feud simmering between McGinnity and Mathewson in 1907 is purely conjecture. However, there were rumors that McGinnity might be traded to the Cardinals or that he might choose to just quit. The big house on Seneca Street in McAlester finally was finished. He hinted that he might just retire to a life of leisure there.

All of that was laid to rest in early February when McGinnity announced he was ready to play for the Giants again in 1907. He dispatched a note to team secretary Fred Knowles, telling him that as the team headed for Los Angeles, it could stop and pick him up somewhere along the way, possibly in Kansas City or Dallas. "I am in good shape," his note concluded. "Hope we will have the best of success.... Yours as ever, Joe McGinnity."[9]

He was there in Kansas City when the team's train passed through on February 25. Knowles told the *New York Times*: "From my personal knowledge, McGinnity never protested the treatment he had received at the hands of the New York club, and I am positive that Manager McGraw never had an idea of trading him."[10]

After the Giants and Philadelphia Athletics had met in the World Series in 1905, plans had been made for the two teams to stage "a second World Series" during the spring prior to the 1906 season. Because the Giants had so many problems — Mathewson's illness, the numerous injuries, *etc.* — the series was postponed a year. Now they were scheduled to meet in spring training 1907 in New Orleans as the two clubs made their way back east to open the season.

McGinnity won the first game of the special series, 4–3, on March 27 but things began to get ugly in the second game the next day. McGraw and Bresnahan became so vocal and belligerent in protesting what they thought was a balk that umpire Charlie Zimmer asked police to forcibly remove the manager and the catcher from the ballpark. McGraw took his entire team out the door with him and Zimmer awarded the game to the Athletics on a forfeit.[11]

The next day, McGraw refused to play again if Zimmer was involved and the umpire again declared the Athletics the winner by forfeit. However, a huge crowd had gathered and rather than disappoint the fans — and lose the gate receipts — the two teams played a game with a substitute umpire. Philadelphia won, 7–0.

That was enough for McGraw. He called an end to the series and back at the hotel later that day he got into a shouting match with Philadelphia owner John Shibe.[12] He took his team home to New York.

The tone for the entire season had been set. It was a campaign filled with even more temper tantrums than usual by McGraw. Early in the season, the volatile manager got into a fight with a security guard following a game in Cincinnati.[13] Another time he tossed a cup of water in the face of umpire Bill Klem.[14] He was ejected from games seven times during the season.

And the season began with another bizarre forfeit on opening day. New York police commissioner Theodore Bingham had decreed that the city's officers no longer would be allowed to be on duty for sporting events held on private grounds. It was becoming too costly to pay the large number of officers needed. So there was no police presence at the Polo Grounds when the Giants opened the season on April 11 against the Phillies.[15]

A crowd of 17,000 turned out despite the fact that New York had been the scene of a spring snow shower just a day earlier. The snow was simply shoveled off to the side so that the game could be played.

In the seventh inning, with Philadelphia leading, 3–0, some of the fans decided to move for the exits and brazenly took a shortcut across the field. Klem, the home plate umpire, tried in vain to stop the flow of humanity and he refused to resume the game until every fan was outside the restraining ropes.

He was booed and jeered by the crowd and, as the *New York Times* noted, "In the last inning the ringleaders evidently thought it would be good sport to defy his authority."[16] When the Giants came onto the field for the top of the ninth inning, another wave of fans—at least 1,000 people—flooded into the right field area.

Klem ordered them to leave but a few hundred more fans joined them. Players and ushers implored the fans to clear the field, but they refused. Klem threatened to forfeit the game to the Phillies and some fans clustered around him and laughed at him. They began pelting him with snowballs, and Klem finally had no choice. He declared the Phillies the winner.

Bingham finally sent four officers into the stadium to disperse the lingering crowd. They arrested two fans for disorderly conduct.[17] The next day, there were police officers patrolling the stands at the Polo Grounds.

Something else happened in that April 11 opener that was even more far-reaching in its impact. Bresnahan took the field wearing something no one had ever seen before—shin guards. He had a set of cricket shin guards modified for his own use to provide added protection behind the plate, but some fans in the crowd at the Polo Grounds jeered him . Pittsburgh manager Fred Clarke, who wasn't even there that day, later filed a formal protest. After considering the matter for more than a month, Pulliam denied the protest and approved Bresnahan's innovation.[18] It wasn't long before every catcher was wearing them.

Despite all the disputes and emotional fireworks, the Giants got off to their usual fast start. McGinnity won a game against the Reds, 1–0, in 12 innings on May 13 and a few days later shut out the Cardinals, 4–0, in the second game of a doubleheader to extend the Giants' winning streak to 16 games.

Things were going so well that McGinnity and the Giants even were being nice to the umpires. When the home crowd became incensed with veteran umpire Bob Emslie during a May 21 game at the Polo Grounds, McGinnity stepped in and threw his arms around Emslie to protect him and "talking in a loud voice to the crowd, begged them to desist." According to one report, he even deflected "several blows aimed at the ump's head."[19] League president Harry Pulliam was so grateful, he dispatched a letter to McGinnity praising his actions.[20]

The Giants' winning streak reached 17 games before they finally lost to

McGinnity remained a durable pitcher in 1907 although for the first time in his major league career he failed to win 20 games (Baseball Hall of Fame Library).

St. Louis on May 20. They were 24–3 at that point. But they couldn't shake the Cubs, who were nearly as hot. By the end of May, the Giants had a very impressive 28–10 record but they were in second place, a game back of Chicago. When the Giants went 8–11 in June, the Cubs pulled away, opened a double-digit lead and never looked back. McGinnity, after starting well, had a stretch of nearly three months in the middle of the season in which he won only three games. It wasn't always his fault. In his 18 losses that summer, the Giants scored only 36 runs.

The frustration started to really show in the final weeks of the season. The Giants were swept by the Reds in Cincinnati on September 22 with McGinnity losing a 1–0 duel to Bob Spade, who was making his major league debut. The Giants also dropped the second game, 2–1.

Bresnahan was kicked out of the first game by Bill Klem for arguing a strike call, but he played in the second game. However, when the Giants showed up to play in Pittsburgh the next day, Bresnahan was informed by Klem that he would not be allowed to play again until league president Harry Pulliam said he could. When McGraw turned in a lineup card that included Bresnahan's name, Klem reiterated the ruling. The start of the game was delayed for 12 minutes while McGraw argued.[21]

As Klem stood by the Giants bench insisting that a change be made, McGraw finally told Frank Bowerman to take over as catcher. At that moment, someone threw a splash of water into Klem's face. He didn't know who had done it although McGraw was sitting there in front of him holding an empty tin cup.[22]

Klem didn't take any action at that point, but he got his chance during the game. In the sixth inning, the Pirates' Ed Abbaticchio hit a line drive down the third-base line that Klem called fair. McGraw stormed out of the dugout and was kicked out of the game. He went under the grandstand and continued to run his team from there until Klem found out and had him forcibly removed from the premises by police. In the next inning, he kicked Giants third baseman Art Devlin out of the game, too.[23]

The Giants ended up losing their last seven games to finish in fourth place at 82–71, 25½ games behind the Cubs.

For the first time in his major league career, McGinnity did not win 20 games and did not have a record above .500. He went 18–18 although he again led the league in games pitched (47) and saves (4). Taylor, Wiltse and Ames didn't win or save as many games, but all had better earned-run averages and they all were quite a bit younger. McGinnity may not have realized it yet, but John McGraw already was thinking about possibly phasing out an old friend.

16. One Final, Wild Season

In 1908, the Giants found a new spring training site in Marlin, Texas, about 25 miles southwest of Waco. They had tried a variety of sites through the years—Savannah, Memphis, Los Angeles—and other teams had tried Marlin. The White Sox trained there in 1904 and the Reds used it as their training base in 1907.

The Giants built their own facility there, including a little stadium in which they could hold exhibition games, and they used it for the next 11 years. The facility sat alongside some railroad tracks, about a mile south of the Hotel Arlington, where the Giants stayed, and they hiked to and from the field along the tracks twice each day.[1]

Hot springs had been discovered in Marlin in 1893, and it became a minor tourist attraction for visitors looking to relieve their aches and pains in the steambaths that popped up around the town. The Giants used them almost daily to relax after a tough day of practice.

McGraw liked Marlin because it was off the beaten track, close enough to Waco, Dallas and other towns where the Giants could find quality competition, but not *too* close. He had grown tired of his players breaking training and treating spring training as a vacation. He figured they couldn't find much mischief in a sleepy little town of 4,000 people. As Mathewson later wrote in his book, it was "no setting for a pleasure party."[2]

As the team made its way north, it was scheduled to make a special stop at McAlester. The plan called for the Giants to play exhibition games there on Saturday and Sunday, April 4 and 5.

McGinnity was in no shape to play in his adopted hometown. He was suffering from a mild case of malaria and had such a severe groin pull that he was having trouble even walking. He pleaded with McGraw to let him go on ahead to McAlester ahead of the rest of the team, but McGraw wouldn't allow it.[3]

There was a gala atmosphere when the Giants arrived in Oklahoma, which had just become the 46th state. Mary had the majestic house at Seventh and Seneca decked out in purple and white for the occasion. The Brooklyn Cup was displayed in the window of one of the downtown stores. There were pictures of Iron Man and McGraw everywhere. On the day the Giants arrived, the town's band went to their hotel four different times to entertain the players. Fans were coming from a 50-mile radius and a crowd of more than 6,000 was expected for each of the two games.[4]

There were two problems: McGinnity couldn't play. And it wouldn't stop raining. What were supposed to be the first major league games ever played in McAlester never happened. As the club continued north, McGinnity stayed behind under Mary's care to try to get healthy.

Joe, Mary and Marguerite arrived in New York a few weeks later with Mary's younger sister, Lula May, accompanying them, as she often did in those days. Lula May, the second youngest of the 12 Redpath children, frequently lived with the McGinnitys to help take care of Marguerite. She was a young widow who briefly dated second baseman Larry Doyle,[5] another former Illinois coal miner who had been purchased from the Springfield club of the Three-I League in the middle of the 1907 season.

When McGinnity rejoined the Giants in late April, it didn't take long to see he didn't figure prominently in McGraw's plans. The manager had gone to a four-man pitching rotation of Mathewson, Taylor, Wiltse and Ames, and when Ames struggled, he replaced him with Otis "Doc" Crandall.

McGinnity didn't get his first start until May 10. He held the Pirates to two runs and two hits through seven innings, then gave up three runs in the eighth and lost, 5–2. The Giants made four errors behind him, two by Doyle and one especially costly one by first baseman Fred Tenney.

For a few weeks, there was almost constant speculation that McGinnity would be traded. McGraw and Brush actually put him on waivers once, but he wasn't claimed.[6] Attempts were made to work out deals with both Cincinnati and St. Louis, but no one wanted to take on his oversized salary.

In the midst of all this, he pitched some of the best baseball of his career. He beat the Dodgers, 5–0, on May 30 and with the trade rumors at their peak, he quieted them by throwing a six-hit shutout against the Cardinals on June 8, much to the tongue-in-cheek delight of W.W. Aulick of the *New York Times*: "The talk of Mr. McGinnity's projected release by the boss of all the Giants reached the ears of the Iron Man only yesterday, being somewhat delayed in transmission. 'Oh well,' quoth this wondering marvel. 'If they feel like that about it, I'll give them something to release me for.' So he fanned seven scarlet socks because they seemed unduly heated, and shut out St. Louis neat and systematic. If we don't want pitchers who practice this sort of specialty, now's our chance to make an advantageous deal. Who wants McGinnity? A neat dresser on and off, and we pay fares. Let's hear the bids."

McGinnity even delivered a ringing double in the third inning and scored the first run of the game. "What're you going to do with a fellow like that?" Aulick asked.[7]

He threw another shutout on June 26, beating the Braves, 2–0. This time he allowed only three hits and again scored one of the runs himself.

In spite of his revival, the Giants couldn't shake the persistent Cubs, who were again a source of frustration for Giants backers. That double-play combination of Tinker, Evers and Chance wasn't prolific in the number of double plays it turned but they always seemed to do it against the Giants at the most crucial moments, so much so that *New York Globe* columnist Franklin P. Adams penned an enduring poem about them that first appeared on July 10, 1908:

McGinnity continued to pitch well in 1908 despite being relegated to a part-time role amid frequent speculation that he would be traded (Charles W. Brown, Jr., collection).

>These are the saddest of possible words,
>Tinker-to-Evers-to-Chance.
>Trio of Bear Cubs fleeter than birds,
>Tinker-to-Evers-to-Chance.
>Ruthlessly pricking our gonfalon bubble,
>Making a Giant hit into a double,
>Words that are weighty with nothing but trouble,
>Tinker-to-Evers-to-Chance.[8]

The two rivals played a bizarre game on July 16. Frank Chance tried to psych out the Giants by electing to have his team bat first—home teams were given the option of doing this until 1951—but the Giants got a strong pitching performance from Crandall and had a 4–1 lead going to the ninth inning. The victory appeared so certain that Mathewson went to the clubhouse, took off his uniform and jumped into the shower.

But Crandall was tiring and walked three straight batters. When McGraw turned and called for Mathewson to relieve him, he was stunned to find his ace was nowhere in sight. Instead, he put McGinnity into the game and he walked in a run. The Giants began stalling as someone ran to tell Mathewson to get out of the shower. Larry Doyle even went so far as to get thrown out of the game to buy time.[9] Mathewson didn't even take time to towel off. He threw on his uniform with his street shoes—he apparently could not find his spikes—and trotted out to the mound dripping wet without a hat, without proper footwear, and retired the next two batters to preserve the win.[10]

The incident indicates how much McGraw had come to rely on Mathewson and how much his faith in McGinnity had slipped. McGinnity wasn't the only Giants pitcher who was beginning to fade. Taylor was in decline, too. Wiltse had one of his best seasons, including a 10-inning no-hitter against the Phillies on the Fourth of July in which he retired the first 26 batters in succession, but Mathewson was the horse. He won a career-high 37 games that season and pitched a dozen shutouts.

McGinnity lost a crucial game to the Cardinals on August 16—it was Mathewson's turn in the rotation but it was Sunday—but he then defeated Cincinnati on August 22 in a nine-inning relief appearance after Ames walked the first two batters of the game and was pulled. That win came just a few hours after the Reds rejected yet another trade offer for Iron Man.[11]

He won again against Boston on September 4 and on September 18, a huge crowd at the Polo Grounds watched the Giants seemingly bury the Pirates' pennant hopes with a double-header sweep. Mathewson pitched a shutout for his 33rd win in the first game, and Wiltse and McGinnity teamed up to win the second game, extending the club's winning streak to 11 games.

Five days later, they faced the Cubs in what would come to be viewed as the most controversial game in baseball history. And McGinnity, though no longer pitching as frequently as in the past, was right there in the middle of it.

The Cubs had swept a doubleheader the day before and this game, at the Polo Grounds, was of vital importance to the Giants. McGraw made a key lineup change, replacing ailing first baseman Fred Tenney with a talented 19-year-old rookie named Fred Merkle, who had been with the team most of the season but hadn't played much.

It was standard procedure at the old Polo Grounds in those days that when a game ended, the ushers would open the gates and allow fans to come out onto the field to mingle with the players, patting them on the back if they won or perhaps chewing them out if they lost. The players got into the habit of racing to the clubhouse in right center field the second the game ended to avoid the rush. Fred Snodgrass, who was a rookie with the team that year, recalled that the benchwarmers were especially aware of this because it was a long run all the way from the dugout out to the clubhouse.[12] Merkle and the other subs had become expert at eluding the post-game crush.

But now, given a chance to play, Merkle came up with a big hit in the ninth inning of a tie game, stroking a single down the right-field line that sent Moose McCormick racing to third with two outs. Shortstop Al Bridwell then rifled a single to right center that got between the outfielders and rolled to the fence. McCormick trotted home with the apparent winning run, the ushers opened the gates and Merkle veered off to go to the clubhouse while he was still 30 feet from second base.

Years later, Merkle told an interviewer that Mathewson actually stopped him on the way and took him back to base umpire Bob Emslie to make sure he hadn't done anything wrong. Emslie supposedly told them the game was over.[13] He and home plate ump Hank O'Day allegedly also hurried to their dressing room behind home plate to avoid the crowd.

It seems as though there may have been only two men who fully understood that the game was not really over until Merkle touched second base. Cubs second baseman Johnny Evers realized it. So did the crusty, crafty 37-year-old ex-coal miner who was coaching third base for the Giants.

According to the most credible accounts of the incident, Evers began screaming at centerfielder Artie Hofman to get the ball. Hofman, like almost everyone else, thought the game was over and hadn't retrieved it. Now, at Evers' urging, he got the ball and threw it back toward the infield. The ball got to Evers about the same time McGinnity did, and the two men wrestled for possession of it. Evers was among the toughest, scrappiest men ever to play the game, but he weighed only 125 pounds and he was grappling with a 200-pound Irishman who was every bit as tough.

In the days and years that followed, dozens of conflicting accounts of the incident were related. The exact details have been muddled and blurred through the decades by the posturing accounts of the participants. A century later, it's still not exactly clear what transpired.

McGinnity insisted that he ended up with the ball and threw it into the left-field seats. In a letter written many years later, in 1926, he tried to claim that he did so in jubilation because he believed the game was over.[14] No one bought that story.

Evers insisted that McGinnity did not get the ball and he somehow produced a baseball amid the chaos of thousands of happy spectators. He stepped on second base to force out Merkle, negating the winning run.

The accounts of the game in the New York papers the next day—and there were about a dozen of them then—all were different.

A few of them had McGinnity being tackled by three Cubs players—Evers, pitcher Jack Pfiester and catcher Johnny Kling—as he scooped up the ball. Another story had Pfiester hitting McGinnity's arm as he tried to throw the ball out of the stadium with the ball landing harmlessly in shallow left field, where a fan picked it up. Cubs third baseman Harry Steinfeldt supposedly wrestled for possession of the ball with the fan before teammate Floyd Kroh came over and punched the fan in the nose, causing him to drop the ball. Steinfeldt then threw it to Evers for the forceout.[15]

The *Chicago Tribune*'s Charles Dryden reported that Kroh had to fight off six fans and that Steinfeldt handed the ball to shortstop Joe Tinker, who took it to Evers. Dryden also wrote that Mike Donlin was frantically trying to get Merkle to go touch the base.[16]

According to the *New York Evening Journal*, Cubs catcher Johnny Kling got his hands on the ball after Hofman's throw hit Tinker in the back, but the paper said Merkle was standing on second base by then, having been escorted there by Mathewson.[17]

Several accounts of the play have Mathewson being carried off by jubilant spectators. Some of them don't even agree on where McGinnity was prior to the play. A few had him coaching first base while others had him stationed at third.

As the years passed, the principals became more and more fuzzy—or creative—in recounting the episode.

McGraw wrote a column many years later for the Christy Walsh Syndicate in which he said McGinnity wrestled with Kroh, not Tinker or Evers.[18]

O'Day told *Sporting Life* six years later, in 1914, that it was Pfiester who first grabbed the ball when Hofman threw it back to the infield and that McGinnity wrestled it away from him, firing it into the seats. He said Steinfeldt retrieved the ball, ran back and handed it to Evers.[19] O'Day's hand-scrawled report to the league office written the day of the incident doesn't mention any of that. In it, he reported that Emslie did not see if Merkle touched second base and it was he who told him that Merkle had not. He said it was Emslie who then called Merkle out. O'Day also said that the game could not be continued because it would have been dark by the time the fans were cleared off the field.[20]

About 20 years later, Evers told *Time Magazine* yet another tale, claiming that Hofman's throw sailed over his head and that it was Tinker who wrestled with McGinnity. He repeated the story about Kroh getting the ball from a fan and said Kroh then handed the ball to him. Evers said that he then stepped on second base and that O'Day was still on the field to call Merkle out.[21]

Mathewson was quoted in a couple of papers after the game as saying that Merkle returned and was standing on second base before Evers got the ball,[22] although Matty later changed his story when quizzed about it in a formal hearing. The *New York Sun* reported that Merkle realized his blunder and tried to get back to second base only to be tackled by Chicago players.[23]

Chance claimed that he went to the umpires and told them they needed to make a ruling. He told them that since Evers touched second base while in possession of the ball, Merkle was out, the run didn't count and the game should be declared a 1–1 tie. Moreover, since there was no way to clear all those fans off the field and resume the game, and since McGinnity clearly interfered while the ball was still in play, the game should be forfeited to Chicago.[24] O'Day, in his 1914 interview with *Sporting Life*, claimed he called Merkle out not because of the force play but because of McGinnity's blatant interference.[25]

It appears as though Emslie and O'Day may not have even agreed on what should be called, but at the end of the day Fred Merkle was called out.

The final decision was not made until about 10 P.M. Rumor had it that McGraw went to the Coney Island boarding house in which Merkle lived, woke him up and took him back to the Polo Grounds so he could step on second base. The thinking was that in the legal wrangling that was sure to follow, Merkle could at least testify that he did in fact touch second base on September 23. The story likely is fiction, a tale fabricated to embellish the McGraw legend. Larry Doyle, who lived in the same boarding house, said Merkle refused to eat dinner and locked himself in his room for the rest of the night.[26]

Chance was doing everything he could to swing the decision his way. He had his team report to the Polo Grounds earlier than usual the next day and sent his team onto the field at 1:30, the normal starting time for a doubleheader. He had pitcher Andy Coakley throw a few pitches from the mound and insisted that his team should be declared the winner by forfeit because the Giants had failed to appear for the continuation of the previous day's game.[27]

O'Day had been involved in a similar play between the Cubs and Pirates a few weeks earlier and had ruled against the Cubs that time, but he admitted publicly that the baserunner should have to continue on to touch the next base. This time, he called the game a tie, and his decision was supported by National League president Harry Pulliam.

Of course, Pulliam had been undercut by the league's board of directors before, especially where McGraw was concerned. The board gathered in Cincinnati on October 5 and heard testimony from the umpires and others involved. Merkle reportedly told them he had touched second base before being tagged out or forced out. The directors deliberated all day without reaching a decision, hoping the pennant race would resolve itself and they wouldn't need to decide. Finally, on October 6, they upheld Pulliam's decision and ruled that if the Cubs and Giants finished in a tie for the pennant, they would replay the game on October 8.[28]

That's exactly what happened. The Giants swept a three-game series from the sixth-place Braves to finish the season, with McGinnity winning the next-to-last game in relief of Ames. The Giants and Cubs both finished with 98–55 records and the fast-finishing Pirates nearly made it even more confusing, ending up at 98–56. There would be a one-game playoff between the Giants and Cubs at the Polo Grounds.

The visiting Cubs had to make the long trip to New York through the night on what the *Chicago Tribune*'s Harvey Woodruff described as "the fastest train ever taken by a baseball club." It cost Cubs owner Charles Murphy a bundle of money to charter the Twentieth Century Limited, but it was scheduled to get the players there 10 hours quicker than they would on a normal train.[29] Even at that, they would only reach New York a few hours before the start of the game.

When they arrived, they waded into one of the most hostile atmospheres any team ever has faced. The New York newspapers only fueled the fury of the fans. The *Times* reported: "Never before has a club been compelled to play for a championship after once winning it, for despite the decision regarding the tie game, the Giants really won the game that was protested, but lost it through a technicality. It was the result of a grievous and inexcusable blunder of a New York player, and may result in the loss to the Giants of the National League championship."[30]

Thousands of fans jeered the Cubs as they stepped off the train in Penn Station. At the Polo Grounds, they encountered thousands more who had been turned away at the gate. The place was full by 1 P.M. for the 3 P.M. game. There were 35,000 people inside the stadium, but there also were fans standing on the roof of the grandstands and lined up on nearby Coogan's Bluff just to get a glimpse of the historic game.

Fans piled off the elevated trains at the 155th Street station by the thousands, and some of them couldn't even get near the stadium. They stood along the tracks of a railroad viaduct and tried to peer in over the left-field wall. A New York fireman named Henry McBride fell to his death from the viaduct and, as the *Times* noted, "his vacant place was quickly filled."[31] Another man fell 15 feet from the top of the right-field bleachers and broke his leg.[32]

The *Chicago Tribune* reported that a gang of boys broke a hole in the fence behind the grandstand and began crawling into the stadium only to be met by a security guard. "They were ordered back through the hole but one of them held out a quarter in temptation of the near cop, and it worked. Every kid that could raise a quarter gave it over and they were allowed to climb to the roof of the grandstand."[33] Other boys tried to climb a fence to get into the stadium and were turned away with fire hoses.[34]

"There is no record of a sporting event that stirred New York as did the game of yesterday...," the *New York Times* added. "Perhaps never in the history of a great city, since the days of Rome and its arena contests, has a people been pitched to such a key of excitement as the New York fandom yesterday."[35]

The Cubs had to fight their way through the crowd and arrived too late to take batting practice. With the stadium already overflowing and in a frenzied state, it was decided that the game would begin 15 minutes earlier than scheduled, leaving the visitors even less time than usual for infield practice. They had been loosening up for only a few minutes when they heard the bell ring signaling that they had to clear the field. The man ringing the bell was McGinnity, who walked over to Chance and ordered him to get his team off the field.[36]

It was all part of a plan to get the Cubs first baseman and manager ejected from the game before it even began. Depending on what version of this story you believe, McGinnity called Chance a bunch of names, spit on him, stepped on his toes or hit him in the chest with a bat—possibly all of the above— with the intent of provoking him into a fight. Chance, who Mathewson later wrote was actually a "very good friend" of McGinnity's,[37] didn't bite on any of it. According to the *Sporting News*, Chance said: "McGinnity, I am going to let you get away with this now, but if I ever meet you on the street, you had better get on the other side or I'll knock you there."[38]

The insanity didn't stop there. Dr. Joseph Creamer, who had served as the Giants' team physician all season, walked over to umpires Bill Klem and James Johnstone just before the game, pulled out an envelope and showed them that he had $5,000 in it.[39] Six months later, a three-man committee chaired by John T. Brush himself recommended that Creamer be banned from major league parks for life for offering a bribe.[40]

When the game finally began, Mathewson was pitted against Pfiester in a rematch of the same pitchers from the Merkle game. Mathewson retired the Cubs in order in the first inning, but Pfiester lasted only five hitters. He plunked Tenney and walked rookie Buck Herzog. Bresnahan struck out and Herzog was picked off first, but Mike Donlin doubled in Tenney with the game's first run. When Cy Seymour walked, Chance had seen enough. He pulled Pfiester and brought in Mordecai "Three-Finger" Brown, his ace.

Brown, a future Hall of Famer, had lost one-and-a-half fingers on his throwing hand in a childhood farming accident, but it gave his curve ball a peculiar spin. In truth, he may have been a larger nemesis to the Giants than the double play combo made famous by Franklin P. Adams' verse, and he handled them again when it counted most. The onslaught that began against Pfiester came to a grinding halt against Brown.

The Cubs scored the tying run in the third when Tinker tripled over Seymour's head in center field and was brought home seconds later. The Cubs broke loose for three more runs in the inning, the last of them scoring on a booming double by Chance.

The Giants managed just one seventh-inning run off Brown, and the Cubs won, 4–2, to take the pennant.

The hardest part of the day remained for the Cubs. They had to fight their way through an angry mob that Brown later described as a "lunatic asylum."[41] Chance was punched in the throat and Pfiester sustained a minor knife wound,[42] but the Cubs, escorted by a battalion of armed officers, finally reached the safety of the locker room and quietly slipped out of town.

The Cubs went on to win the World Series, beating a Detroit team managed by Hughie Jennings, and Fred Merkle's name went into history as a synonym for scatter-brained.

In the years that followed, Merkle was haunted by his mistake, taunted by unsympathetic fans and ridiculed by vaudeville comedians. The story of his *faux pas* has been written, rewritten, scrutinized and analyzed. A century later, his name is still known to baseball fans because of one momentary lapse in judgment.

In 1950, he told an interviewer "I suppose when I die, they'll put on my tombstone, 'Here Lies Bonehead Merkle.'"[43] When he did pass away six years after that, his grave was unmarked at his request.

McGraw was extremely supportive of the rookie. He told him he hadn't cost the Giants the pennant. He even gave him a modest raise for the following season, something McGraw almost never did without a squabble. The ebullient manager had gold medals made for each of his players, engraved with the words "The Real Champions 1908."[44]

In the wake of all the madness, mayhem and Merkle-bashing, no one quite realized they had just seen something else of significance in October 1908—the end of Joe McGinnity's major league baseball career.

17. Newark

If it hadn't been obvious to McGinnity at the start of the 1908 season that he didn't figure prominently in John McGraw's future plans, it certainly had to have been clear to him at the end of the season.

As the 1909 season approached, McGinnity knew he had to find another place for himself in the baseball world. The Giants had tried to send him to Indianapolis of the American Association as partial payment for pitching phenom Rube Marquard, but McGinnity refused to go.[1] He also had no desire to play for any other major league team.

He and an old friend from Springfield named H. Clay Smith hatched another plan. In late February, McGinnity asked for and was granted his release from the Giants. The next day, it was announced that he and Smith, who was referred to in stories as "a Chicago millionaire," had purchased the Newark Indians of the Class A Eastern League for $50,000.[2] It was the highest price ever paid for a minor league team at that time although some sources have listed the price as only $30,000.[3]

McGinnity had looked into buying the Buffalo team in the same league, but when he heard that owner Frank Farrell was looking to get out in Newark, he jumped at the opportunity.

It was not uncommon for retired ballplayers to buy minor league teams in that era. Jack Dunn, who played with McGinnity in Brooklyn, owned the Baltimore Orioles of the Eastern League. Bresnahan owned the Toledo Mudhens from 1916 to 1924. It was a way for players to stay close to the game after they were no longer able to play it.

But McGinnity had no intention of calling it quits as a player. It was announced that he would be both the team president and a workhorse starting pitcher.[4] He rehired the club's previous manager, a rough-and-tumble ex-major league third baseman named Harry Wolverton. Despite a penchant for getting into accidents, Wolverton was McGinnity's kind of guy—hard-nosed, relentless, tough. His own eight-year major league career had included its share of scuffles, including a fistfight with teammate Tim Donahue (McGinnity's old Kansas City catcher) during spring training in 1900.[5] While playing for the Phillies in 1901, Wolverton had been standing on the steps of a Philadelphia streetcar as it rolled down the street and ventured a bit too close to a light pole. He was struck in the head and sustained a fractured skull. It barely caused any interruption in his career. He was back playing the next season as though nothing had happened. A few years later, he would spend one unsuccessful season managing the New York Highlanders, also owned by Frank Farrell. (He was destined to meet it his demise in an accident in 1937, when he was struck and killed by a hit-and-run driver on the streets of Oakland, California.)[6]

McGinnity moved his family into the Continental Hotel on Broad Street in Newark, and he and Wolverton began assembling a team comprised primarily of players who either had been in the major leagues once or who would get there eventually. Included were shortstop Baldy Louden, who went on to spend four years as a starting infielder at the major league level; first baseman Bud Sharpe, who was the Braves' starting first baseman the following season; and third baseman Eddie Zimmerman, who later started for Brooklyn in 1911. Outfielder Jake Gettman had played three seasons in the National League in the late 1890s and, at age 33, was still scratching out a living in the minors.

On April 11, the Indians played a preseason exhibition game against the Highlanders (later to be known as the Yankees) and claimed a 6–1 victory behind the pitching of John Frill (who was to join the Highlanders the following season) and Arthur Mueller.

The next day afforded McGinnity an opportunity for personal redemption. The Indians ventured up to the Polo Grounds for an exhibition against the Giants, and he was taking the mound himself. The outcome wasn't what he had hoped for. The Giants managed only four hits off him, but they tagged him for three runs in the first inning and won, 4–0. McGinnity's old pal, Larry Doyle, did much of the damage, ripping a run-scoring triple in the first and adding a home run in the sixth. McGinnity bristled throughout the day, complaining loudly to the umpires several times. He also may have been dismayed by the disinterest of Giants fans in the matchup. The game was played in front of what the *New York Times* called "a small gathering of the most faithful followers of the sport."[7]

The Indians opened the Eastern League season 10 days later in front of a much larger crowd. About 12,000 people filed into Weidenmayer Park, but the result was similar. McGinnity again allowed only four hits but suffered a 2–0 loss to a Toronto team managed by his old Brooklyn teammate, Joe Kelley.

The Indians hung around the middle of the pack for much of the season. They were in fifth place in the eight-team league in early August. They were dead even at 48–48 on August 7, then won eight straight games to climb into second place behind John Ganzel's Rochester Hustlers. Frill pitched a 1–0 shutout against Montreal for the eighth consecutive win in spite of the fact that McGinnity, Wolverton and three other players were ejected from the game.[8]

Led by their 38-year-old team president, the Indians spent the next month applying the heat to Rochester. On August 18, McGinnity shut out Providence, 2–0, in the second game of a doubleheader. On August 23, he blanked Rochester on five hits to move the Indians to within two games of the lead. The next day, they beat the Hustlers, 7–4, to trim the lead to a single game.

On August 27, McGinnity resorted to his old Iron Man tactics. He pitched both games of a doubleheader in Buffalo and won them both, 4–2 and 4–1. The Bisons scored two runs in the first inning of the first game, then got just one more run off McGinnity in the next 17 innings.

McGinnity was depicted on a trading card for the Polar Bear tobacco company while playing for Newark in 1909 (Charles W. Brown, Jr., collection).

On September 12, a crowd of 15,000 wedged into Weidenmayer Park for yet another doubleheader with the Jersey City Skeeters. (Because of an unusually rainy summer, the Indians played 31 twin bills that season.) McGinnity worked in relief in a 2–1 loss in the first game, then hurled a 3-hit shutout in the nightcap.

Five days later, Rochester's lead was down to one game again, but the Indians couldn't get any closer. They finished five games off the pace.

Just for the heck of it, when Newark and Rochester met in a doubleheader on the final day of the season, McGinnity worked both games again. He lost the first one, 3–2, but won the second, 7–1. He gave up only 10 hits in the two games.

It was an impressive finish. The Indians went 37–18 after August 7 and McGinnity was a big part of it. He worked 422 innings in 55 games, went

29–16 and recorded a career-high 195 strikeouts. He even took over management of the team down the stretch. Wolverton was injured late in the season and unable to go on the final road trip with the club, so Iron Man handled the reins.

That brief run of success late in the season showed McGinnity that he could also be a manager and when the 1910 season began, he took on that role full-time. Wolverton, who no doubt found it awkward to have his boss also serving as a member of his pitching staff, landed a job with Oakland in the Pacific Coast League.

The Newark players soon learned that Iron Man ruled his team with an iron fist. Any player who was out of shape was likely to be fined. Several years later, he banned his players from smoking cigarettes during spring training because he felt it might impair their vision.[9] Any player who asked for time off for any reason was likely to be ostracized. Players were forbidden to bring their wives with them to spring training[10] although McGinnity likely had a double standard in this area. Mary almost always seemed to go with him on such trips. Gettman, a reliable center-fielder and cleanup hitter for Newark in 1909 and 1910, once asked for a couple of days off because his wife had pneumonia and he needed to take care of her. McGinnity called Gettman "yellow" and refused his request. Gettman simply quit the team instead.[11]

But McGinnity's hard-nosed tactics seemed to work. The Indians held onto first place for nearly 3½ months in 1910 with much the same everyday lineup they had used in 1909. The pitching staff struggled at times, though. McGinnity was forced to try another of his Iron Man efforts on July 30 in Buffalo. He pitched a shutout in the first game, getting the best of his old Giants teammate, Dummy Taylor, but he lasted only six innings in the second game and lost, 8–5.

He tried to bolster the staff by signing Bob Spade, the young kid who out-dueled him in his major league debut during the 1907 pennant race. And after Rochester slipped past the Indians into first place in August, McGinnity took a chance by signing Rube Waddell.

Waddell was an immensely talented lefthander, who led the National League in strikeouts six years in a row. He once struck out the side on nine pitches in 1902, but he also was among the most wild and eccentric men ever to play the game. There were reports—undoubtedly exaggerated—of him racing off the mound to chase a passing fire truck in the middle of games or being late for games because he stopped to play marbles with some neighborhood kids. He was a notorious drunkard who sometimes showed up for games with a snoot full. In 1909, he had collapsed on the mound in a drunken stupor during a game and in the middle of the 1910 season, the St. Louis Browns finally released him.[12]

He and McGinnity hadn't exactly been friendly as players. Iron Man never forgot how Waddell knocked him cold when he kneed him in the head during the 1900 Pittsburgh-Brooklyn post-season series. But McGinnity was in a fight for the pennant and he needed help. He signed Waddell on August 11 and immediately threw him into an important game with the Montreal Royals. Waddell won, 7–1, and the *Newark Star* reported "Rube had everything that he possessed in his palmist days. His curves had baffling breaks, and his speed was marvelous."[13]

Waddell had been cut by Connie Mack and the Philadelphia Athletics earlier in his career and was replaced by a pitcher named Rube Vickers. On August 20, McGinnity gave him a chance to go head-to-head with Vickers, who was then pitching for Baltimore, and Waddell was masterful, winning, 4–0. During the six weeks or so that he played for McGinnity in 1910, Waddell apparently behaved himself. He pitched in 15 games, worked 97 innings, and posted a 5–3 record. Waddell never made it back to the major leagues, however, and he died just three years later of tuberculosis.

Despite the added pitching help, the Indians couldn't quite catch Rochester again as Jack Dunn's third-place Baltimore club delivered some crushing blows in the final weeks. The Orioles swept the Indians in a September 12 doubleheader with McGinnity losing the second game, 3–2, and two days later, a kid named Harry Kroman tossed a two-hit shutout for Baltimore against Newark in his pro debut.

McGinnity had another superb season on the mound, winning 30 games while pitching 408 innings in 61 games. But Rochester won the pennant by 4½ games.

As the 1911 season approached, McGinnity continued to round up promising, young players while also dredging up useful, old ones. He signed a career minor leaguer named Johnny Nee, who was a grandfather as well as a competent second baseman.

He already had one good catcher on his roster, Lew McCarty, who was destined to spend nine years in the National League with the Dodgers, Giants and Cardinals. And on the recommendation of scout Larry Sutton, he also signed a young catcher from Henry County, Illinois, where McGinnity had been born.[14] Forrest "Hick" Cady caught 136 games for Newark in 1911 and had the best offensive season of his career.[15] He made it to the major leagues the following season and played in three World Series in his first five years with the Boston Red Sox.

But McGinnity supposedly passed on a chance to sign one more catcher who would have been his greatest find. Legend has it that three friars from a Baltimore orphanage approached him and said they were trying to find a place for a burly young catcher who they thought had great possibilities. They didn't even tell McGinnity that the kid was a lefthanded catcher, which really would have discouraged him. McGinnity refused anyway, telling them he already had two good catchers and didn't need any more. The story is somewhat dubious since the kid didn't sign his first pro contract until more than a year after McGinnity left Newark. But it was still fun to tell people in later years that he passed up a chance to sign Babe Ruth.

The 1911 season started badly for McGinnity and never got much better. In March, he was turning the crank on his newest toy—an automobile—when the crank broke loose and spun around, breaking the radius bone in his right wrist.[16] Manager McGinnity suddenly had lost the services of his best pitcher for close to two months. Since he had just turned 40, there was some doubt as to whether he ever could pitch effectively again.

A month later, in an April 22 game against Montreal, McGinnity was arguing the umpires' interpretation of a ground rule and carried his case to league president Ed Barrow, who was seated behind the Montreal bench. As he was talking to Barrow, a Montreal player named William Nattress spit in his face. McGinnity momentarily raised his right hand to punch Nattress, then remembered that the arm already was broken. He decked him with a left instead.[17]

He returned to action on May 21 and pitched very well in a complete-game effort at Rochester, allowing just six hits. But as so often happened in his Newark years, he didn't get much offensive support and lost, 3–0.

McGinnity worked 422 innings for Newark in 1909 and 408 more in 1910. His 195 strikeouts in 1909 were a career high (Charles W. Brown, Jr., collection).

The Indians were in seventh place by the time he came back, barely ahead of last-place Providence, and they never made any sort of run for the pennant, which was won again by Rochester. The Indians finished 57–95 and for the first time since his disastrous 1894 season at Kansas City, McGinnity's own record was below .500. He pitched in 43 games and worked 278 innings, but he registered just 12 wins with 19 losses.

The season also had not been a financial success for the ballclub and McGinnity was discouraged, ready to give up and move on. He and H. Clay Smith entered into negotiations with local real estate magnate William J. McManus for the purchase of the team. McManus was offering $65,000, but he wanted everything involved with the team. While McGinnity and Smith were ready to sell, Frank Redpath, McGinnity's brother-in-law, had been granted a five-year lease on the concession rights and he wouldn't budge.[18]

The deal fell through. There were more negotiations with other potential buyers but none of them went anywhere.

The *Syracuse* (New York) *Herald* intimated that the team was being mismanaged, claiming that McGinnity was drawing a salary of $10,000 to serve as team president and another $3,000 to pitch.[19] Barrow came to his defense, telling the *Herald* in a November 10 article that McGinnity and Smith had gone about things in "a businesslike way."[20]

They never did sell the team although they did take in some new investors. McGinnity unsuccessfully tried to get McGraw to put some money into the team and did find a willing partner in Brooklyn Dodgers owner Charles Ebbets.

McGinnity and Smith were the majority stockholders when the 1912 season rolled around, but Newark now found itself in a new league. Under Barrow's direction, the Eastern League changed its name to the International League and moved up to being a Class AA organization.[21]

That brought an influx of even more ex-big leaguers. Former teammate Cy Seymour, who nearly won a Triple Crown for Cincinnati in 1905, joined the Indians in an effort to resurrect his career. McGinnity reacquired Eddie Zimmerman, who had been the starting third baseman for the Dodgers the year before, and at mid-season he added Bert Tooley, who had been the starting shortstop. He also added catcher Harry Smith, who spent 10 seasons in the majors with the Pirates and Braves.

But Newark still wallowed in the middle of the standings for most of the season. In mid–August the Indians were four games below .500 and in fifth place in the eight-team league.

Nothing seemed to go right for McGinnity around that time. On August

13, he had his car stolen. By now he had moved his family into a house at 143 Meeker Avenue, near Weequahic Park, and he left the car at a garage down the street. A 17-year-old named Herbert Johnson and two other men took it for a joy ride, smashed it into a tree and wrecked it.[22]

On the field, the Indians put on another late rush reminiscent of the charge they'd made in 1909. They won 19 of their last 28 games, but finished third in the league behind Toronto and Rochester.

Along the way, McGinnity turned in one more of his signature Iron Man stunts. On July 23 at Rochester, he won the first game of a doubleheader, 4–3, as the Indians rallied for four runs in the seventh to overcome an early deficit. The second game was no contest as McGinnity hurled a five-hit shutout. He held the three-time defending league champions scoreless for the last 14 innings of the afternoon.

His pitching record was much better than it had been the previous year—16–10 with 261 innings pitched—but he worked much less frequently as the season wore on. He had one last splash of glory with a 1–0 shutout of Providence on September 8.

However, it was clear that his time in Newark was coming to a close.

On August 29, Charles Ebbets quietly took in two new partners, contractors Stephen and Edward McKeever, to provide him with some extra capital to help in the completion of a new ballpark he was building for his major league club. It was an omen of things to come. Ebbets held 45 of the 233 total shares in the Newark franchise, and now he and Ed McKeever engineered what amounted to a takeover of the team. Each of them bought half of H. Clay Smith's 50 shares, which made Ebbets the majority owner. McGinnity, seeing what was happening, sold his 45 shares to McKeever. After all the maneuvering, Ebbets and McKeever each had 70 shares, vice president George L. Solomon had 45 and there were another 48 distributed among minority shareholders.[23]

McGinnity received $8,000 for his shares, resigned as president and manager, and was granted his unconditional release. Harry Smith was named the manager with Solomon assuming the title of team president.[24]

McGinnity issued one last statement addressed to "the baseball public of Newark":

> At this opportunity I beg to express my deep gratitude and appreciation to my many friends and patrons in Newark for their kindness during the past four years of my connection with the Newark Baseball Club.
>
> It has been the one aim of my work and the height of my ambition ever since I became interested in the Newark team, not only as a baseball magnate, but as a participant in the game as well, to give the city of Newark a

team far superior to any other and my efforts to attain this end has no doubt merited the appreciation of the public in general.

Owing to circumstances entirely beyond my control, I am compelled with deep regret, to sever my association with the Newark Baseball Club. It is my firm belief that the baseball enthusiasts of Newark are ever on the alert in the support of a good team, and my experience has fully convinced me that the city of Newark is the best paying baseball city in the minor leagues.

To the players on the Newark team, I also wish to express my sincere appreciation, individually and collectively, of their hearty cooperation and earnest endeavors to give the fans of Newark a class of ball unequaled to that of any other team and though their efforts and mine have not met with the success for which we were striving, it cannot be said that it is due to indifference on our part, as all of the players worked very faithfully to present Newark with a pennant.

As to my future plans, I cannot say much regarding this at the present time, but the probabilities are that I shall not retire from the game but later center my interests in some other team. In the meantime, I shall take a few week's vacation, for after four years of hard striving to please the baseball fans of Newark in my endeavor to give them a winning team, I very much feel the necessity of a short rest.

Mr. Henry C. Smith and myself are retiring from the Newark Baseball Club with the deepest regrets and we leave our best wishes for the future welfare and success of the team under the new control.[25]

Newark finally got its pennant the following season, but by then Joe McGinnity was 3,000 miles away.

18. Tacoma

After selling his shares in the Newark team, McGinnity had no shortage of other opportunities. The Topeka Jayhawks of the Western League wanted him and the terribly named Terre Haute Terre-irs of the Central League also extended an offer.[1]

His old teammate, Hughie Jennings, serving as manager of the Detroit Tigers, stated in an interview with the *Newark News* that he wanted McGinnity as his pitching coach and possibly as a relief pitcher.

"When I heard that McGinnity had secured his release I wasted no time in informing President Navin, of our club, that Joe would be a valuable addition to our pitching corps, and Mr. Navin got into communication with the Iron Man," Jennings told the newspaper. "We could use McGinnity to advantage in more ways than one. There isn't a man in the country who can pitch to batters like Joe. I don't mean by this that in case we landed the twirler that he would be used for that purpose, but he would give our players confidence when they advanced to the plate because McGinnity has always been noted for the manner in which he can control the ball and get his offerings over the plate. He varies the ball but very little and it is the balls that go over the plate that we want our men to hit and not to go after every ball served up. I consider McGinnity still able to pitch good ball and as a relief twirler, one who can jump into the game cold, he has never had an equal. I would sooner have McGinnity on this team than a dozen youngsters who only show flashes of form."[2]

McGinnity apparently liked being his own boss, however, because he turned down all those offers and in November secured a 30-day option to buy the Class B Northwestern League team in Tacoma, Washington.

George Shreeder had owned the club until the middle of the 1912 season but when he became ill, Edd Watkins took over as team president. Watkins was instrumental in wooing McGinnity to a part of the country he'd probably never even seen and he reportedly accepted a lower offer from Iron Man because he believed someone with his star power had a better chance for success.[3]

After visiting Tacoma in December, McGinnity said the people there treated him like "a prince." He said they were "crazy" about baseball and talked of nothing else. "Everyone seems to have a hospitable way about them and I am sure that the town will be one of the best in the circuit with any kind of winning club," he added.[4]

He and his 31-year-old brother-in-law, Frank Redpath, became partners, paying a mere $8,500 for the franchise.[5]

While he was there in December, McGinnity attended the league meetings in Tacoma and fought hard to get better schedule dates for his new team. The Tacoma Tigers had played only 58 home games the previous year but for the 1913 campaign, they were scheduled for 96, including 20 Sunday games plus home dates on Memorial Day, the Fourth of July and Labor Day.[6]

McGinnity took the train back to Newark feeling as though there was no way the Tacoma franchise could be anything but a huge success. He arrived back in Newark on New Year's Eve, collected his family and was bound again for Washington less than two weeks later on the Lehigh Valley Railroad's Black Diamond Express. A handful of cheering Newark fans saw him off.[7]

Part of his plan was to have a new ballpark built in Tacoma only about a five-minute walk from the downtown area, close enough for workers to stroll over to games at the end of the business day. He couldn't get a piece of land that was large enough, however, and he ended up paying $20,000 to buy Athletic Park, a rundown ballpark in the southwest part of the city. He received assurances from the Tacoma Railway and Power Company that it would provide adequate transit service to the park. He planned to sink about $50,000 into renovating the 6,000-seat facility, putting up new grandstands, bleachers, dugouts and clubhouses, and completely resodding the field.[8]

McGinnity also bought a large 11-room house on south L Street that cost nearly as much as his new ballclub. He had tucked away a nice bundle of money during 10 years in the major leagues and four years in Newark, and he was pouring it all into his Tacoma venture, certain that it would pay off.

Before leaving New Jersey, he signed several of the best semi-pro players in the area, including pitchers Harry "Kid" Kurfess and Abe Weisher, infielder Charley Rothfuss and catcher John Foley, who gave up a good job as a police officer to follow McGinnity across the country. McGinnity also offered a contract to George Boice, a pitcher from his 1911 Newark club, and hoped to sign more prospects on the way to Washington.[9]

McGinnity wasn't a complete stranger to his new situation. The president of the Northwestern League was Fielder Jones, who had been his teammate with Brooklyn in 1900 and an adversary in the early days of the American League. He also knew Daniel Dugdale, the president of the Seattle team, who had played against him in the Southern League in 1893 and who owned and managed the Peoria team in the Western League just before McGinnity got there. There were many others involved with the league who he had played with or against.

As he was preparing for the season, he also bumped into Adrian "Cap" Anson, an old Chicago White Stockings superstar of the 19th century who was touring the Pacific Northwest performing a vaudeville act. Anson told the *Tacoma Ledger* he had no doubt that McGinnity's club would win the Northwestern League pennant and assured the local fans that Iron Man's "famous Old Sal curve is equal to all of the fadeaways and other new-fangled shoots when it comes to deceiving the batter ... it is one of the hardest balls in the world to hit."[10]

The Tacoma Tigers opened the season on April 15 wearing some garish new uniforms. McGinnity borrowed an idea he had used back in Newark and outfitted the club in brown army khakis, arguing that they were "warmer and more serviceable than the ordinary kind."[11] The Tigers wore red stockings and red caps with green bills. The word Tacoma was spelled vertically down the front of the shirts.

Unfortunately, their play on the field never was quite that flashy. They lost their opener to Vancouver, 4–1, and McGinnity suffered a 7–0 loss in the second game of the season. Kurfess finally secured the first win, allowing one hit in the first eight innings and holding on for a 5–4 win over Vancouver, but the Tigers hovered around .500 for most of the first few weeks.

One place they did excel was at the box office. The *Sporting News* reported on May 22 that Tacoma was leading the Northwestern League in attendance.[12] In fact, having a former major league hero around was helping to draw crowds everywhere. With Portland struggling to attract fans, league president Fielder Jones proposed that it try to spike attendance by holding a special day to honor McGinnity when Tacoma came to town.

"The acquisition of Joe McGinnity, the Iron Man, former star pitcher of the New York Giants, as owner of the Tacoma Club has not only strengthened the national game in Tacoma, but has also been of benefit to the league generally," Dugdale said in an interview. "A man of his standing can not but help any league with which he becomes associated."[13]

McGinnity was making new friends all around the league. When a 21-year-old youngster from Oklahoma named Carl Mays came up with a sore arm while pitching for Portland, he sought McGinnity's counsel, and the veteran pitcher taught him how to throw underarm to save wear and tear on his arm.[14] Mays eventually won 207 games in the major leagues with that same sweeping motion although he is best remembered as the man who threw the pitch that killed Cleveland shortstop Ray Chapman in a 1920 game.

The Tacoma Tigers, led by player-manager Joe McGinnity (second from left), had high hopes when they embarked on the 1913 season (Marc H. Blau collection).

Meanwhile, McGinnity was struggling to get his own team to perform up to expectations and he wasn't showing much patience. He released starting catcher Dick Crittendon less than a week into the season and brought in a replacement. He was bringing in new players every week and experimenting with different combinations. Kurfess ended up playing almost as much at shortstop and center field as he did pitching.

And McGinnity couldn't ever seem to find enough good pitchers. He found himself utilizing his own hurling skills more than even he would have liked, working in 24 games and throwing 144 innings over a span of 40 days in the middle of the season.

His own right arm seemed to be one of the few things he could rely on. On April 26, he shut out Seattle on four hits, 6–0. On May 29, he blanked Victoria for nine innings, then lost the game on a run in the 10th inning.

On June 14, he did something he'd never done before for any team at any level, clubbing a home run in a 9–5 victory at Spokane.

He was doing everything he could in every phase of the game to try to win and light a fire under his club. In another game in the same week in which he hit the home run, he got on base, stole second, stole third and then scored on a sacrifice fly. It was a remarkable sequence for a 42-year-old pitcher.

"But the burst of speed was too much for the veteran's wind," the *Sporting News* reported. "He returned to the box in the next inning and lost his game because he was all in. A man of McGinnity's experience should know it is not good for a pitcher to run himself out on the baselines."[15]

It was indicative of the way he was pushing and prodding and driving his team. The *Sporting News* reported that he was alienating some of his players by employing many of the same demanding methods he'd used in Newark, "fining his men for everything imaginable."[16]

The Tigers never got higher than third place in the six-team league all season and they finished fifth at 75–96, 26½ games behind the pennant-winning Vancouver club. McGinnity appeared in a career-high 68 games and threw 436 innings, 99 more than any other pitcher in the league. His record was 22–19. He even batted .176, rapping out 27 hits and scoring 13 runs.

But it had been a season of almost constant turnover in personnel. The *Tacoma Times* reported that "McGinnity overestimated the league at the beginning and was forced to change all the time."[17] There was a veritable revolving door at some positions. McGinnity used eight different first basemen, 10 different shortstops, nine different catchers and 15 different outfielders. Only six players who opened the season with the Tigers finished the season with them.

McGinnity was determined that things would be different in 1914. He brought close to 40 players to training camp, which was scheduled to begin on March 23. The players were so eager to get started that they played a game the day before camp officially opened, defeating a touring Japanese team, 5–1.

McGinnity ran a rugged camp with two practices every day, at 11:30 A.M. and 3:30 P.M.[18] There were exhibition games against all sorts of competition, from local high school teams and the Cushman Indians (a local semipro outfit) to the Chicago American Giants, one of the strongest Negro League teams in the country.

It didn't seem to matter who they played. The Tigers were crushing everyone by scores such as 21–1, 14–2, 13–2 and 13–0. They beat the American Giants, led by the immortal Rube Foster, 7–4, on April 5. Foster brought his team back for a rematch on April 10 and it was worse. The Tigers pounded out 17 hits and won, 15–6. McGinnity's club seemed primed to make a run at the championship of the six-team Northwestern League.

He returned many of the players who finished the previous season with the Tigers. He had very high hopes for a reliable Iowa-born first baseman named Frank West and a promising 22-year-old second baseman from California named Fred McMullin. Besides himself, he had four returning pitchers—Dick "Izzy" Kaufman, Dave Kraft, Jerry Girot and Kurfess, the only one of his New Jersey recruits who actually made it. He also still had catcher Skin Harris and two good outfielders—Cy Neighbors, who had played one game in the major leagues with Pittsburgh six years earlier, and a native Washingtonian with an intriguing name—Ten Million. Two new recruits also had some major league experience. Center-fielder Ody Abbott played 22 games with the Cardinals in 1910 and third baseman Bill Yohe saw action in 21 games with the Washington Senators in 1909.

The Tigers looked like a sure contender and opened with an 8–7 conquest of the Vancouver Beavers amid a gala atmosphere. Despite intermittent showers, the two teams rode around the ballpark in Fords before the game and Washington governor Ernest Lister threw out the first pitch.[19]

The Tigers didn't get off to quite the outstanding start that everyone hoped for, though. They played .500 ball for most of the first six weeks. On April 25, McGinnity was hit in the head by a line drive and sustained a nasty gash above one eye that kept him out of action for a week.[20]

On May 16, after he lost a 1–0 pitcher's duel to Seattle's Alva Gipe, the *Tacoma Times* reported that "McGinnity is pitching much better so far this year than he did last."[21]

He was still as ornery as ever, as evidenced by a May 20 battle with an umpire named Schuster, who seemed to be having trouble keeping track of the ball and strike count. The *Tacoma Times* referred to Schuster as "a cross-eyed, wooden-headed son of a pirate."[22]

"Being Irish, the Iron Man ... spoke to Schuster," the *Times* reported. "He spoke harshly. He doubled up two bunches of knuckles suggestively. In clear, lucid tones, he conveyed to the unhappy Schuster the intense pleasure it would give him to change the topography of the said Schuster's map. He said other things, too—shocking words that are not repeated in our circle."[23] McGinnity ended up being suspended by league president Fielder Jones, who also fired Schuster and brought in some new umpires.

The Tigers were not doing great at the gate, but they weren't the only ones. Attendance for a late–May series opener at Portland was so bad that McGinnity suggested the remaining games of the series be played in Tacoma instead. Portland manager Walter McCredie politely declined.[24]

On June 7, Spokane pitcher Lou Stanley took a page out of Iron Man's book and pitched both ends of a doubleheader against Tacoma. He actually went McGinnity one better, throwing shutouts in both games.

McGinnity was the losing pitcher in the first game in what was the start of a horrific month for the Tigers. They were 22–26 and hanging onto fourth place at the start of the month, but they went 5–26 in June and fell into the cellar. The Tacoma newspapers began the inevitable sniping that McGinnity was not fit to be manager, that he used himself on the mound too often and left himself in a little longer than he should.

In late June, he responded to the whining of the fans and the newspapers by stepping down as manager and putting 42-year-old Russ Hall in charge.[25] Hall had had a very brief major league career—only 40 games—but he had been a player and manager for Seattle in the Pacific Coast League for many years. He also was active in trying to improve the plight of players. He had been the first secretary of an organization called the Association of Professional Baseball Players of America. He had a softer, gentler touch than McGinnity. In the modern-day vernacular of the sport, he would be known as a players' manager.

Hall's first game as manager on June 28 was greeted with a brass band and one of the largest crowds of the season, and the Tigers whipped first-place Vancouver, 9–6. Hall began remaking the roster, bringing in at least 10 new players in a matter of weeks, including a pair of 20-year-old phenoms named Bender and Stevens, who became available when the Fresno team of the California State League folded. The Tigers began to play better baseball. In a July 13 game in Spokane, McGinnity pitched seven strong innings but things began to unravel in the eighth when he dropped a pop-up he should have caught, walked a man and gave up a double.

"Ordinarily, Joe would have stayed in the box until the Colts were about three runs ahead..." the *Times* reported. "With Russ Hall on the job yesterday, things went different. He yanked McGinnity before the damage had gone too far.... Hall's good judgment pleased the fans who have seen game after game go by the boards that should have been won as certain as yesterday's, had there been good management at the helm."[26]

Under Hall, the Tigers strung together an eight-game winning streak in July. In the eighth game, they banged out 11 hits against their old nemesis, Alva Gipe. The *Times* loved it: "The Tigers are just demonstrating what they would have done all through the season with proper management. Russ Hall is given credit for the winning streak—even the players pass the praise along to the jovial Kentucky manager—and our only regret is that Russ did not take charge of the Tigers when the season opened." The same story noted: "McGinnity believes that he made the best move of his life when he hired Russ Hall."[27]

Hall also came up with the idea to have a "Carnival of Baseball," a weeklong celebration of the sport, to attract fans to the ballpark. Each day of the week was to be devoted to a local group—the Elks Club or the Conversation League or the Ad Club—in an attempt to spike attendance. Fielder Jones called it "a splendid idea."[28]

Struggling to pitch and manage at the same time, McGinnity turned the managerial reins over to a more player-friendly boss, Russ Hall. The positive impact was immediate but temporary (Marc H. Blau collection).

The Tacoma franchise was not making money although the *Times* reported that the team was not in as much danger as the Portland franchise, which had recently moved to an old Scandinavian neighborhood of Seattle and become known as the Ballard Colts.

McGinnity seemed to prosper without the weight of having to manage the team. He ended up winning 20 games again although this time he managed to lose 21. He also worked 326 innings.

But the Tigers, after their initial surge into fourth place under Hall, leveled off and faded to fifth, finishing ahead of only the financially-strapped Ballard club. They were 38–43 under Hall but only 64–93 for the season, finishing 34½ games behind Vancouver.

The season was not over for everyone. Fred McMullin, one of the team's steadiest players for two years, joined the Detroit Tigers late in the season. In 1916, he would begin a five-year run as a key utilityman for the powerful Chicago White Sox. His career was terminated after the 1920 season when he and seven teammates were banned from baseball for throwing the 1919 World Series. (McMullin batted only twice as a pinch-hitter in the series and got one hit, but he was banned anyway.)

McGinnity's season was not over either. He signed on to pitch for manager Hap Hogan and the Venice (California) Tigers, who were trying to make a late run at the Pacific Coast League title.[29] He won his September 25 debut but in eight games with Venice, he went only 1–3.

Meanwhile, back in Tacoma, the honeymoon clearly was over. The local newspapers had been rough on McGinnity all season and now they speculated that he might not even be back for the 1915 campaign.

"Fans in Tacoma are now wondering what we will do for baseball next season," the *Times* reported on September 14. "Joe McGinnity has lost much of his popularity, and it is confidently rumored that he will not attempt to manage another Tacoma team. His repeated sale of good players, just when his team was beginning to show class, has discouraged patrons of the game. Tacoma's infield has been admirable most of the season, and the team had looked good on paper, but Joe wouldn't pay money for pitchers, and he was repeatedly breaking his lineup by selling his best players.

"Tacoma will support a good baseball team, even in an off year. It's a safe bet the Tigers would not have lost money this year if the fans had not been disheartened by McGinnity's desire to make money rather than to make a team."[30]

But McGinnity wasn't ready to quit. He returned for the 1915 season and again enlisted Hall to serve as the manager. "I will not step in to interfere with him," McGinnity promised.[31]

To gain more operating capital, McGinnity and Frank Redpath began selling stock in the Tacoma Tigers during the 1915 season (Marc H. Blau collection).

The team was now on unsteady ground financially, and McGinnity and Redpath sold stock in the team to acquire some operating capital. There were rumors that George Shreeder, the old owner, was interested in buying the club back. Shreeder denied it.[32]

The Tigers opened with McGinnity pitching a 3–1 victory over Seattle and the team held onto first place for the first few weeks of the season. As was the case late in the 1914 season, McGinnity seemed to pitch better without the weight of having to call the shots from the dugout. On April 25, he gave up only four hits in a 1–0, 11-inning loss to Seattle. On April 30, he shut out Aberdeen, 1–0.

"Poor old Joe McGinnity, whose obituary notices were printed during the winter, pitched another shutout game the other day, holding Aberdeen to three hits," the *Sporting News* reported.[33]

On May 20, McGinnity engaged in a rematch with an old adversary. Back in 1904, Bob Wicker had been pitching for the Chicago Cubs and hurled a no-hitter for nine innings to snap McGinnity's season-opening 14-game winning streak. Wicker now was the player-manager of the Spokane Indians, and he and the Iron Man hooked up in another duel. Wicker won again, 2–1.

This time he had a one-hitter for eight innings before Tacoma strung together four hits in the ninth to score its only run. The two old-timers rattled off the game in an hour and 12 minutes with McGinnity allowing only seven hits and not issuing a single walk.

They were scheduled to square off again three days later, on May 23, but Wicker had a sore arm. McGinnity, who claimed to never have had a sore arm in his life, pitched and beat Spokane 6–4. Frank Calhoun wrote in the *Sporting News* that "McGinnity has started his 22nd season in baseball like a house afire."[34]

But it didn't last. After a few weeks, Vancouver edged past the Tigers in the standings.

Even before that happened, it was clear that the Tacoma fans weren't embracing their team. It wasn't the only club doing poorly at the gate. In late July, the Aberdeen and Victoria teams folded, leaving the league with only four teams.

At about that time McGinnity announced that he also would give up his franchise if attendance didn't turn around very soon.[35] As it was, he and Hall were carrying only 12 players on the roster to save expenses.

The community rallied briefly around the team with the impetus coming from an unlikely source. Many of the ministers in Tacoma arranged to have a "booster day" for the team, and they implored their congregations in Sunday morning sermons to go out to the ballpark. It worked. On July 31, the Tigers drew an overflow throng of 12,000, the largest crowd in the history of the Northwestern League.[36]

McGinnity's players did their part, too, voting unanimously to take a 10-percent pay cut to help the team make ends meet.[37]

The Tigers briefly dropped all the way into last place, then staged a furious rally in the final weeks and finished only four games behind first-place Seattle at 85–73. McGinnity, who worked 355 innings and went 21–15, had one of the most dominant stretches of his career in that final rush, pitching shutouts against Spokane on September 12 and 16, and holding Vancouver scoreless on September 19. He allowed only two hits in the victory on the 12th and on the 16th he again out-dueled Wicker.

But the Tacoma fans barely noticed. And as a result, most of those late heroics took place on the road.

As the season wound down, the Tigers still were struggling financially and taking a beating in the local media. On September 6, the *Times* reported that "baseball in Tacoma is becoming a joke. It's better than a Sunday colored comic supplement." The team had played a benefit game on September 4 with the local YWCA being promised 15 percent of the gate. YWCA sup-

The Tacoma Tigers of 1915 were joined by a pair of clowns for a group photo. McGinnity is in the back row, second from the right. To his right is his brother-in-law, Frank Redpath. Next to him, also in street clothes, is manager Russ Hall (Marc H. Blau collection).

porters turned out and helped put on the game, but received only $15.50 after expenses.[38]

With so little support at home, McGinnity made a controversial maneuver, one that was not unprecedented in that era but which brought down the wrath of the Tacoma community nonetheless. He accepted a $1,000 guarantee to play 12 straight games in Spokane near the end of the season rather than playing them in Tacoma.[39]

"McGinnity has departed," the *Times* reported in yet another personal attack. "Four games are scheduled to be played in Tacoma before the end of the season. If someone will bid two bits, maybe McGinnity will consent to keep his team away from home the remainder of the season."[40]

It was all smoothed over somewhat after the season when the city gave a banquet in honor of McGinnity and his team "in which it was agreed to bury the past disastrous season with all its bickerings." The fans pledged to be more supportive of the club in 1916.[41]

But McGinnity's financial scars wouldn't ever heal. He reportedly had lost $27,000 in three years in Tacoma.[42] The initial novelty of having a former major league star in town had worn off and it finally was time for him to move on. He and Frank Redpath pretty much gave the franchise to Hall. On February 21, 1916, it was announced that they had sold it to Hall for $365.75, the exact amount of the team's outstanding debt.[43]

By then, the *Tacoma Times* had changed its tune slightly and was a bit more sympathetic to the plight of minor league baseball owners: "McGinnity is to be complimented on his gameness. Realizing that he could not handle the Tacoma club of the Northwestern League any longer, he sent a letter to Hall Saturday admitting the fact and offering Hall the club."[44]

Another column in the newspaper, entitled "Peter's Piffle," added: "Regardless of everything that has been said of Joe McGinnity, we have to show our respect for him over the graceful manner which he gave up the Tiger team. Only a man of pretty good sporting blood could admit defeat in such a straight-forward manner. It's a whole lot easier to win at anything than to admit that you are beaten."[45]

19. Montana

Joe McGinnity had been a part of minor league baseball as an owner for seven years through an era of explosive growth in the lower levels of the sport. By 1914, there were 42 leagues sanctioned under the auspices of the National Association of Professional Baseball Leagues,[1] more than twice as many as there are today.

But a downturn in the trend was coming. A third major league, the Federal League, briefly cut into the talent pool in 1914 and 1915, and then clouds of war gathered in 1916. When the United States officially entered World War I in April of 1917, the minor leagues really began to stagger.

This war, with its global ramifications, was even more of a distraction to baseball fans than the Spanish American War had been and players began to enter the armed services in bunches. By 1918, there were only nine minor leagues in operation and none of them played beyond mid–July that summer.[2]

McGinnity and Frank Redpath didn't see all that coming, though, when they jumped into another venture in the Northwestern League in 1916.

The league had been reorganized and reenergized. The Victoria Bees had gone out of business and so had the Aberdeen Black Cats, who had replaced the struggling Portland/Ballard franchise. For the first time since 1903, there were two new franchises in Montana—in Butte and Great Falls—and McGinnity was to have a hand in shaping both of them.

It was a natural fit. His roots in Montana extended back to before he was even born. His grandfather, John Denning, had followed the wagon trains to Virginia City, Montana, in the 1860s and McGinnity's Aunt Elizabeth and her husband, Brown Ferrell, still lived in Pony, Montana, about 40 miles southeast of Butte. Several cousins were scattered through the southwest part of the state.

McGinnity and Redpath were developing a coal mining operation of their own near Box Elder in the northern part of the state.[3] They now became the driving forces behind the new Butte team, which was sometimes known as the Miners, but was more often referred to as the Ironmen, after its famous new manager.

Butte should have been a splendid place for a minor league franchise. It was a thriving metropolis at that time, the boomtown of the copper industry. Its population was then about 100,000, triple what it is today. The city had 14,500 miners who toiled each day in underground shafts.[4] Ballgames in the late afternoon sunshine should have been the perfect diversion.

Working with the directors of the Butte Baseball and Athletic Association, McGinnity and Redpath leased a piece of land from the Great Northern Railroad in the southeast part of town, between First and Second Streets, just east of Oregon Avenue. A new wooden ballpark was hastily constructed on the site, patterned largely after the stadium back in Newark. It included chairs instead of bleacher seats in the grandstand and had seating for 4,500. The local newspaper, the *Butte Miner*, estimated that 175,000 feet of lumber were used in the construction of the park.[5] It wasn't anything as grand as the double-decked palace in which Dan Dugdale's team played over in Seattle, but it seemed functional enough.

It included something else that owners hadn't had to worry much about before — a parking lot. America was becoming an increasingly motorized society and the new owners wanted to have enough room for 300 vehicles beyond the left-field fence. The clubhouses, equipped with all the modern amenities, were situated in the right-field corner.

To make room for the larger-than-usual parking lots and clubhouses, the outfield fences were brought in much closer to home plate than in almost any other park in minor league baseball. The cozy dimensions and perpetually gusting winds of Butte Community Field — also known as Hebgen Park — were going to make for some astronomical scores in the next two years.

In the beginning, there was a great deal of harmony in the franchise. The *Butte Miner*, speculated that it seemed "too good to be true,"[6] but there actually were all sorts of nagging little problems. There was one man perpetrating a scam by telling people he was selling fence signs at the ballpark and then pocketing the money. A group of children got together a petition protesting that the ballpark was displacing a playground even though, according to the local newspaper, there had not been a playground on that land for many years.[7] And McGinnity eventually would find that the board of directors of the Butte Baseball and Athletic Association were a tight-fisted bunch unwilling to spend the kind of money he wanted to develop facilities and upgrade the team.

He wasn't yet aware of that when he gathered his team for spring training in Puyallup, Washington, just south of Tacoma, on April 10. It's not entirely clear why McGinnity chose Puyallup as a training site. It may have been because he still owned a house in nearby Tacoma. It certainly wasn't because of the Washington weather.

The team worked out at the Western Washington Fairgrounds, which had a new baseball field with 3,000 seats and also had a large building—100 feet by 280 feet—that could be used for indoor workouts when the weather was not suitable to play outside.[8] It ended up being used much more often than the outdoor field.

On April 16, McGinnity took his first pitching turn of the spring against a semi-pro team from Tacoma. Sportswriter Ned C. "Spike" Haynes wrote in the *Butte Miner*: "Joe McGinnity loosened up his old reliable propeller shaft and held down the mound for four innings, during which the visitors got three singles. Joe said he could have finished the game but he didn't want to overwork his famous old wing."[9]

About a week before the team was to return to Butte, Joe, Mary and Marguerite went out to the theater one night and as they returned home to their house in Tacoma, they found two men escaping out the back door. McGinnity grabbed a rifle and took off after them but was unable to catch up with them. They had taken close to $300 in jewelry. Most of it belonged to Marguerite, but also included was a special watch given to McGinnity nearly 20 years earlier by members of the Watch Factory team in Springfield. "Guess we will be safer on the road and in Butte," he told Ned Haynes.[10]

The Butte ballclub that opened the season was very young. McGinnity was the only player over the age of 30, but Haynes reported that the team had plenty of speed and loads of hitters.[11] In fact, it was destined to have three of the top four finishers in the league batting race that season.

Center-fielder Ed Kippert, who had played two games with the Cincinnati Reds in 1914, batted .358 and right-fielder Eddie Johnson hit .345. Roy Grover, the team's scrappy leadoff man and second baseman, batted .342 and actually finished the season with the Philadelphia A's. He was destined to start for them the following season. At least 10 players on the 1916 Butte club—including Kippert, Johnson, Grover and four other starters—had been with McGinnity the year before in Tacoma, an indication that his leadership style, though harsh and demanding, appealed to many players of the era.

McGinnity seemed optimistic that this would be the team that finally would bring him a pennant as a manager.

"My club, playing in Tacoma last year, finished second in a hard race .... and we are going to do better this year," he told Ned Haynes. "We have a great infield, a hard-hitting outfield and the pitchers are all that could be desired in a minor league."[12]

The season opened April 27 at Seattle amid controversy. There was a driving rainstorm and McGinnity refused to pitch, but umpire Garnet Bush was equally stubborn and refused to call off the game. The Ironmen went down to an 8–2 loss in front of a crowd of about 1,600.[13] The next day, after the rain had stopped, McGinnity threw a five-hitter but committed two errors in the field and Seattle won, 4–0.

On May 1, the Ironmen played in Tacoma and found that 12 carloads of fans had made the trip over from Puyallup to support them. McGinnity left the game in the seventh inning on the short end of a 6–4 score, but the Ironmen scored two runs in the ninth to tie it, then won the game in the 11th.

The gala home opener in Butte was scheduled for May 16 against Tacoma. Most of the players—with the exception of McGinnity and pitcher Rex Hydorn—had never even seen the city they were representing and there were all sorts of festivities to welcome them.

There was a huge pre-game luncheon at the Butte Grill that was attended by 300 people and included speeches by several politicians and dignitaries. Among the speakers was McGinnity, who told the throng "It's the team that makes a manager, not the manager who makes the team. I'll let my boys speak for me this afternoon and what they do on the diamond, good or bad, is no indication of what they can do. I know they can play baseball and I hope they will continue."[14]

The luncheon was followed by an automobile parade that took both teams to the ballpark. Montana governor Samuel Stewart and Butte mayor Charles Lane both were there. So was an announced crowd of 4,977 although the *Miner* said it was more like 6,000.[15]

The only negatives of the day were the fact that Tacoma won, 7–3, and that the weather, somewhat marginal all day, turned terrible in the ninth inning. By the time the game ended, it had degenerated into a small blizzard.

The Ironmen, with Kippert and first baseman Gil Stokke injured, stumbled through the first few weeks. McGinnity didn't get his first win until May 18 when he beat Tacoma, 12–5. He defeated his former team again on May 21 although he hardly was dominating, allowing 14 hits in a 15–10 victory.

On May 30, in the second game of a Memorial Day doubleheader in Great Falls, he hit a home run, something he had done only once before in his pro career. He always was a good hitting pitcher, but he seldom hit for power. This time, he hit a line drive into the right-field power alley that took a weird bounce and rolled to the wall as he circled the bases.[16]

It became apparent very early that while McGinnity had a pretty good team, he couldn't match the bunch that abrasive manager Nick Williams had assembled in Spokane. Williams had three players on his club who were destined for lengthy major league careers. Dutch Ruether would win 137 games in 11 years in the big leagues. Earl Sheely would bat .300 in nine seasons in the majors. And Ken Williams, who had spent half the previous season with the Cincinnati Reds, would become a major star with the St. Louis Browns, becoming the first major leaguer to collect 30 home runs and 30 stolen bases in the same season in 1922.

Another thing that became very apparent very early in that season was that McGinnity never was going to get along with Garnet Bush, a former National League ump who had forced Seattle and Butte to play in a driving rainstorm on opening day. That was only the start of a running feud.

Bush also kicked McGinnity out of a game in Great Falls on May 28. And on June 4, against Spokane in front of the home fans in Butte, he kicked him out of *two* games. McGinnity pitched the first five innings of the first game of a doubleheader, but when he accused Bush of favoring the other team, he was ejected. According to the *Butte Miner*, the home fans grew increasingly dissatisfied with Bush as the day progressed and when McGinnity also was kicked out of the second game, the crowd was in a frenzy. One fan threw a rock that opened a gash in Bush's head.[17]

League president Robert Blewett felt McGinnity had helped to incite the crowd and he fined him $100 and suspended him indefinitely. Needless to say, that brought another angry outpouring from Butte. Ned Haynes branded it a "mighty unjust decision" and Mayor Lane sent a telegram to Blewett complaining that Bush was discriminating against the Ironmen.[18]

Blewett fired back on June 7, saying he would not allow McGinnity on the field until he received assurances from the Butte management that he would behave himself. "McGinnity acted unbecomingly on the field Sunday and he deserves to be punished the same as any other player," Blewett said. "He cannot expect the league to be kept clean and orderly by pulling the stuff which he did and the sooner he finds it out the better. I have more than the umpire's word for what was done and said in the attack on the umpire by the Ironman and I know that I am right in taking the action which I did."[19]

He also said he would not grant Butte's request for a meeting of the league's board of directors on the issue. But the meeting was called anyway and set for June 15 in Seattle.

In the meantime, McGinnity was temporarily reinstated. In his first game back, on June 10, he "scattered" 16 hits in a 19–4 victory over Great Falls.

At the meeting to determine his fate, the representatives of the six clubs haggled for eight hours over how to resolve the McGinnity-Bush dispute. At the end of the day, they reduced McGinnity's fine to $25 and levied a $25 fine against Bush for "indiscretion."[20]

The feud didn't go any further. A few weeks later, Bush walked off the job in the middle of a July 4 doubleheader at Vancouver and was fired by the league.

McGinnity, now fully reinstated, began to win. He claimed three victories in the span of a week in June, going 13 innings to win the last one at Seattle.

Throughout June and July, his Ironmen battled to catch up with first-place Spokane but never could seem to get any closer than six or seven games. On August 2, McGinnity beat the league leaders, 2–1, and Butte won the first game of an August 6 doubleheader in Spokane. But the Indians won the second game, 3–1. In the eighth inning of that game, the Ironmen loaded the bases and McGinnity took himself out of the game, sending first baseman Frank Guigni up to pinch hit for him. Guigni struck out rather feebly to end the threat.

Following the game, McGinnity accused Guigni of conspiring with Spokane and striking out on purpose, and he immediately gave him his release. Nick Williams was livid, claiming that McGinnity should be barred from baseball for making such an accusation.[21] He then signed Guigni to play for his team. Guigni seemed to rediscover his hitting stroke with the Indians, and a few weeks later he went 5-for-5 and hit for the cycle against Tacoma.

The day after releasing Guigni, the Ironmen returned to Butte for a very long homestand to take one more shot at catching Spokane. But the fickle winds and cozy dimensions of Hebgen Park worked against them.

On August 9, they defeated Vancouver, 17–12, with McGinnity pitching 8⅔ innings in relief, but a 15–13 loss the next day dropped them into third place. On August 12, McGinnity was hit in his pitching hand by a line drive for the second time in a month and was unable to pitch for about a week. Without him, Butte gave up runs in even larger numbers in its little ballpark, losing one game to Seattle, 24–8. When the Ironmen finally snapped a five-game losing streak, they did so with a 27–12 victory.

After a 13–5 loss to Seattle on August 18, the team's frustrations bubbled over. Catcher Skipper Roberts was upset at being removed from the game, and he and McGinnity engaged in a brief fistfight in the clubhouse. A day later, Roberts was fined $25 and given his outright release.[22]

McGinnity also was still being haunted by his accusations against Williams and Guigni earlier in August. Williams lashed out against McGinnity in an August 23 story in the *Seattle Times*, announcing that he and Guigni planned to sue McGinnity and Redpath.[23]

"McGinnity kills baseball in every town in which he has anything to do with the management of baseball," Williams said. "He did it (in Tacoma). He did it in Newark, and he is doing it in Butte. Every time he loses a game, someone is cheating him. He has gone too far in this matter by trying to make Guigni and myself crooks. Honesty is the foundation of baseball and a player that has been branded as McGinnity attempted to mark Guigni is barred from organized baseball. We are going to take this case to the highest courts of baseball and force McGinnity and his brother-in-law, Redpath, to prove the charges they are making so freely. More than that, we are going to bring civil action against them and force them to pay for the libelous statements they have been making."[24]

There is no record of Williams and Guigni ever filing any legal action, however. The issue was supposed to come before the league's board of directors at its winter meeting, but Guigni failed to show up to present his case and the matter was dropped.

With Spokane firmly in control of the pennant race, the Ironmen went through a few weeks near the end of the season in a veritable daze, prompting Ned Haynes to write: "There isn't any life and still there isn't a solitary thing on which to make an accusation. The gang appears to be willing enough but they don't deliver. We'll admit the cripples, an astonishing number of breaks for every club that comes here and all that sort of stuff but when a club like Seattle or Vancouver can drop around these parts and romp home day after day, there's a reason."[25]

The *Seattle Times* wasn't done taking shots at Iron Man either. It printed an item on August 29 in which it depicted the Butte fans and newspapers as a veritable lynch mob. It said McGinnity had lost control of his players. It said the team's board of directors had given him a "free hand" and he had failed to deliver. "The ragging, scrapping tactics of the Butte manager in handling his players and conducting the club on and off the field, have resulted in an open breach between players and managers, and there is an absolute lack of harmony between McGinnity and the Butte players...."[26]

If the players were in mutiny, as that story indicated, they had an odd way of showing it. On the day the story appeared, McGinnity pitched a 9–0 shutout over Great Falls, which had surged into second place. The Ironmen won five straight games against the Electrics with McGinnity again beating them on September 2 on Eddie Johnson's game-winning home run in the ninth inning.

Butte finished 12½ games behind Spokane in the final standings, but it held a comfortable margin over the rest of the league at the end of the campaign. McGinnity had pitched in 43 games and registered the 14th (and final) 20-win season of his career, going 20–13.

Ned Haynes wrote a lengthy wrap-up of the season in the September 6 *Butte Miner*, in which he noted "the club is not going to make any money this season. That's a bet. But a start has been made and with everybody pulling together baseball will next season undoubtedly be better established than ever."[27]

Numbers released by the league a few days later indicated that Butte actually was one of three Northwestern League clubs—Spokane and Tacoma were the others—that turned a profit during the season.[28] However, the season left McGinnity, Haynes and others wondering what might have been had they not experienced so many injuries and bad breaks. Haynes pointed out that the pennant-winning Spokane club had hardly any injuries or adversity all season.

"McGinnity as a manager has done excellent work with his material, has played the game hard and is entitled to a lot of credit," Haynes wrote. "Joe is popular here and before any member of the Butte management goes to Spokane to attend the league meeting, some decision should be reached as to the leadership of the club next year. Personally, we favor McGinnity. Joe might be a little too rough with his gang but he generally gets results, knows the game and hasn't got any too good a deal since he has been in this league. He's not asking for and doesn't want any sympathy but with all this talk of 'running McGinnity out of the league,' it might be well for the Butte management, if they want him again, to take the bit in their teeth and make themselves known at the forthcoming meeting. The directors and fans as a whole certainly want him."[29]

The board quickly followed Haynes' advice and rehired McGinnity to manage the team for the following season. The *Seattle Times* reacted predictably, noting that "the old boy slipped something over" on his team. "Several club owners professed to believe that Joe would be dropped by the Butte club," the paper added, "but they proved to be poor guessers."[30]

McGinnity and Frank Redpath and their families split the winter months between Box Elder, where they had a coal mining operation, and Oklahoma, secure in the knowledge that they would be back in Butte for the 1917 season.

The Northwestern League held its preseason meeting on March 3 at the Davenport Hotel in Spokane and Guigni's grievance was discarded when he failed to appear.[31] At that same meeting, the Ironmen swung a trade that sent Stokke to Vancouver for a veteran first baseman named Clifford McCarl. It was a deal McGinnity would come to regret several times in the months that followed.

The Ironmen got a late start on spring training, heading back to Puyallup while most of the other teams in the league already were working out in warmer climates, but there were other problems on the horizon.

The war that had been raging in Europe for a few years was escalating and expanding, and the United States was being inexorably pulled into the mess. On April 5, about three weeks before the Northwestern League season was to begin, Congress passed a resolution declaring that a state of war existed with Germany. Within days, almost all college athletic programs were temporarily shelved, and there was talk that baseball and other sports might need to do the same.

The Ironmen gathered in Puyallup on April 9 anyway to begin preparing for the uncertain season. They still had veterans Dave Hillyard and Eddie Johnson in the outfield and Dutch Hoffman behind the plate, but McGinnity had tried to bolster his team with some new acquisitions, many of which did not work out very well. A player he signed on his winter trip back to Oklahoma never showed up. Another player quit the team because his mother was sick. A few enlisted in the service.

Then there was McCarl, a supremely gifted first baseman who couldn't seem to make up his mind whether or not he wanted to play. Four years earlier, he had signed with Spokane, then got married and went on a lengthy honeymoon before reporting to the team. Now he played a similar game with McGinnity. First he said he would play, then he decided to hold out, then he came back, then he quit again, saying he had been appointed assistant city clerk of Fresno, California.[32] McGinnity finally signed Bun Giddings, a journeyman first baseman, to replace him.

The spring weather in the Pacific Northwest was even more unpredictable than usual, and the Ironmen spent much of the first few weeks working out indoors in the large exhibition hall at the Western Washington Fairgrounds, only occasionally getting outdoors to beat up on local semi-pro teams such as the Puget Sound Ministers.

Before the season began, league president Robert Blewett made an attempt to avert some of the dubious on-field behavior he had dealt with the previous season. He issued a mandate that the slightest hint of profanity would not be tolerated in the league. Any players using foul language would be escorted from the premises. Like most leagues in that era, the Northwestern League was endeavoring to market its game to a female audience. Blewett said that "dern" and "dog-gone it" would be tolerated "but nothing stronger."[33]

By all appearances, Blewett may not have had to worry much about the Ironmen, who didn't seem to have many of the same ruffian element on the roster this time.

"The Butte squad is composed of a peppery, clean cut, companionable lot of chaps without a roughneck in the lot," Ned Haynes wrote in the *Miner*. "They are not by any means a crowd of slackers...." He noted that one of

McGinnity's young pitchers was a gifted piano player and several of the players had good singing voices.[34]

But they weren't terribly talented on the playing field. Butte opened the season with three wins over Spokane, but then lost 11 games in a row. McGinnity was almost constantly tinkering with his team. In the middle of the 11-game skid, he released three starting infielders at once.[35] The replacements weren't much better. On May 9 at Vancouver, the 46-year-old player-manager pitched a three-hitter but lost the game, 1–0, when his new second baseman fumbled a routine ground ball.

Haynes wrote on May 9 that either McGinnity or the team's board of directors needed to move quickly to improve the team, warning that "there will be more men at the recruiting offices than the ballpark unless something is done."[36]

He also questioned the commitment of both the directors and McGinnity, citing the fact that Iron Man had not stayed around during the winter and had gotten a very late start on spring training. "There have been unnecessary bickerings and a lack of mutual consideration regarding the team that has played havoc with even the prospect of a club," he wrote. "Who is to blame? Looks like a 50–50 proposition."[37]

The Ironmen played their first 32 games on the road—they actually rallied to go 14–18 in those games—and while they were gone, there were concerns about the quality of their playing field back in Butte. The board of directors had promised to pay to have it resodded, but they now were reneging on that. It was too expensive and they weren't sure how much good it would do. McGinnity told them he feared his players might stage a strike until the playing surface was improved.[38] J.R. Wharton, manager of the Butte Electric Railway, finally stepped forward to donate the necessary sod, having it taken from Columbia Gardens, a large amusement park on the east side of town.

But McGinnity continued to feud with the board from afar. He had been trying very hard to sign a promising shortstop named Tom Fitzsimmons, whom he considered a key to solidifying his team. He couldn't get the board to give him enough money to do it and on May 11, Fitzsimmons signed with Spokane.[39]

He settled for a lesser talent at short—Joe Levin—but on May 20, Levin told him he was quitting the team for "business reasons."[40] McGinnity also was struggling to find quality pitchers. It irked him that Herman Pillette, a pitcher he had cut the year before, had emerged as the league's elite pitcher with Tacoma.

McGinnity found the same solution to the pitching shortage that he had used so often in the past. He simply worked more often himself. On May 12, he did another one of his Iron Man stints, pitching and winning both ends of a doubleheader against Vancouver, 3–1 and 6–2. In the first game, he held the Beavers to just four hits while banging out three hits himself. He gave up 11 hits in the second game, but nine of them were singles.

"This latest feat of McGinnity was the result of a fit of pique," the *Brooklyn Eagle* reported. "His pitching had been going so badly that he became disgusted and told them he would show them up."[41]

Of course, McGinnity also couldn't go through a season without feuding with umpires. His chief adversary this time was an ump named Edward Eckman. On May 22, the Ironmen were locked in a duel with Tacoma that was tied at 6–6 in the 14th inning. It was at that point that Eckman kicked Butte catcher Dutch Hoffman out of the game. McGinnity already had used his other catcher, Frank Kafora, as a pinch-hitter earlier in the game and he was out of players. McGinnity argued and then went to appeal to Tacoma manager Tealey Raymond to allow him to bring Kafora back into the game. Before he could make his case, Eckman forfeited the game to Tacoma.[42]

McGinnity filed a formal protest but it fell on deaf ears. Blewett fined him $100.

Three days later, McGinnity and Eckman were at it again. The umpire ejected Butte pitcher Sash Meikle in the third inning of a game and in the ensuing debate, McGinnity, Kafora and pitcher Ben Hunt also were kicked out and escorted from the Tacoma ballpark by police officers.[43]

Like Garnet Bush the previous year, Eckman didn't last the entire season. He quit on June 18.

On May 29, after more than a month of road games, the Ironmen were scheduled to play their home opener. However, a late-spring snowstorm struck southwest Montana that day and the game was postponed. They finally played the opener on May 31 and it quickly became evident that Hebgen Park, as the year before, was going to be a house of horrors for pitchers. On June 2, the Ironmen lost to Vancouver, 22–4. One June 7, Tacoma hammered out 31 hits in a stunning 31–12 victory over Butte. McGinnity pitched 5⅓ innings in relief in that game and was hit as hard as anyone.

Haynes' story on that game in the *Butte Miner* was very short and sharply critical: "Don't know whether it's a record or not in what is supposed to be a Class B league, but yesterday it was a Class Z league in every department of the game.... The game was a farce and a freak. It's not worth speaking about."[44]

The Ironmen were in last place at 15–29, and McGinnity was almost continuously squabbling with the board now. In early June, he held a series of closed-door discussions with the directors with Blewett serving as a mediator.

On June 8, after the team rebounded for a victory following the 31–12 loss, McGinnity resigned as manager, sold his shares in the team for $3,000 and retired. The *Miner* reported that McGinnity "was willing and perhaps not at all adverse to getting out of baseball."[45]

"He always worked hard in a game, saved many a contest for his club and socially is as fine a fellow as ever walked," the newspaper added.[46]

A few hours after the transaction was completed, something happened on the north edge of Butte, at a place called Granite Mountain, that put the travails of the local baseball club into perspective.

The site was a copper mine operated by the North Butte Mining Company. A mine worker carrying a carbide lamp accidentally ignited a damaged electrical cable, starting a fire shortly before midnight. The flames, transported quickly by underground gases and air currents, swept through a 700-foot shaft that contained 415 men working the night shift.[47]

The accident devastated the entire Butte community and created a scene eerily reminiscent of what McGinnity had seen in Krebs 25 years earlier. He was not directly involved this time, but the familiarity of it must have hit home. As in Krebs, anguished, wailing relatives flocked to the mine site, waiting for bodies to be recovered, hoping against hope to see one of their loved ones come out alive.

A makeshift morgue was set up at the site and it took two weeks to unearth all the bodies. The mining company had to hire extra workers to handle the flood of telegrams that came in from around the country, inquiring about the status of loved ones. The final death toll was pegged at 168. It remains the worst hard-rock mining disaster in American history.

Out of respect to those affected by the catastrophe, the Ironmen did not play for the next few days. When they finally resumed on June 11, they had an unlikely new manager—Clifford McCarl.

McGinnity left to tend to his mining interests near Box Elder after pitching 92 innings in 13 games and registering a nondescript 4–4 record.

By now, it was obvious that no one involved with minor league baseball was going to finish the season. The war was adversely impacting attendance and luring away players. By the Fourth of July, four leagues—the Three-I, Northern, North Carolina and Virginia—had disbanded for the season. Three-I League president A.R. Tearney urged all 13 minor leagues that were Class A or lower to suspend operations after the Fourth.[48]

Something else happened on the Fourth of July: Joe McGinnity returned to the Northwestern League after less than a month on the sidelines. He seemingly couldn't stand to be away from the game and the competition. He had kept busy pitching for a semi-pro team in Havre, Montana, close to his mining interests. When Great Falls lost pitcher Bert Hall to an injury, manager Herb Hester asked McGinnity if he'd like to begin pitching for the Electrics. He accepted. Again, it was a good fit for him. Great Falls was closer to his mining interests in the northern part of the state.

And Great Falls, unlike Butte, was in a pennant race. The Electrics had been trying to catch Tacoma all season and while they were doing so, Seattle had swept past both of them into first place. It was now a three-team fight to a finish that figured to come much sooner than scheduled.

McGinnity made his debut with Great Falls on July 4 and beat Spokane, 5–3, in the second game of a doubleheader. Three days later, he beat Spokane again, 13–4, and rapped out a couple of hits at the plate.

But the league's owners voted on July 9 to conclude their season after the games of Sunday, July 15. It was hardly unanimous. Seattle owner Daniel Dugdale and Vancouver's Bob Brown, the two most powerful men in the league, had absorbed heavy losses and wanted the season to be over.[49] Brown had said before the season he thought his team and his community would not feel the effects of the war,[50] but now he was feeling it as much or more than anyone in the league. Spokane, mired in last place, was ready to join them.

The two Montana clubs—Butte and Great Falls—wanted to keep going and they seemed to have Tacoma and Russ Hall on their side. However, Dugdale and Brown persuaded the Tacoma board of directors to overrule Hall and vote to end the season.

The remaining schedule was adjusted to minimize travel expenses. Teams were to stay where they were at that moment and play out the schedule at those sites, which meant Great Falls was to finish the season with six straight home games against the Tacoma club it had been battling all season. Seattle played Vancouver.

At the time of the vote, Tacoma was in first place, but it led Seattle by only half a game and Great Falls by one game. Seattle beat Vancouver in five of those last six games, but Great Falls swept six straight from Tacoma to cop the pennant. McGinnity provided one last bit of heroics, hurling a 4–2 win over Tacoma on July 12. In his only three regular-season starts with Great Falls, he pitched three complete-game victories.

The Montana teams were not willing to just let the season die. A plan was hatched to have Great Falls and Butte keep playing in an altered league in which the players from Tacoma and Spokane would relocate to two Montana cities—Billings and Lewistown.⁵¹ Forget Dugdale and Brown. They were going to keep playing.

But the plan fell apart. In the cold, hard light of financial reality, Billings and Lewistown backed out.⁵² Butte and Great Falls continued to play one another every day for one extra week with Butte winning three games, Great Falls two and one game ending in a tie. In the first game, McGinnity pitched a 2–1 victory over his old team and did it in just an hour and 10 minutes—the quickest minor league game ever played at Great Falls' Earling Park. He pitched once more in the series, losing the final game, 6–5.

It was the last gasp of the Northwestern League for 1917.

20. Northwest Encore

The Northwestern League wasn't completely dead. It came back to life in January of 1918, with the help of a former superior court judge and U.S. congressman named William Wallace McCredie. He had been backing teams in Portland, Oregon, for many years with his wife, Alice, and his nephew, Walt. Alice generally served as ticket manager and Walt, who played part of the 1903 season with the Brooklyn Dodgers, served as player-manager.

The McCredies had been part of the larger, more prestigious Pacific Coast League for a few years, but the California teams that dominated the league were trying to reduce travel costs and after the 1917 season they essentially evicted the non–California franchises. The McCredies opted instead to become part of the Northwestern League, which W.W. McCredie insisted upon renaming the Pacific Coast International League. The move infuriated Pacific Coast League owners, which probably was the whole point.[1]

The McCredies also renamed their own club. Portland teams for years had been known as the Beavers, but they changed it to Buckaroos to avoid confusion with Vancouver, which also was known as the Beavers.[2] Portland and the Aberdeen Black Cats replaced Butte and Great Falls in the revamped PCI.

The league seemingly was doomed from the outset. The clouds of this new "world war" were growing too dark for the new PCI—or any other minor league—to survive. Secretary of War Newton Baker and General Enoch Crowder, the United States' provost marshal, had issued a "work or fight" order, decreeing that all adult male citizens in some way contribute to the war effort.[3] Playing ball was not considered an essential activity, and there was considerable pressure to shut down leagues for the duration of the war. August Herrmann, chairman of the National Baseball Commission, reported in June that 17.1 percent of the players in the major leagues had enlisted and another 11.8 percent had been drafted.[4] Many players began taking factory jobs to avoid the service and the PCI was quickly stripped down by players going to work in the shipyards that were scattered throughout the Pacific Northwest. Roy Grover found work in a shipyard. So did Nick Williams and Alva Gipe. Herb Hester enlisted.

McGinnity, too old to become a solider anyway, initially had no intention of being part of the revamped league. He planned to stay home and tend to the mining business. But as more and more young players were lured away by "work or fight," quality pitchers were in short supply. And, as so often happened with McGinnity, his competitive juices yearned for an outlet.

The *Sporting News* reported the predictable news in mid–May: "Joe McGinnity just can't keep out of it. The gray-haired veteran has left his coal business in Montana to take another fling at the game with the Vancouver team. Joe says he is in fine shape, that he had a great winter, feels his youth renewed and knows he can have a profitable and pleasant season pitching ball for Bob Brown."5

Brown, known as "Mr. Baseball" in Vancouver, had been operating the league's only stable Canadian franchise for years, playing shortstop, batting seventh in the batting order, calling the shots on the field and managing to make ends meet with a shoestring budget. With travel costs rising fast, there had been some sentiment for cutting Vancouver out of the league along with Butte and Great Falls, but Brown had succeeded in keeping his franchise. It was now a "community-owned" franchise with many Vancouver townspeople pitching in to keep it going.

McGinnity joined the Beavers 15 games into the season, but it was as though he'd never been away from the game. In his second game, on May 24, he went the distance against Seattle, allowing only five hits in a 1–0 loss. He shut out Portland on four hits on June 6 and won in relief the next day. He went 10 innings in a loss to Seattle on June 16 and 11 in losing to Aberdeen on June 20. The old, McGinnity fire was still there. When his left-fielder misplayed a fly ball during Seattle's game-winning rally on June 16, the *Seattle Times* reported that "old Joe McGinnity was ready to murder" him.6

He was as strong as ever, but the PCI was weakening fast. Less than a month into the season, on May 26, it became a four-team league when Spokane and Tacoma both disbanded their clubs. Tacoma, under Russ Hall, had one of the best teams in the league but received almost no fan support. The *Sporting News* reported that "some people are mean enough to say it is the rottenest city of its size in the country when it comes to baseball."7 In retrospect, McGinnity's brief financial success in Tacoma a few years earlier looked pretty good.

Vancouver was the one box office success in the league. The Beavers drew 6,000 fans for their home opener and regularly attracted good crowds by playing "twilight" games, which began at 6 or 6:30 P.M., allowing more working men to attend. The *Sporting News*, in its June 27 issue, published an article by A.P. Garvey lauding Vancouver's continued strength as "remarkable." "President Brown stands out alone as the one magnate in this part of the country who is running along smoothly with little fear of facing the bankruptcy courts. The fans are flocking to the park night after night...." The article added that "Vancouver is on the baseball map to remain and the fans are solidly behind Brown."[8]

Ironically, Vancouver, British Columbia, was unceremoniously expunged from the baseball map at about the time that article hit the newsstands.

Brown and Seattle owner Dan Dugdale, who had been allies in shutting down the Northwestern League the year before, were now bitterly at odds. In a May 31 league meeting to discuss what to do in the wake of the departures of Spokane and Tacoma, Dugdale had argued to terminate the season only to be shouted down by Brown and his fellow owners. The *Seattle Times* said the owners voted unanimously to continue the season only because Dugdale was "shamed" into voting that way.[9] The discussion grew so heated that Dugdale at one point walked around the table and kicked Brown. Charles Sullivan, a Seattle police officer who moonlighted as the president of the Aberdeen club, quickly separated them.[10] Another rumor had Dugdale and Blewett coming to blows during the meeting.[11]

As the league's financial situation worsened in the weeks that followed, the other owners came over to Dugdale's side of the argument and Brown became the victim of an insidious power play.

With only four teams remaining, Dugdale and McCredie pushed through an altered schedule that called for Vancouver to play a weeklong series in Portland at the end of June. While Vancouver was drawing well at home, Portland wasn't drawing anything. Brown proposed that the games be played in Vancouver instead. McCredie said he only would do so if Brown guaranteed him $800. Neither owner would budge, and the *Seattle Times* pronounced the league to be on life support. "The Pacific Coast International League is so nearly dead that the physicians in attendance have cranked up their cars and are ready to drive away," the paper reported.[12]

The league's board of directors met again and declared that Brown was to be stripped of his franchise since he refused to follow their altered schedule. The franchise was then moved to Vancouver, *Washington*, just across the Columbia River from Portland, and the company team of the Foundation Ship Building Corporation was substituted in place of Brown's club. Brown's Vancouver Beavers played their final game on June 22 and three days later, the shipyard team, which included a handful of former minor leaguers, took their place.

"Never in the history of baseball has a league done such an outlandish thing as this," the *Seattle Times* reported. "The PCIL has cut off the city that has been its bread and butter all season and taken in a city that has never even supported semi-professional baseball before."[13]

Another meeting was arranged for June 26, at which time Brown was to argue his case, but the *Seattle Times* reported that the Vancouver owner "spoiled the fun" by not showing up.[14]

The shipyard team didn't provide much competition, and a week later it was replaced by a different team from the Columbia-Willamette Shipbuilder's League. The *Sporting News* wasn't exaggerating a bit when it called the entire situation "a joke."[15] The league struggled on for two more weeks with Seattle and Aberdeen playing one another every day and Portland having its way with the shipbuilders, winning 14 games in a row.

On July 7, the league closed operations for the year,[16] as did every other minor league in the country. Even the major leagues cut short their seasons so that players could "work or fight."

McGinnity pitched in only nine games, going 2–6 before Vancouver was evicted from the league. His 11-inning, 6–3 loss to Aberdeen on June 20 was his final appearance. Within a week after that, he, Mary and Marguerite returned to Montana and ultimately to Oklahoma. He finally had seen enough of the politics of baseball in the Pacific Northwest.

21. Working for Staley

After the premature end of the 1918 baseball season, Joe McGinnity went back to work at the Union Iron Works in McAlester, Oklahoma, but he didn't stay there long. In early May of 1919, he received another offer that must have seemed too good to be true—a chance to again become involved in baseball while also retaining a somewhat normal lifestyle back in Decatur as an employee of the A.E. Staley Manufacturing Company.

A.E. "Gene" Staley was the ultimate self-made man. He had grown up on a farm in North Carolina and received very little formal schooling. He taught himself to read and found he liked talking to people more than the hard labor that went into running a farm. His father died when Staley was 16 and he seized the opportunity to do something else with his life. Before long, he had made big money selling tobacco and other items to small grocery stores all over the Carolinas. He noticed that the most consistent seller was corn starch and decided that was a good business into which to sink the money he had made.[1]

He heard about a vacant mill in Decatur that would be perfect for his growing enterprise, convinced many of his old grocery clients to buy stock and purchased the plant in 1912.[2] With the help of an energetic engineer named George E. Chamberlain, he built a business that brought new prosperity to Decatur and changed the face of the town.

The *Staley Fellowship Journal*, his company newsletter, described the company in 1920 as "one of the largest producers of corn products in the world. It grinds 30,000 bushels daily. Products include starch, syrup, gluten, feed, meal and oil."[3]

Staley never had been an athlete himself, but he loved sports and soon seized upon athletics as a way to build company morale, enhance productivity in the workplace and promote the company name outside the confines of Decatur. The Staley Fellowship Club began sponsoring athletic teams, starting with a baseball team in 1917.

Within the next few years, the company would add teams for football, basketball, track and bowling, and Staley was determined that each of them would be among the best in the country in their individual sports. The baseball team enjoyed immediate success, winning city and league championships in 1917, but two years later Staley saw an opportunity to upgrade the program even more by hiring one of the most famous pitchers in the history of the game.

He no doubt heard the local townsfolk talk about the local guy who had made it big in the majors earlier in the century and he may also have heard that the same guy was looking for a new opportunity. With very few minor leagues in operation and a dwindling number of job opportunities in that area, it didn't take much to persuade Joe McGinnity to take on the dual role of starch factory worker and baseball coach. Over the course of the next few years, he also would find time to help tutor the pitchers of the University of Illinois team under new coach Potsy Clark.[4] And, of course, he had one other role: He still planned to get out on the field and do some pitching.

"Just how active a part Joe will take on the ball team remains to be seen and depends much on his condition," the *Decatur Review* reported, "but he will undoubtedly pitch some of the games and if in the right sort of shape, may pitch the bulk of them."[5]

The move back to Decatur was a welcome change for McGinnity in many ways. He still had family there. His daughter, Marguerite, now a young adult, would be back in the city in which she was born. And McGinnity, for the first time in 20 years, had a job that didn't keep him on the road for weeks and months at a time.

He rented a house at 1606 E. El Dorado, in the same block in which he had lived 25 years earlier, and only a few blocks down the street from the Staley plant and its adjoining athletic fields at 22nd and El Dorado. It was an exceptional athletic facility for that era—a nice playing field, bleacher seating for 1,500 fans, a spacious locker room with modern shower facilities. McGinnity had endured worse facilities with many of the professional teams for which he'd played.

Before he even arrived, plans were set in motion to add even more seats to Staley Field. By the time the renovations were completed, the field was to have a capacity of 3,500.[6]

McGinnity's homecoming quickly evolved into a gala celebration. Sunday, May 18, was declared McGinnity Day and the returning hero was scheduled to pitch for Staley's that day against the Sangamo Electric Co. of Springfield.

The Decatur papers reported that hundreds of old friends and fans from Springfield planned to make the trip over to Decatur by train for the game.[7] The *Review* added: "Not only will the usual number of present day fans be present but so will several hundred old timers who have almost forgotten the game but have never forgotten Joe. Nor has Joe forgotten them."[8]

Both Decatur papers printed a special invitation from McGinnity to his old cronies to come out and see him: "The Staley baseball club has kindly honored me in my first appearance here Sunday by naming it McGinnity Day. Therefore, we'll make it a good old reunion. All of my old friends of years back are invited to the game and to come out on the grounds, shake hands and have a little chat. Don't be backward. Just walk out on the grounds any time before the game and I'll be glad to see you. Yours truly, Joe M'Ginnity."[9]

A crowd of about 1,500 turned out and the Staley's team rewarded the fans with a 6–3 victory. McGinnity pitched the first six innings, allowing two runs on three hits. The score was tied at 2–2 when he went to the bench, but his team rallied in the late innings to win.

"The Staley team is already giving signs of the course of training that McGinnity is giving them, playing with more snap and putting across some new ideas," the *Review* observed.[10]

The team already was pretty formidable when McGinnity arrived and with his help it got even better. With his name and reputation, he was able to recruit good players from all over Central Illinois. Just a week after his arrival, Staley's went down to a 3–1 loss to a town team from nearby Mount Olive, thanks largely to a spectacular sixth-inning catch by a left-fielder named Eller. Immediately after the game, young Eller was easily persuaded to come to work for Staley's.[11]

However, arguably the best player on the Staley's team was one who was already there when McGinnity arrived. Charlie Dressen grew up in Decatur, the son of a German saloon-keeper, and he had quit school at the age of 14 to start playing semi-pro ball. At 5-foot-5, 146 pounds, he was unimposing but quick, athletic and as tenacious as any athlete McGinnity had been around since his days with McGraw. In truth, McGinnity probably saw a lot of McGraw in Dressen, who went on to play eight years as a third baseman in the National League and to manage five major league teams. In 1952 and '53, he won NL pennants as the manager of the Brooklyn Dodgers although in his first year in that job, 1951, he had openly boasted that the Dodgers had the pennant won, only to have the Giants overtake them on Bobby Thomson's historic home run.

Dressen was only 20 years old when he began playing for Staley's and he quickly emerged as perhaps the best all-around athlete in the company, a reliable infielder on the baseball team and the quarterback of the football team. He even was the best bowler around, carrying a 180 average.[12]

Led by Dressen, Staley's continued to dominate the Central Industrial Baseball Association, which also included the Indian Refining Co. Havolines of Lawrenceville, Illinois; the Samson Tractors of Janesville, Wisconsin; the Fairbanks Morse Fairies of Beloit, Wisconsin; the Simmons Bed Co. of Kenosha, Wisconsin; and Republic Trucks of Alma, Michigan.

The Staleys also played other strong company teams such as Sangamo Electric, Armour and Co. of Chicago and Briscoe Motors of Jackson, Michigan, plus several town teams, representing Mount Olive, Atwood, Champaign, Bloomington, Maroa, Cowden, and Joliet. Every now and then, they would face a minor-league team such as McGinnity's old Peoria club and on rare occasions they even squared off with a big-league team.

One of those occasions came within his first few weeks on the job when the powerful Chicago White Sox stopped off in Decatur for a game on May 29. No one could have known it at the time, but this was destined to become the most nefarious ballclub in baseball history. The Sox breezed to the American League pennant that summer, then many of their best players conspired with gamblers to intentionally lose the World Series to the Cincinnati Reds, evoking a scandal that shook the sport to its roots.

But in the spring of that season, the Sox were heroic figures and their visit to Decatur guaranteed the biggest crowd ever for a Staley's game. The team included some of the game's brightest stars—left-fielder Shoeless Joe Jackson, third baseman Buck Weaver, second baseman Eddie Collins and pitcher Eddie Cicotte. Another star, catcher Ray Schalk, did not come to Decatur, opting to go home instead to be with a sick child. The Sox roster also included Fred McMullin, the young infielder who had played for McGinnity in Tacoma.

Staley's tried something new for the occasion, employing a local celebrity named Al Freeman to serve as a public address announcer so that the local fans would know who the White Sox players were.[13]

A crowd of about 3,000 turned out to see the Sox win, 7–4, in a sloppily played game that included plenty of clowning. The *Herald* indicated that the Sox could have won by a much larger margin had they applied themselves.[14]

McGinnity started on the mound and his brightest moment came in the second inning when he picked the Sox' Chick Gandil off second base. But by the fourth inning the major league club was hitting him hard and he was replaced on the mound by Jim Lambrecht. Dressen probably left the strongest impression on the visitors, hitting a long home run over the railroad tracks in left field in the third inning off veteran pitcher Grover Lowdermilk. Staley's also managed to get a couple of runs on errors by the Sox in the sixth inning and Eller singled in a run in the ninth.

White Sox center-fielder Hap Felsch, one of eight players who later was involved in throwing the World Series, was injured in the contest. As he was running back to pursue Dressen's home run in the third inning, he stepped on a broken pop bottle, cutting his foot. He was carried off the field although he only was sidelined for a few days.[15]

In 1920, McGinnity's second year with Staley's, the company's athletic programs took an even more decided upturn with the addition of a tough-minded young Navy veteran from Chicago.

George Halas had been an outstanding end on the football team at the University of Illinois and was trying to make it as an outfielder with the New York Yankees in 1919 when he injured his hip sliding into third base. After only 12 games and 22 at-bats (and only two hits) with the Yankees, Halas was sent to play for St. Paul in the American Association for the remainder of the 1919 season. He was released at the end of the campaign and went back to Chicago, using his engineering degree to land a $55-a-week job with the Chicago, Burlington and Quincy Railroad.[16]

He had been in that job less than six months when he was contacted by A.E. Staley and visited by his righthand man, G.E. Chamberlain. They offered Halas a job working in the Staley millhouse, playing for the company baseball team and coaching the company football team. And he'd only have to take a pay cut of $5 a week.

Something obviously felt right about the situation because Halas jumped at it. In later years, he said he saw the opportunity to do something big in football, but he admitted that another part of the allure was a chance to be around someone who epitomized the sort of toughness and durability he admired. He was looking forward to working with Joe McGinnity.[17]

Halas played for McGinnity's baseball team in 1920, being forced into action at the unfamiliar position of shortstop for much of the season. He also began to assemble a great football team, importing players he knew through his days at Illinois and at the Great Lakes Naval Air Station. It helped that he was able to not only offer full-time jobs in the plant but guarantee that two hours out of each work day would be spent practicing football.

In the fall of 1920, he and Canton Bulldogs coach Ralph Hay and the leaders of some of the other top semi-pro teams around the country banded together into one of the first professional football leagues. The representatives of the teams gathered in Hay's Huppmobile dealership in Canton and put together plans for standardized rules and a coordinated schedule.[18]

Meanwhile, Halas' drive to build a better football team also helped McGinnity's baseball team because they were able to utilize some of the same athletes. Not only did Halas himself have major league baseball experience, but he recruited a pair of linemen, Bob Koehler and Guy Chamberlain, who both had played some baseball. In turn, Halas also made good use of Dressen's skills, found a reliable halfback in catcher Walter Veach and discovered that pitcher Ranney Young had been a standout tackle during his days at Millikin University in Decatur.

Halas' first Decatur Staleys football team went 10-2-1 in 1920 with the only losses coming against its two most bitter rivals—the Rock Island Independents and the Chicago Cardinals.

The day after the football team fought Akron to a 0–0 tie in Chicago to finish the season, McGinnity and other representatives of the Central Industrial Baseball Association met at the Sherman Hotel in Chicago to begin planning the 1921 baseball season.

Major league baseball had been torn apart by the revelations of what the White Sox (now beginning to be referred to as Black Sox) had done in 1919. McGinnity likely was very distraught by the throwing of the World Series, partially because one of his former protégés (Fred McMullin) was among the accused and because the gambler who allegedly bankrolled the fix, Arnold Rothstein, was a former business associate of John McGraw's. As the *Decatur Review* pointed out many years later, the idea of losing a game on purpose was totally foreign and completely repulsive to McGinnity: "There never would have been a baseball scandal if the White Sox of 1919 had been made up of McGinnity's for Joe wouldn't trade a win for all the money you could stack in a building."[19]

McGinnity and the rest of the industrial league leaders were anxious to make sure they didn't fall victim to the same sort of corruption. They put forward a resolution to deal just as harshly with unscrupulous players as the major leagues were beginning to. They agreed that they would not "knowingly harbor nor play against any club harboring any player who by his conduct has proven himself unworthy of recognition in the sport." Their attitude toward gambling was that "this association will redouble its efforts to stop this evil."[20]

The one thing the league's teams weren't going to be able to stop that season was McGinnity's Staley's baseball club. The Staley's players were so eager to get going that they played some games indoors on a makeshift field at the YMCA during the winter of 1920–21.

Almost every player from the 1920 team had received at least some sort of professional baseball offer, but very few of them had accepted. Harry Rush, another Navy veteran, accepted an offer to try out for the St. Louis Browns, and Jim Lambrecht was getting a shot with the Cardinals, but almost everyone else was back.

It was a power-packed team with Halas, Walter Meinert and Ray Demmitt forming a superb outfield. Demmitt had seven years of major league experience and had led the American League in outfield assists as the starting right-fielder of the St. Louis Browns in 1918. The infield was equally potent with hard-hitting Otto "Lefty" Pahlman at first, Buster Woodworth at second, young Charles Schaffer at short and Eddie Hemingway, who had been wooed away from the Fairbanks Morse team, at third. There were three good catchers—Veach, George Watkins and Avery McGlade. And there were so many good pitchers that it didn't appear as though the team's 50-year-old manager was going to need to take the hill very often. Young and Clyde Seib were hard throwers, Ray Summers had a lively spitball and McGinnity filled his need for a lefthander by bringing in local product "Happy Jack" Kotzelneck, who had spent a few years in the Cardinals' farm system after winning 32 games and throwing four no-hitters for the inaugural Staley team back in 1917.

"Unless we miss our guess about a mile, Joe McGinnity is going to pilot one of the strongest industrial baseball teams ever assembled this season and one that will eclipse the 1920 nine at least 20 percent," the *Staley Fellowship Journal* predicted in its April issue.[21]

Howard Millard, writing in the *Decatur Review*, was equally emphatic: "With the club McGinnity has in the making, it looks like 1921 is going to be the biggest baseball year in the history of the game in Decatur."[22]

One other key member of the team was trainer Andy "Windy" Lotshaw, who had filled in as an outfielder-first baseman the previous year but whose primary role now figured to be as an occasional umpire.

Halas recalled many years later in his autobiography that Lotshaw was not always entirely impartial in that role. In a game against Lincoln, the Staleys trailed, 1–0, in the ninth inning with two runners on and two out. Halas worked the count to 3-and-2 but then watched helplessly as a perfect curveball swept directly over the plate.

"Ball four! Take your base!" Lotshaw called out.

The next batter singled in the tying and winning runs.

"Andy knew that his job as trainer for the football team was secure," Halas said.[23]

But in 1921, the Staleys didn't need much help from umpires. They probably were better than many minor league clubs that year. Halas recalled that he batted .320 and that he wasn't even close to being the best hitter on the team. Demmitt batted .383 and almost all the starters were over .300. Included in the season was a 29–0 rout of the Missouri Valley White Sox in which the Staleys declined to even finish their final at-bat.

McGinnity wasn't pitching that often, but he was having fun. On March

19, he celebrated his 50th birthday by pitching in an intrasquad game between the "Rooks" and the "Rookies." In four innings against the Staley starters, he allowed only two infield hits. The *Staley Fellowship Journal* noted that "Joe is still capable of stepping into the box and twirling good ball."[24] In another game with the Rail Lights, he not only was the winning pitcher but he stole a base.

Such was the stature of the Staley's program that it attempted to line up a game with a major league team that would have been an even bigger draw than the White Sox. Howard Millard reported in the *Decatur Review* in the spring of 1921 that McGinnity and Halas, who now had the title of athletic director, were trying to woo the New York Yankees and Babe Ruth to Staley Field for a game.[25] The Yankees were scheduled to wrap up a series with the St. Louis Browns on May 25, then had two off days before their next game. Decatur would be an easy stopover.

Ruth would have been a huge draw. He had broken baseball's single-season home run record in 1919 by clubbing 29 in a season despite only playing the outfield about half the time. He had nearly doubled the record by smashing 54 in 1920 and he was destined to hit 59 that season. Millard butchered Ruth's nickname in his story, referring to the Big Bambino as the "Bamboo King," but he was undoubtedly accurate in his assessment of the appeal of such a game: "The appearance of the famous Babe would jam the local park to capacity for fans within a radius of a hundred miles would travel here to see him lift one over the lumber pile in Ray Demmitt's field."[26]

It never happened. Halas and McGinnity couldn't quite pull it off. But the fact that Staley's would even consider such a move is evidence of how strong a team it had and how much clout its manager had in professional baseball circles.

With the Yankees game falling through, Staley's instead played an exhibition game on May 26 against the famous House of David team, a barnstorming ballclub based in a religious colony in Benton Harbor, Michigan, that traveled the country playing a variety of opponents. Its trademark was that all its players wore long beards, but it apparently wasn't much of a team. Staley's beat them, 7–2, in front of a crowd of 2,800.

"Their hitting was weak, their fielding slow and their knowledge of the pastime lacking," Bill Penhallegon wrote in the *Decatur Herald*. "However, they meant well and were out there trying, so you have to give them credit."[27]

A couple of weeks later, McGinnity crossed paths with an old adversary when Staley's took on the Havolines, a formidable industrial league team out of Lawrenceville, Illinois. Among those pitching on a regular basis for the Havolines was Mordecai "Three-Finger" Brown, the old Cubs star who beat the Giants in that hotly-contested 1908 playoff game. Brown was 44 and five years removed from the major leagues, but he had hurled a complete-game shutout the week before against a local town team. It was announced that the two old stars would meet in a head-to-head pitching duel on June 12 in Decatur.[28]

They did just that although neither of them stayed around long enough to figure in the outcome. McGinnity only pitched the first two innings, allowing just one hit and facing the minimum six hitters. Brown only worked three innings and went to the sidelines after giving up a two-run home run to Demmitt in the third. The Havolines eventually broke through against Seib, Young and Kotzelneck, and won the game, 9–4.

It was a rare loss for that 1921 Staley's team. Halas, in his memoirs, gave the team's record for that season as 52–31.[29]

Not quite everything went right in McGinnity's life during that time period. He received word that his mother had died on March 31 in Los Angeles, where she was living with his younger brothers, John and George, and his sister, Hannah. She was buried the very next day, before Joe could get there for the funeral.

But just about everything else in his life was rosy. He had found a niche, found a job he could hold for the rest of his life. He could grow old developing baseball teams for Staley's.

Or maybe not.

The nation's economy was beginning to take another turn for the worse and even the most stable companies were feeling the pinch of a recession. In late June of 1921, Staley's announced extensive wage cuts for almost all of its 500-plus employees. A.E. Staley himself and his plant superintendent, George E. Chamberlain, both reportedly took 40-percent cuts in their own pay. Common laborers making between 35 and 55 cents per hour took five-cent cuts and skilled workers making between 65 and 90 cents per hour were dropped by a dime. The *Decatur Herald* reported that the plant had the highest wages in the city before that.[30]

"Practically every employee of the plant is taking a reduction," Staley announced. "And that takes me in, too."[31]

Obviously, in that sort of fiscal crisis, the athletic teams became more of a luxury than a necessity, and A.E. Staley began to realize how much money he was pouring into his sports programs. The football team, in particular, had become very expensive. The team reported a net loss of $14,406.36 for the 1920 season and in 1921, things got bad enough that Staley couldn't bear the losses any more.[32] He simply gave the football franchise to Halas, handed him $5,000 and recommended that he move it to Chicago,[33] where it had a better chance to succeed financially. It was good advice. The Chicago Staleys prospered in spite of the economy, and a year later Halas renamed them the Chicago Bears. That little league that he and Hay and their friends had thrown together in Canton became the National Football League.

Meanwhile, Staley had to figure out what to do with the other athletic programs. The dreaded announcement came in the March 1922 issue of the *Fellowship Club Journal*. After five years of glorious on-field success, the management was eliminating all athletic teams.[34]

"This action is part of a systematic campaign of retrenchment by which it is hoped to lop off every element that might cause direct waste, and to pare down our manufacturing costs to a non-reducible limit."[35]

In other words, athletics had fallen victim to budget cuts.

"Mr. Staley is meeting a desperate situation gallantly and successfully," the *Journal* reported. "Every employee of the company feels himself enlisted as a valiant defender of the business which supports him and his family."[36]

The same story noted that the news was not received very well by some of the athletes, but they were being encouraged to remain loyal to the company.

"Our winning teams have made us known the length and breadth of this vast country," the piece continued. "They have formed for us valuable friendships. They have furnished recreation and interest to the members of our organization. Let us hope that the brilliant sun of prosperity already creeping above the horizon may restore to us our well-beloved and sadly missed athletics.

"And they will be missed. More than one bright eye dimmed, more than one pretty lip trembled at the untoward announcement. A fine bunch of fellows, they were—genial and upright, clean-minded, hard-working and loyal to the team and company. A few—too few—will stay with us. To the others, we wish a hearty God-speed. May health and prosperity attend you. We extend the hand of the Staley organization in the strong grasp of affection."[37]

Not surprisingly, Joe McGinnity was among those who left the Staley company shortly after that announcement. They had taken away the one thing he loved more than anything except perhaps his wife and daughter. They had taken away baseball.

22. Back to the Minors

Joe McGinnity probably thought he was done forever with minor league baseball. No more seemingly endless train rides through the night to get to the next town. No more scraps with umpires and opponents. No more day-to-day worries about how many fans were going to stroll through the turnstiles.

He had settled into a job with Staley's and slowed his life to a more leisurely pace. He got to see much more of Mary and Marguerite. He had gotten to see Marguerite grow into a young woman who was soon to be married and settle down in Decatur herself.

Then Staley's discontinued its sports programs. And then the directors of the Danville Veterans of the Three-I League tempted him into a comeback.

Danville, a town about 80 miles east of Decatur near the Indiana border, had re-entered the league and was making big plans under manager Charles O'Day and an ambitious board of directors that included McGinnity's old business partner, H. Clay Smith.

The team had taken over the baseball grounds at the Old Soldiers Home[1]—hence, the nickname Veterans—and brought in an assortment of players, many of them cast-offs from major league clubs. Pitcher Henry Fine had gone through a tryout with the Red Sox. Tom Pyle supposedly had gotten a look from the White Sox. Clarence Brown had been in camp with Brooklyn.

But the team was disorganized and the talent didn't look quite as strong as it had been billed. On April 9, O'Day was fired only a month after taking over. Outfielder Pete Knisely took over on an interim basis.[2]

On April 11, McGinnity came over from Decatur to look over the team. He did it mostly as a personal favor to Smith, who now was working for Allith-Prouty,[3] a company that manufactured locks, pulleys, sliding doors and other metal devices.

McGinnity wasn't really sure he wanted to get back into the minors as either a player or manager, but he consented to help Smith out, take over the team for a few weeks, whip the recruits into shape and utilize his contacts to find better players. According to the *Danville Commercial-News*, he was given "carte blanche in the matter of signing new players and disposing of those on hand."[4]

Before long, he got caught up in the rebuilding effort. O'Day had set up only a couple of preseason exhibition games and McGinnity tried to change that as he also tried to find some players. A touring team from Hamilton, Ontario, played the Veterans on April 16 in a game that O'Day had arranged, and McGinnity invited Hamilton to come back for nearly a week later in the month to work out with and play against the Veterans.

Within a few days, he cut four players and began bringing in new ones, moving some of the old players to new positions in an effort to assemble a decent team. Among the new imports was Charles Schaffer, who had played shortstop for him with Staley's the year before. He also called many of his old friends and acquaintances in baseball—McGraw, Jack Dunn, even Ban Johnson—in an effort to round up prospective players who were better than the ones he inherited.

On the eve of the May 2 opener with the Peoria Tractors, McGinnity actually sounded optimistic.

"Though not yet as fast as I expect the club to be, the locals have surprised me by their progress the past few days," he told the *Commercial-News*. "There are some mighty sweet ballplayers on the Danville team, and while there are some weaknesses, I hope to overcome much of this during the next few days. It is a mighty big task to build up an entirely new team."[5]

According to the paper, he even did a few things to ward off bad luck. Danville fans had an idea that the city's franchises of the past had been jinxed. So, McGinnity carried an old horseshoe into the shower room and the *Commercial-News* reported that "the groundskeeper drove a cross-eyed Negro off the infield during early practices."[6] But it was going to take much more than a couple of superstitious rituals to help this team.

Like most minor league cities in that era, Danville had a whole array of festivities connected to the opener. There was a parade that started at the Aetna Hotel, where the Peoria team was staying, at 1 P.M. There was a band concert on the field at 2. Earl F. Bowers and Louise Faulkner were married at home plate at 3, and the game started shortly thereafter.[7]

Everything went wonderfully until the game began. Then it became evident it could be a long season. Peoria won, 12–1.

On May 4, McGinnity took the mound himself, pitched seven scoreless innings and held on for a 5–3 win over Peoria. It would be the only pitching victory he had with the Veterans.

The team's pitching was OK, but the club was last in the league in both hitting and fielding from the very beginning.

And it didn't take long for the fans to grow impatient. A traveling salesman from Chicago passed through town, watched the May 7 game and was astonished at how the local fans were treating the legendary pitcher who was now serving as their manager. The salesman expressed his dismay in a letter to the *Commercial-News*: "I was much surprised ... at the lack of support given Mr. McGinnity. It was very apparent to me that he played the game and used unusual judgment in making the change of pitchers at the time he did. It seems to me that the fans should remember that the full management of the club rests upon the shoulders of the manager and he never should be criticized openly by the home fans for the reason that this criticism has a bad effect upon the players under his control, and often is the cause of losing games where loyal support, even though the fans think he may be wrong, pulls many a game out of the fire."[8]

A few weeks later, the Veterans traveled to play the Decatur Commodores on the Staley Field upon which Iron Man had spent so much time the previous three years. Decatur fans declared the May 27 game "McGinnity Day." Forty Staley employees, led by G.E. Chamberlain, marched onto the field before the game and presented McGinnity with a basket containing five dozen roses and a purse containing some gold coins. The *Commercial-News* reported that there was $100 in gold inside.[9] In reality, there was only $26.[10]

Chamberlain made a speech: "My fellow employees of the Staley Manufacturing Company have asked me to present this gift to you as their remembrance. The presentation is not made because you are a Decatur product and learned to play ball on the sandlots of the city; neither is it because of that fact that you are one of the most famous baseball pitchers who has ever lived; nor is it because you are one of the best preserved athletes the United States has known, but the presentation is to indicate to you that we men who know you best and have been in daily touch with you admire you most for your lovable traits of character, and these gifts are to indicate to you our love and affection for you."[11]

Peter Brilley, the director of the Decatur Fans Association, then presented McGinnity with a raincoat and a sweater. McGinnity was noticeably moved by the acts of kindness.[12]

Several Danville fans also had made arrangements to go over to Decatur for the occasion, but most of them didn't get there in time to see the shower of affection. Two different train accidents made them late and it's just as well they missed the start of the contest. McGinnity gave up five runs in the first inning and eight in all before taking himself out. Decatur won, 9–0.[13]

On June 13, the Veterans lost to the Bloomington Bloomers, 5–2, in a game that included an assault on an umpire named Lawler although details of the incident varied greatly depending on which newspaper you read. The *Commercial-News* reported that Bloomington catcher Pat Harkins struck the umpire "several times" in the sixth inning. Lawler did not even eject Harkins until McGinnity protested and threatened to file a complaint with league president A.R. Tearney.[14] The *Bloomington Pantagraph*, however, reported that McGinnity and one of his players grabbed Lawler and slung him around in the first inning. It said Harkins grabbed Lawler in the sixth but only to get his attention.[15]

McGinnity continued to bring in new players every week, sometimes adding four or five fresh youngsters to the roster at a time. Sportswriter Curley Anderson of the *Moline Daily Dispatch* wrote that "The Iron Man has had three teams practically all season, one coming, one playing and another leaving."[16] The *Bloomington Bulletin* also delighted in the revolving door and the inexperience of the new recruits. "Iron Man McGinnity must be dealing in futures from the wealth of young blood on his team. Danville is dreaming of a pennant in 1927."[17]

Some of the moves paid off. He brought in first baseman Otto Pahlman, another of his old Staley protégés, and he emerged as one of the premier hitters in the league. Later in the season Pahlman clicked off a 50-game hitting streak that stretched from mid–July into early September.

Despite all the player moves, McGinnity couldn't get the team going. It was in the second division of the eight-team league throughout the first month and as June wore on, it sagged into the cellar. A rumor circulated that McGinnity was planning to resign when the team returned from a road trip to Rockford, but members of the board of directors said they knew nothing about it. Some admitted they wouldn't mind if he quit.[18]

If McGinnity was about to quit, he had an odd way of showing it. He missed the first game of the Rockford series so he could go over to Chicago and look over some semi-pro players that might be able to help him.[19]

On June 28, with the team still on the road, the *Commercial-News* told of a special report compiled by a sub-committee of the board of directors. The committee's conclusion was that the team's problems did not center around McGinnity. The problem was the players.[20]

"The majority of the players now here are castoffs from some other club, Danville getting them after some other club was through with them," the report stated. "A pennant cannot be won with such a team. Joe McGinnity has labored hard to make the team a winner. He is a big stockholder in the local club. He has spent his own money, working hard with the lads. He came here and found but one ball player. That was right at the start of the season. He has done remarkably well to get together even so good a team as he has, considering the fact that he had but little time and no money at all on which to build."[21]

The report also indicated that the players liked McGinnity and "with one or two exceptions, work hard for him. Disturbers on the team will be disciplined."[22] It may have been only a coincidence, but the next day, the team released Knisely, one of the best hitters on the club, and outfielder Joe Cvengros.

But that didn't change much. On July 6, the Veterans suffered their eighth straight loss and extended their streak of consecutive scoreless innings to 28. They were 21–43, 19½ games out of first place, 5½ games behind the seventh-place Moline Plowboys.

For McGinnity, it must have felt like déjà vu of 1914 when his Tacoma team went into an uncontrollable tailspin in June and he finally had to hand the managerial reins over to Russ Hall amid talk that he was less than adequate as a manager.

The Danville players, in a meeting with the directors, said McGinnity drove them too hard and was too demanding. McGinnity said some of the players didn't play with enough fire and seldom delivered in the clutch. He offered the Danville fans association a deal. He would take a week off, go on "vacation," go scouting for new players, and turn the team over to Avery McGlade on a temporary basis. If the team's fortunes improved, he would resign. If they did just as poorly, he would return to the job.[23]

Over the next week, the Veterans went 1–6, clearly indicating that their record was the result of bad players, not bad management. Nevertheless, on July 12, the board of directors voted 15 to 3 to release McGinnity from his contract.[24] Catcher Roy Gillenwater, a player John McGraw had sent to Danville on the eve of the season, took over as interim manager although O'Day eventually was brought back to run the team for the rest of the campaign.

The board members and McGinnity both declined to comment on his dismissal, and the *Commercial-News* reported that Iron Man would go back to Decatur and resume working for Staley's.[25] It was wrong about that.

23. A New Challenge

If Joe McGinnity thought the Danville team he was leaving was bad, he was about to join a club that was even worse.

When the proprietors of the Dubuque team in the newly formed Class D Mississippi Valley League heard that one of the greatest names in baseball was available, they made him an offer to become the manager and part owner of the team.

The Dubuque franchise went by many different names in that era—Dubs, Climbers, Mullenites (after deposed manager Larry Mullen). No matter what you called them, they were among the poorest minor league clubs in the country.

Nevertheless, within a week after being dismissed in Danville, McGinnity took on the task of managing a team that had lost 31 of 32 games in one stretch.

The *Dubuque Telegraph Herald* lauded his arrival and announced that Sunday, July 29, had been declared Joe McGinnity Day to formally welcome him to the Mississippi River town. "With his face and neck bronzed by the blistering sun which has beaten down during the diamond campaigns of three decades, and possessing a massive chest and broad shoulders which show no traces of the grueling strain to which they have been subjected by 'iron man' stunts, McGinnity is a formidable figure on the ballfield," the newspaper reported.[1]

His new team wasn't formidable at all. He almost immediately pronounced it a "hopeless case."[2]

"It's really too late to go anywhere now," he added, "but I'll try to lift them off the bottom."[3]

He recruited a couple of players off the Columbia (now Loras) College team to plug a few holes and also picked up a fast infielder who had just graduated from the University of Dubuque, Johnny Armstrong.

The team finished last in the league and the day after the season ended McGinnity gave the entire team its outright release.[4] He would start over from scratch the following spring.

When the Climbers reported to camp for the 1923 season, McGinnity had used his contacts to round up 40 players from which to choose. The *Telegraph Herald* described some of them as "relics of the pastime."⁵ It was not the most physically gifted bunch of players, but many of them had the smarts and aggressiveness that McGinnity had learned to covet from his days with McGraw.

Dubuque didn't have much of a baseball tradition. It had won the Three-I League back in 1905 and finished second in 1913, but more often it found itself at the bottom of the standings. Its 1907 team went 22–109 with a team batting average of .188, and there had been similarly lean years since.

But 1923 would be a year to remember.

McGinnity's most noteworthy discovery was Armstrong, who had been an athlete of almost legendary proportions at the University of Dubuque, lettering in four different sports. He was the star forward and leading scorer on the basketball team. He did just about everything in track—pole vault, hurdles, 100-yard dash, discus and javelin. He was the quarterback of a football team that won one game by a 125–0 score. In fact, he also played pro football in the early days of the NFL with the Chicago Bears' archrival, the Rock Island Independents. He was one of those natural athletes who could do anything. He also was an excellent bowler and golfer, and was nearly unbeatable in a billiards parlor.⁶

He became McGinnity's starting second baseman and was the swift, aggressive hitter and baserunner that he needed in the No. 2 slot in his batting order.

McGinnity also brought in Chief Meyers, who had become the New York Giants' starting catcher right after Iron Man left the team. Meyers had spent nine solid seasons in the National League and although he was now 42 and five years removed from his last game in the majors, he provided savvy and experience.

Upon taking over a downtrodden Dubuque team in 1922, McGinnity almost immediately pronounced it "hopeless." A year later he found his greatest moment of redemption (Charles W. Brown, Jr., collection).

The Climbers also had plenty of that in their 52-year-old manager.

"McGinnity was always known as a fighter," the *Telegraph Herald* reported a few years later. "When he entered a ballgame he had but one objective in mind—a victory. He was aggressive. He fought for his team and a player who did not show a disposition to fight for the club had no place in Joe's heart. There were times when many thought he went too far with his aggressiveness. But that was McGinnity's style of play and it won him ballgames. Off the field he was a different type of man, but once in that uniform he was all baseball, first, last and all the time."[7]

McGinnity was popular not only in Dubuque but elsewhere around the league. The fans in those rugged river towns admired his toughness and stubbornness. He was still a pretty effective pitcher, too. And, as always, he was an incredibly fast worker.

On May 24, he pitched a four-hit shutout against Marshalltown, winning 1–0 on a terribly windy day. He set a league record by getting the game over with in an hour and eight minutes.[8] On June 3, he blanked Waterloo, 2–0. On June 15, at Douglas Park in Rock Island, he pitched another shutout that was completed so quickly the newspapers measured the time in fractions of minutes. The *Moline Dispatch* said the time of the game was 1:03½.[9] The *Davenport Times*, from just across the Mississippi, listed the time as 1:04½.[10] Either way, it was another new record.

Suddenly, he found himself back in the national spotlight to some degree, not for pitching quickly but for pitching at all at the age of 52.

After his swift victory over Rock Island, he received a congratulatory note from Michael H. Sexton, president of the National Association of Minor Leagues: "Really, Joe, I am beginning to believe that you will never grow old."[11]

Paul Mallon of the United Press was among those who gushed about his exploits, noting that Iron Man "has lost none of his cunning" and "still is contributing his share in the battle to establish the ultimate supremacy of age over youth."[12]

New York Herald reporter Frank J. Price Jr. heard Iron Man was still pitching out west and he went to see him throw against Cedar Rapids in July. McGinnity lost the game, 7–1, but still impressed the eastern journalist, who pointed out in his story that McGinnity not only was still pitching winning baseball but he was batting .269.[13]

McGinnity told Price there was no "dark secret" about how he was able to last so long. He took good care of himself and stayed away from "things I knew wouldn't help my ball playing any."[14]

Price wrote: "I confess that I never have seen a man of his age, or much less, look as well as Joe does. There are lines, of course, but his face has that healthy color that comes only with life outdoors and clean living."[15]

McGinnity told him his arm felt great, too. "Of course, I haven't the speed I used to have, but I've got all the stuff I ever had, and when I'm going right, with control, I'd say I'm as effective as I ever was."[16]

Price asked if he thought he was pitching well enough to still be in the big leagues. "Son, I've pitched games this year when I could do anything at all with the ball, that would have made any club work hard to score." Price said the former Giant hero was "sturdy as an oak, with a waist not a fraction of an inch larger than in his Giant days." McGinnity did concede that he was starting to feel it in his legs, though.[17]

Wilton Floberg also did a lengthy piece on McGinnity for the August issue of *Sporting Life*, in which Iron Man noted "I don't feel old. Of course not. The idea seems absurd to me. I am able to take my regular turn on the mound and I expect to do that for many years yet. Baseball is too fine a game to give up, ever."[18]

The Dubs led the Mississippi Valley League all season and finally clinched the pennant on September 4. They defeated Marshalltown, 9–0, in the first game of a doubleheader, and they were in the second inning of the second game when they learned that Cedar Rapids had beaten second-place Ottumwa, assuring them of the pennant.

Before the game resumed, there was a brief ceremony. Both teams stood near home plate as John Chalmers, a local attorney who also was the football coach at the University of Dubuque, spoke to the crowd, praising the work McGinnity had done in giving Dubuque the pennant for which it had waited for so long.

The *Telegraph Herald* reported that Iron Man seemed uncomfortable as he listened to Chalmers sing his praises. Once he put on his game face, it was hard for him to shed it so quickly for a ceremony of this sort. He pawed at the ground with his spikes and didn't seem to know what to do with his hands. Upon completing his remarks, Chalmers handed him a bouquet of flowers. Then, McGinnity knew exactly what to do. He walked over to the nearby box seats and handed the flowers to Mary.[19]

The crowd burst into applause and the game resumed although McGinnity removed himself from the game at that point. The Dubs clobbered Marshalltown, 9–4, to complete a perfect day. The next day, they completed the season with a 16–7 rout of Marshalltown amid a giddy atmosphere. McGinnity allowed five different players to pitch, including Armstrong, and an umpire named Deweese worked the entire game behind the plate wearing cowboy garb.[20]

There was some sentiment for continuing the season beyond that point. The Decatur Commodores had rolled to the Three-I League title by winning their last 11 games and there were some who wanted to see the "Commies" take on the Mississippi Valley League champs from Dubuque. McGinnity appears to have been the one who came up with the idea. He proposed that the two clubs play each other six times, three times in Decatur and three times in Dubuque, and if a seventh game was necessary to decide the outcome there would be a coin flip to determine the site for that game.[21]

The folks back in Decatur, where McGinnity still lived in the off-season, didn't think much of the idea. "There would be nothing to gain from such an affair," the *Decatur Herald* opined on September 7. "The Mississippi Valley loop is a class D circuit and the Three-I a class B, hence there would be no credit for winning such a series. Too, there is little likelihood that it would be a good 'gate' attraction. Aside from the fact that Joe McGinnity, a Decatur resident, manages the Valley pennant winners, local fans would view a Commy-Dubuque series with little interest and President Gene Wylie of the Decatur Fans Association yesterday expressed the opinion that the series proposed by McGinnity would not pay expenses."[22]

McGinnity didn't have anything more to prove anyway. He had pitched in 42 games and compiled a 15–12 record, and perhaps for the first time, he was recognized as more than just a great pitcher. It was sweet redemption for the 1914 and 1922 seasons, in which many people openly questioned his managerial skills. It was clear now that, given a modicum of talent with which to work, he could be a superb field manager.

As the *Telegraph Herald* reported many years later, "Joe McGinnity was a leader. He possessed baseball cunning. He knew inside baseball and he was tricky. He never asked of his fellow players anything he couldn't do himself. That is the reason why he pulled over a pennant in 1923 with a club that hardly could be rated as the best all-around club in the league. There were better hitters on the other clubs. There were better pitchers. But the other clubs had not been taught the game so well. Joe had a well-coached team. There was teamwork. He knew what was coming in practically every play. The team did, too."[23]

Less than two weeks after Dubuque's season ended, McGinnity turned up elsewhere in Iowa pitching for the Des Moines Boosters in a Western League game with St. Joseph. The Boosters had dropped into the second division and needed something to spike attendance for a late-season Sunday doubleheader that was played on a cold, damp day so they invited a 52-year-old legend to pitch the second game. McGinnity didn't look very legendary, giving up 13 hits and 12 earned runs before removing himself with nobody out in the third, effectively squelching rumors that he might possibly make a return to the major leagues.[24]

Des Moines Register sportswriter Sec Taylor, destined to become a legend in his own right, was less than kind in his description of Iron Man's outing, noting that he "should have been at home toasting his shins in front of the fireplace ruminating over the glories of yesteryear or, at the most, reading of the prowess of younger and more hardy athletes." He did point out that McGinnity struck out three batters—all on quick pitches—and he expressed admiration for his courage, but he said the veteran never had a chance, especially in the adverse weather conditions: "Joe just couldn't get the old soupbone warmed up and the Saints had no pity for old age."[25]

That game may have played a role in influencing McGinnity to do what he told Wilton Floberg he would not do. More likely, though, it was Mary's faltering health that led him to retire as an active player. In January, he announced he was turning the team over to Johnny Armstrong and taking a job as a millwright with Staley's back in Decatur.[26]

"I've been at it long enough," he said. "I want to settle down, stay in one place. Sure, I'll go to the game, but only as a spectator."[27]

He offered a bit of advice to young pitchers trying to make a name for themselves, telling them that curve balls "save wear and tear on the arm if the pitcher does not snap his wrist in throwing them. I've been pitching curves ever since entering the game and I've never had a sore arm. Control is a pitcher's asset. It depends on holding the ball right. Don't grip your fingers together. Spread them and get three equal points of contact. Throw with a full-arm motion. Roll the ball off your index finger. That's my advice to young pitchers who want to preserve their arms."[28]

Less than a month later, it looked as though he might get right back into the game. It was widely reported on February 2, 1924, that he was going to become McGraw's pitching coach in New York. Roger Bresnahan recently had sold his interest in the Toledo Mudhens and he was in line to become the Giants' chief scout. The old battery mates would be back together again and working for their mentor.[29] McGinnity also had an offer from Christy Mathewson to help coach the Boston Braves' pitchers during spring training. Big Six had purchased a large piece of stock in the Boston team a year earlier and was serving as the team president. The *Sporting News* reported that McGinnity would go to St. Petersburg, Florida, to tutor the Braves' pitchers.[30]

But McGinnity ended up backing away from all those jobs. On February 23, he announced that he would not be officially involved with any major league teams that season.[31] Through the years, he and Mary had rented several different houses in the area between downtown Decatur and the Staley's plant. They had lived at 1606 E. El Dorado, 1647 E. El Dorado and 1703 E. El Dorado. Now they bought a home of their own only a block south of those other houses at 1603 E. North Street. They paid $5,000 for a nine-year-old, two-story home that was a mere shadow of the grand homes they had owned in McAlester and Tacoma.[32]

McGinnity seemed to have finally settled into retirement. He still worked for Staley's and he still threw a few semi-pro games around Decatur and Springfield. He would help Armstrong recruit some players and perhaps even help him coach the Dubuque team in spring training. He even did some scouting for Brooklyn, occasionally showing up at ballparks in Peoria, Springfield, Decatur, Danville, Bloomington and other towns to check out talent for Wilbert Robinson.

But there still were a few competitive juices flowing. A year later, in February of 1925, it was announced that McGinnity was returning to Dubuque to partner with the 27-year-old Armstrong in running a team that had finished second in the Mississippi Valley League under Armstrong's guidance in 1924. Armstrong would become the team captain with McGinnity taking over as manager.[33] And, of course, he planned to continue pitching on a regular basis, noting in one interview that he expected to pitch at least 35 games that season.[34]

"McGinnity's decision to return to the game is not expected to cause much surprise," the *Telegraph Herald* reported. "Despite the fact that he announced his retirement after piloting Dubuque to the pennant in 1923, many of his friends predicted that he would be back in uniform sooner or later."[35]

The story noted that McGinnity and Armstrong already had been busy lining up players for the coming season.

The team would now be universally known as the Dubuque Ironmen, in McGinnity's honor. Another amateur team in the area adopted the nickname McGinity's Giants, fracturing the spelling of his last name, as so many others did through the years.

McGinnity and Armstrong worked with city manager O.E. Carr to make improvements to the city's aging ballpark, and McGinnity and Armstrong did much of the actual labor themselves, repairing the grandstand and improving the playing surface.[36]

They also tried to assemble a quality team although there were signs before the season even began that they were not succeeding. The Ironmen looked horrible in a loss to an amateur team, the Maquoketa Independents, and the Telegraph Herald gave its readers a pep talk on the eve of the season to keep them from losing hope.[37]

The Ironmen beat Burlington, 6–4, in the season opener, pulling off a pair of double steals, and there was that 7–3 victory over the Ottumwa Cardinals on May 12 in the home opener, in which McGinnity defeated the 18-year-old kid, John Welch. The fact that Welch was a rising talent who signed with the Chicago Cubs later in the season made it all the more impressive that a 54-year-old man beat him, reaping national notoriety.

The club also won a stirring victory on May 14 as McGinnity had a pair of hits and the Ironmen scored six runs in the last two innings to beat Rock Island, 7–6.

Three days later, Dubuque celebrated another "McGinnity Day,"[38] but less than two weeks into the season, it was apparent this was not going to be a pennant-winning team.

"During the past few days, many unpleasant things have been said about the club," the *Telegraph Herald* reported. "And there were certain individuals who took pleasure in broadcasting their little pet peeves. It's a fact that the team has not been doing well, as a matter of fact they looked weak at times. McGinnity and Armstrong realize this. They know they have not been going the way they should. The material on hand

In 1925, at the age of 54, McGinnity pitched Dubuque to victory over an Ottumwa pitcher a third his age (Charles W. Brown, Jr., collection).

that had the earmarks of real ballplayers in many instances have failed miserably, while others have not gotten their strides. Fans can rest assured that Bosses McGinnity and Armstrong will bolster the club. They will have a team right up in the running before the gong of September."[39]

The Ironmen defeated the Cedar Rapids Bunnies, 5–1, behind Blacky Blackburn on McGinnity Day. McGinnity and Armstrong each were presented with a basket of roses before the game by Charles McCarthy, the president of the Dubuque Boosters Association.[40]

But the club never did get going the way it had in 1923 under McGinnity and in 1924, when it was under Armstrong's direction. In the first week of July, the Ironmen were 22–38, in last place, and there was a growing tension between McGinnity and Armstrong. They were different kinds of men, of different generations. They thought differently, acted differently, treated players differently.

"Two men can not operate a club successfully," McGinnity said, "especially when the methods favored are directly opposite." The *Telegraph Herald* noted that there had been "earmarks of friction on the team for weeks," adding that it was "the master against the student."[41]

On July 8, the master decided to get out of the way. McGinnity resigned as manager and sold his interest in the club to Armstrong.

He hadn't pitched horribly, going 6–6 in 15 games, but his old-school managerial methods hadn't been as well-received with the young players on the club in 1925 as with the grizzled veterans who populated his 1923 team. He grew tired of the arguments and disputes. As the losses mounted, the gate receipts fell. He'd had enough.

Armstrong said he had been willing to step aside in favor of McGinnity, but when Iron Man offered to be the one who sold out his interests, Armstrong accepted.

The parting wasn't nearly as tense as some of McGinnity's earlier ones, however. He wasn't fired, as he was in Danville. He wasn't lambasted in the press, as he was at the end of his Tacoma tenure. The 1925 season hadn't gone very well, but the Dubuque fans never could forget what he'd done for them in '23.

Armstrong said he hoped their parting would not affect what had once been an "unusually pleasant" relationship between the two men.

The *Telegraph Herald* reflected the mixed emotions of the community: "To him we extend our heartfelt sympathy. Baseball has been the veteran's life work. He has done nothing else. Now this shining star has dimmed. He steps from the ranks as a baseball player.... We have the deepest respect for McGinnity. He's a mastermind in baseball. He's from the school of hard knocks. He knows baseball, he knows every angle of the pastime. But his policy in handling a club of young men was not accepted. We are sorry that this familiar figure is passing from Dubuque."[42]

McGinnity spent most of the rest of the summer playing in exhibition games, capitalizing on the fame he had obtained by pitching into his 50s.

He was the star attraction for a team of Springfield old-timers in a game against the Springfield Senators of the Three-I League on July 28. Pat Wright, Sammy Gibson, Gabe Ford and Bill Cadigan, McGinnity's old battery mate, also played in the game. The *Illinois State Register* reported that the old-timers rode into the ballpark on "a spring farm wagon drawn by a pair of prancing steeds" and hardly took the game seriously. They brought along a keg of beer and several batters walked to the plate with a bat in one hand and a mug of "pre-war" brew in the other. The game was supposed to go three innings but with the old-timers leading, 3–1, after two innings, they instigated a "mock riot" that brought the game to a premature conclusion.[43]

Afterward, Springfield player-manager Dave Lamb signed McGinnity to a one-game contract and let him pitch in the regular-season game against Bloomington that followed the old-timers game. The Senators were buried in last place in the Three-I League anyway. It seemed like a harmless stunt. But owner Bill Jackson didn't like the decision. McGinnity was pounded for five runs in less than five innings[44] and a week later, Jackson traded Lamb to Peoria, taking over management of the team himself.

McGinnity made his way out east and pitched in a game against a semi-pro club called the Bushwicks at Dexter Park in Brooklyn. He also pitched in Newark for a semi-pro team called the Meadowbrooks, claiming a 6–2 victory over the Hilldale Colored Giants, who were led by Hall of Fame third baseman Judy Johnson and who won the Negro League World Series that year.[45]

Those were some of the last games he ever pitched. This time his retirement as a player would stick.

24. The Final Years

By the end of 1925, it was apparent that one of the longest and most successful pitching careers in the history of the game finally was at an end. McGinnity would be 55-years-old by the time the next season rolled around. He still loved the game and his arm might still have had some life left in it, but his legs were gone.

"The pins get wobbly," he said in one interview, "but the old wing is still there."[1]

On December 10, 1925, it was announced that he had signed on to help coach Wilbert Robinson's pitchers in Brooklyn in spring training at Clearwater, Florida. Uncle Robbie was bringing in a whole new coaching staff, including former Brooklyn catcher Otto Miller and another old Orioles teammate, Joe Kelley. McGinnity originally was brought on board only for the spring but Robinson said that if he could impart his decades of wisdom to the young pitchers on the team, it could be a full-season job.[2]

Robinson was eight years older than McGinnity and he had been finished as a player long ago, in 1902. He had begun serving as a coach under McGraw in spring training in 1909—around the time McGinnity left the Giants—and became a full-time coach in 1911. He had been instrumental in the development of Chief Meyers as a catcher and in the success of young pitchers such as Rube Marquard as the Giants won three straight pennants from 1911–13.

He had a falling out with McGraw in 1913, however, when McGraw, in a drunken stupor at a party, berated Robinson for coaching mistakes he made during the recent World Series. He fired Robinson on the spot and, according to some accounts, Robinson responded by dousing McGraw with beer. The two men did not speak to one another for 17 years.[3] They still weren't speaking in 1926 when McGinnity went to work for Robinson. It would be another four years before McGraw and Robinson finally reconciled their differences at the National League's winter meetings.

It's surprising they had stayed as close as they did for as long as they did. McGraw could be a conniving, scheming sort, who frequently tiptoed along the edge of the rules. Robinson was much more virtuous. He could be a fiery competitor on the field, but there wasn't a devious bone in his rotund body.

Casey Stengel, who played for Robinson, said he was "the finest man I ever knew in baseball."⁴ Columnist John Kieran called him "as honest as the sunlight."⁵

Within a month after Robinson left the Giants, he was hired as the new manager of the Brooklyn Dodgers and became so popular that during his years as manager, the team often was known as the Robins. He had some success, winning a pennant in 1916, but he was much better known for his robust personality than any sort of managerial genius.

Robinson's most famous moment came during spring training in 1915, when he was challenged to catch a baseball dropped from an airplane. In 1908, Washington Senators catcher Gabby Street had caught a ball dropped from the Washington Monument and Robinson agreed to try to top that. To do so, he enlisted the help of a female aviator named Ruth Law, who was to drop a ball from her plane as it flew overhead. According to one story, Law got to the airfield to take off and realized she had forgotten to bring the baseball that she was to drop. Instead, she took a grapefruit from the lunch box of one of her crew members and used it instead. She dropped the grapefruit and it splattered all over the bewildered Robinson, who toppled to the ground with his eyes clenched shut, momentarily thinking he had been badly injured. He began yelling that he was covered in his own blood until he saw everyone laughing. It was only then that he realized it was grapefruit juice.⁶

In the mid–1920s, Robbie was looking for someone to help him turn his Dodgers in the right direction and even though McGinnity was still friendly with McGraw, he hired the Iron Man to instill some toughness and moxie in his pitchers.

McGinnity's short time with the Dodgers came during a period punctuated by moments of extreme sadness. Christy Mathewson had died the previous fall in Saranac, New York. Matty had been exposed to mustard gas while serving in the Army in World War I and that led to tuberculosis, which ended his career and ultimately took his life. Although McGinnity and Mathewson had traveled in different social circles, there was a connection between them as pitching partners that was insoluble. Mathewson was laid to rest in Lewisburg, Pennsylvania, in the middle of the 1925 World Series in a massive funeral that attracted the entire Bucknell College student body and hundreds of dignitaries from across baseball.

Near the end of March 1926, as the Dodgers were wrapping up spring training, McGinnity received more bad news. His father-in-law, John Redpath, had died of a stroke back in McAlester. John had lingered near the edge of death for a few days, long enough for almost all his children — including Mary McGinnity — to hurry back and be at his bedside when he passed away.⁷

In late June, McGinnity was the recipient of the worst news yet. Mary had been in poor health herself for a few years, and the strain of her father's death hit her hard. She also fell ill and remained in McAlester at her mother's home for three months rather than going back to Decatur. Now she, too, was failing and Joe took a leave of absence from the Dodgers to go back to Oklahoma to be with her. He was there on June 23 when she died at her parents' home.[8]

Joe laid her to rest alongside Rebecca in Oak Hill Cemetery. For nearly 33 years, she had been the constant in his life. Through all the moves, through the long struggle just to make it in baseball, through all the hopping from one team to the next, through all the battles and abuse, there always had been a smiling face and a soothing voice at the end of the day. She had graciously accepted the role of the ultimate baseball widow, shuffling around the country to be near him or simply waiting at home in Decatur or McAlester for the arrival of autumn. Now, Joe was the one who had been widowed.

He seemingly resorted to the only sort of therapy he knew: Baseball. Less than two weeks after her death, he was back in New York. On July 7, he pitched in an exhibition game at the Polo Grounds as part of "Matty Day." Hooks Wiltse, Roger Bresnahan, Rube Marquard, Fred Merkle, Frank Bowerman, Johnny Evers, Fred Clarke and many other former players also were part of the 3-inning exhibition, which raised $25,000 for charity.[9]

Then it was back to work with Robinson. Despite having one of the best pitching staffs in baseball, the Dodgers never really got going that season and finished sixth in the National League with a record of 71–82, four games behind the fifth-place Giants and 17½ games behind Rogers Hornsby's pennant-winning Cardinals.

While McGinnity had been a marvelous pitcher and a fine manager, he wasn't a rousing success as a coach. Veteran sportswriter Tom Meany wrote in 1952 that the young pitchers on the Brooklyn staff didn't seem inclined to take Iron Man's advice. During spring training and as they worked their way north, the Dodgers played a series of games against the Yankees, who then had Babe Ruth, Lou Gehrig and one of the most dynamic batting orders in history. McGinnity kept telling his pitchers to feed the power-packed Yankees off-speed stuff to set up their fastballs, but they ignored him and kept trying to throw hard stuff past Ruth and Gehrig. The Dodgers lost every game. Meany wrote that "McGinnity suffered the common fate of being an anachronism. He hadn't pitched in the majors since 1908, 18 years earlier, and the players he was trying to instruct simply couldn't believe that the fat old guy had ever been a star pitcher."[10]

McGinnity didn't help his image with the youngsters with some of his comments. In a United Press article in early May, he noted that major league teams carried too many pitchers and the only thing that kept modern hurlers from working as frequently as he had were psychological barriers.

"Take a look at the bench of any major league club now and you will see it all cluttered up with pitchers," he said. "It is not unusual to find 10 regular pitchers on a club roster and in our day a club was rich that had four good pitchers. With so many pitchers to work, a manager has to arrange some sort of a regular schedule for his starting pitchers so that they may keep themselves on the proper edge. The manager may start them in order and tell them they are to work every fourth or fifth day and if there are enough relief pitchers around to act in emergencies the regular pitchers can be worked in regular order. This policy has had a psychological effect upon the pitchers. They have been influenced into the belief that they should not have to work without a long rest and that they can't be effective without that rest. If the pitcher goes to the box with any kind of a doubt in what he has it would be far better to keep him on the bench."[11]

McGinnity was simply being consistent with what he had said throughout his career—that pitchers were better off if they worked often and worked a high number of innings.

"A fellow can't pitch unless he is worked regularly," he had said back in 1912 at the end of his Newark tenure. "A man must go on the rubber often to retain his effectiveness. No pitcher can keep in condition unless he works in games. He might practice until the cows come home, but there is a vast difference between working on the sidelines and working when someone is trying to knock the cover off the ball."[12]

If McGinnity had trouble communicating with and relating to young pitchers, he probably was even less effective as a first base coach for Robinson's team. Players and coaches often wore cardigan sweaters as part of the uniform in those days, and McGinnity would stand in the coaching box with his legs crossed and his hands thrust so deep into the pockets of the sweater that it stretched almost to his knees. On those occasions when Robinson would flash him a sign, he would spring into action, uncross the legs and get down with his hands on his knees. It was obvious to everyone in the ballpark that something was going on. He never had been a good card player and he wasn't able to keep a poker face when the Dodgers were trying to surprise the opponent with a steal or a hit and run.

"Every time I give Joe a sign, it's like ringing a fire alarm," Robinson said. "I don't know if any players are getting the sign, but I know everybody in the park is, including the peanut vendor."[13]

After just one season, McGinnity's coaching career came to an end. In mid–December, Robinson told both him and Kelley that their services no longer were needed.[14]

He went back to Decatur and continued to work for Staley's, as he had in the off-season for many years, although the 1926 Decatur city directory still listed his occupation as "baseball player."[15]

His daughter, Marguerite, had married a watchmaker from Wisconsin named Alloy V. Lappen in 1923, and Joe took up residence with the young couple in the house on North Street. In December 1926, he sold the house to them for $1.[16] A few months later, they sold it to someone else for $1 with the agreement that the new owner would pay off the taxes,[17] which came to $715 for 1927.[18]

Joe, Marguerite and Alloy all ended up moving to Brooklyn and living at 633 E. 16th Street. McGinnity worked for a while in an orthodontic laboratory owned by Dr. John M. Breen at 115 E. 17th Street. He also helped Art Fox coach the Williams College baseball team prior to the 1928 and 1929 seasons.[19]

There were various reports later on that McGinnity might have tried once more to come back as a player, that he went to Rockford, Illinois, and tried to catch on with a minor league club there. A newspaper story written shortly before his death said he played the entire 1927 season with Rockford's team in the Three-League.[20] That's not possible since Rockford did not even have minor league baseball between 1923 and 1947. People in that city continually tried to lure professional teams to relocate there and it wouldn't have been surprising if McGinnity considered such a comeback since his competitive juices seemingly never stopped flowing.

McGinnity in 1926, wearing the trademark cardigan sweater he wore in the first-base coaching box (Frank Williamson collection).

But none of the three Rockford newspapers in existence at that time—the *Star*, *Republic* and *Register-Gazette*—made any mention of him playing for any team in the area. When McGinnity died a few years later, the obituaries in those papers made no mention of him ever having been there.

Of course, McGinnity never stopped thinking about or talking about baseball. Every now and then he would be quoted in a newspaper piece, reliving the old stories or commenting on the current state of the game.

"I would have had a fortune if I had been a star ten or fifteen years after I was at my best," he noted in one interview. "But in my day salaries were not big. When I left the big show and went back to the minors I had a hard row to hoe and I have been at it ever since, but I certainly have got a lot of fun and pleasure out of it. Baseball is a wonderful game and growing better every year."[21]

William O. Trapp reported in the *New York World* that McGinnity spent some time during the summer of 1929 with a group of sandlot kids in the Bronx, showing them some of the tricks he had learned. "Joe spent the entire afternoon with them—just as he had with Matty a quarter century earlier—telling them how to pitch and how to field," Trapp wrote.[22]

His health was beginning to fail, but he seemed to really cherish children, perhaps because he could see in them the pure love of the game that he still carried in his aging heart. Ed Rothberg, the son of Mary McGinnity's sister, Lula May, remembered seeing McGinnity in the late 1920s when he came to visit the Rothbergs in Plainfield, New Jersey. He recalled Uncle Joe as a fun-loving sort who would get out in the yard and throw the ball around with the kids.[23]

On August 27, 1929, McGinnity underwent surgery at Brooklyn Memorial Hospital for what was described as an "intestinal disorder." It actually was cancer of the bladder. Newspaper reports said he had been ailing for several months. An Associated Press story indicated that as he was being wheeled into surgery, he joked "Well, I guess it's the ninth inning for me and I guess they're going to get me out."[24]

Another story at the time reported that

McGinnity (left) watches a game from the stands with his old friend and catcher, Roger Bresnahan (Charles W. Brown, Jr., collection).

he was expected to recover well, but that was wishful thinking. The cancer was very advanced. He had one tumor removed that day and another tumor was soon discovered. It was inoperable. He stayed in the hospital for close to two months.

Finally, near the end of October, he went home to Marguerite's apartment. On October 22, the Associated Press reported, "His surgeons said today that there is little hope for his recovery although he may live 'a month or so' longer. A second tumor has developed and in McGinnity's condition it is considered inadvisable to attempt another operation."[25]

The newspapers back in Illinois began eulogizing him even before he was gone. The *Decatur Review* ran a lengthy piece, written by Howard V. Millard, on October 27 that said "Old Joe, educated in the old school of diamond performers where the players gave no quarter and asked none, is breathing his last out east."[26] The United Press reported on October 28 that his death was "only a matter of hours" away.[27] Once again, someone was underestimating the grit of Joe McGinnity. He gamely clung to life for 17 more days.

Marguerite later said that her father's health never showed any improvement after his August surgery, but she said to the very end he was conscious and alert. She would sit and read him the many letters of encouragement that arrived from all over the country and he comprehended every word.

While he lay there battling the inevitable, the stock market crashed and the start of another economic depression, even more dire than the one he had experienced in the 1890s, enveloped the country. He wasn't going to be around to be affected by it, though.

At 6:07 A.M. on November 14, Joe McGinnity died.

Tributes immediately flooded in from the people and the communities he had touched in his nomadic career. The *Dubuque Telegraph Herald* eulogized him as "one of the squarest shooters" in baseball.[28] The *Rock Island Argus* pegged him as "a mild man off the field but a demon in uniform."[29] The *Sporting News* called him "one of the most unassuming, amiable and gentle mannered men who ever stood on a pitcher's plate."[30]

The *Newark* (Ohio) *Advocate* praised him as a bastion of clean living: "Irregular living, McGinnity said, sent men to the scrap heap, and no athletic ever took better care of himself."[31]

In Butte, a *Montana Standard* editorial took note of the financial beating he absorbed in the Northwestern League and delivered a lefthanded compliment: "As a business man, McGinnity was a mighty good pitcher."[32]

Dick Kinsella, an old Springfield chum who served as a scout for the Giants, called him the smartest pitcher in baseball history. "He was what you might call a natural born baseball pitcher," Kinsella told the *Decatur Review*. "Although Christy Mathewson was a wonder, I think Joe McGinnity knew more about baseball than Mathewson."[33]

McGraw, in a story written by William Hennigan in the *New York World*, gave McGinnity credit for helping to develop Roger Bresnahan as a player and he said Iron Man's rising, underhand curve "was one of the most puzzling things that I ever looked or swung at.

"He loved his baseball and never tired of pitching," McGraw added. "He always kept in good physical condition, and when I was hard pressed for a pitcher in a doubleheader he would come through with one of his famous iron man stunts. And he generally would win both games, for he was that kind of pitcher."[34]

While it was obvious that McGinnity would be buried alongside Mary back in McAlester, the people of Decatur were quick to stake their claim to being his hometown. Earl Obenshain wrote in the *Decatur Herald* that "no matter how far he went, Joe always regarded Decatur as his 'home' town and maintained his connection here" and that if he should be buried there (which he wasn't), a monument should be erected declaring him "Decatur's greatest contribution to American sport."[35]

Millard, in the rival *Decatur Review*, wrote that McGinnity's remains should at least be brought to Decatur "on the way to his final resting place," for some sort of service. "Joe made any number of friends here during his career and the name of McGinnity and Decatur will always go hand in hand when thinking of the deeds of one of the greatest pitchers in the history of baseball."[36]

Roman Catholic services were held on November 16 at 10 A.M. at the Church of Our Lady of Refuge, at the corner of Foster and Ocean in Brooklyn, with about 100 mourners in attendance.[37] It was a modest gathering compared to the Mathewson extravaganza four years earlier, but McGraw and National League president John Heydler were there. So was Abe Yager, the *Brooklyn Eagle* sportswriter who first referred to McGinnity as "Iron Man" in print.

McGinnity's body was then removed to McAlester. A handful of Decatur townspeople—including Marguerite's brother-in-law, James Lappen; John Howley of Staley's; and Pete Brilley of the Illinois Power and Light Company—met the train in St. Louis and paid their respects before it continued on its way.[38] More services were held in Oklahoma on November 18. McGinnity's body lay in state at the local Elks Lodge and members of B.P.O.E. Lodge No. 533 administered the graveside services. His pallbearers were many of the old players with whom he'd first started playing in Krebs nearly four decades earlier—Johnny McGuire, Bill Collins, Billy Powers, Happy Fields, and J.J. McAlester's two sons, Berry and Bunn. Among the half dozen honorary pallbearers was Harry Hokey.[39]

It wasn't an elaborate service. It was simple, basic, straight-forward, no-nonsense, just like the man himself. The bill for the entire funeral came to $23.[40]

25. A Faded Legend

In the years following his death, the legacy of Iron Man Joe McGinnity faded somewhat from public view. He wasn't someone you heard or read much about.

When the Baseball Hall of Fame was inaugurated seven years after McGinnity's death, Christy Mathewson was among the five original inductees, along with Ty Cobb, Babe Ruth, Walter Johnson and Honus Wagner. McGraw went in the next year and both Roger Bresnahan and Wilbert Robinson were inducted in 1945. Finally, in 1946, the Veterans Committee voted McGinnity into the Hall posthumously along with 10 other players, including Tinker, Evers, Chance, Rube Waddell, Eddie Plank and Jack Chesbro.

The Hall of Fame ceremonies were a little different then from what they are now. These days, thousands of people gather outside the stately museum in the heart of Cooperstown, New York, to listen to speeches and to hail the men being inducted. There was nothing like that in 1946. There were a few stories in the newspapers when McGinnity's election was announced in April, but very little fanfare in June when they hung a plaque that barely scratched the surface of the man it honored:

> **Joseph Jerome McGinnity**
> "Ironman"
> Distinguished as the pitcher who hurled two games
> on one day the most times. Did this on five occasions.
> Won both games three times. Played with Baltimore, Brooklyn
> and New York teams in N.L. and Baltimore in A.L.
> Gained more than 200 victories during career.
> Recorded 20 or more victories seven times.
> In two successive seasons won at least 30 games.[1]

After 1946, Iron Man's legacy lapsed back into obscurity. Every now and then, someone would write something about him on the anniversary of his 1903 doubleheaders, but there wasn't the same level of fascination with him as with some of the other deadball heroes.

Perhaps it was because he had no relatives carrying on the McGinnity name. Marguerite did not have any children, so Iron Man had no grandchildren. When he was inducted into the Quad-City Sports Hall of Fame in 1988 in the area in which he was born, the organizers had trouble tracking down a living relative. They found a Chicago priest named Reverend Joseph McGinnity, who accepted the plaque on behalf of his namesake even though he wasn't entirely certain he was related.

Meanwhile, that imposing stone house on Seneca Street in McAlester fell into disrepair. McGinnity had sold it to John Redpath in 1911, and it was sold and resold many times in the years that followed. It was split up into apartments for defense workers during World War II and slowly crumbled from lack of care.[2] It still stands, but it's in much poorer condition than Frank Redpath's wooden house across the street, which was built around the same time.

The city of McAlester also did not do a great deal to tell the world that it was the adopted home of a baseball superstar. The city's water tower proclaims McAlester the home of Carl Albert, a member of congress for 30 years and the speaker of the U.S. House of Representatives from 1971–77. The city also proudly claims to be the birthplace of country music singer Reba McEntire and actress Beverlee McKinsey.

But when someone mentioned to Frank Williamson, an umpire and

The house that Joe and Mary McGinnity built at Seventh and Seneca Streets in McAlester, Oklahoma, remains majestic more than 100 years later although it has fallen into disrepair through the years.

baseball buff in southeast Oklahoma, around 2000 that a baseball Hall of Famer was buried right there in his home area, he didn't believe it. It was true. There in Masonic Section No. 3 of Oak Hill Cemetery on the east edge of McAlester, with a modest headstone, was Iron Man Joe McGinnity.

Williamson, who lives in nearby Wilburton, Oklahoma, became obsessed with McGinnity and began acquiring large amounts of photos and memorabilia of the man. Within a few years, the remaining relatives of McGinnity, led by Charles W. Brown Jr. of Chicago, made arrangements to ensure that the grave was more prominently marked. They erected a modern 3,000-pound headstone at his resting place and dedicated it in a special ceremony on May 9, 2006.

Brown, the great-great-grandson of John and Rebecca Denning, spent months organizing the services. With about 50 family members, friends, townspeople and baseball buffs looking on, a series of speakers—including Brown, Williamson and the author of this book—spoke about McGinnity's life in a ceremony that lasted nearly two hours. One of those presiding over the service was the Reverend Kris Denning of Oklahoma City, a Baptist minister and also a descendant of Iron Man's.

"As you walk through a cemetery, you see a lot of names and you'll see

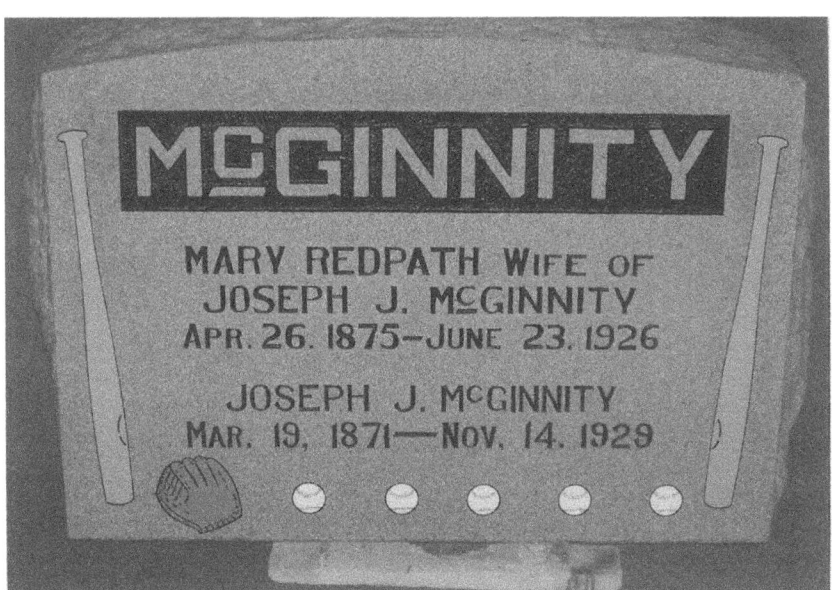

In May of 2006, surviving relatives of McGinnity had a new gravestone made for him and dedicated it in Oak Hill Cemetery in McAlester (Charles W. Brown, Jr., collection).

some dates, too," Denning said during the service. "You may see two dates, separated by a dash. That dash represents a life, but it doesn't tell you anything about that life."

But the new McGinnity tombstone tells you something without even having to read it. There are two baseball bats, five balls and a glove on each side of the marker. The backside includes a covered wagon, which appears on the gravemarkers of members of the Denning family all over the country, and an etching of a baseball game being played in a pasture that was taken from a large wooden bench in the house on Seneca Street. It makes note of his induction into the Hall of Fame. It makes it abundantly clear that one of the unique and special players in the history of baseball lies in the soft Oklahoma soil below.

Appendix A. Statistics

Batted: Right
Threw: Right
Height: 5–11
Weight: 206 pounds
Born: March 20, 1871, Cornwall Township, Henry County, Illinois
Died: November 14, 1929, Brooklyn, New York

Major League Pitching Record

Year	Team	League	W-L	G	GS	CG	SHO	SV	IP	H	BB	SO	HBP	ERA
1899	Balt.	(NL)	28–16	48	41	38	4	2	366.3	358	93	74	28	2.68
1900	B'klyn	(NL)	28–8	44	37	32	1	0	343.0	350	113	93	41	2.94
1901	Balt.	(AL)	26–20	48	43	39	1	1	382.0	412	96	75	21	3.56
1902	Balt.	(AL)	13–10	25	23	19	0	0	198.7	219	46	39	8	3.44
1902	NY	(NL)	8–8	19	16	16	1	0	153.0	122	32	67	9	2.06
1903	NY	(NL)	31–20	55	48	44	3	2	434.0	391	109	171	19	2.43
1904	NY	(NL)	35–8	51	44	38	9	5	408.0	307	86	144	13	1.61
1905	NY	(NL)	21–15	46	38	26	2	3	320.3	289	71	125	14	2.87
1906	NY	(NL)	27–12	45	37	32	3	2	339.7	316	71	105	7	2.25
1907	NY	(NL)	18–18	47	34	23	3	4	310.3	320	58	120	15	3.16
1908	NY	(NL)	11–7	37	20	7	5	5	186.0	192	37	55	7	2.27
Totals			246–142	465	381	314	32	24	3441.3	3276	812	1068	182	2.66

Minor League Pitching Record

Year	Team	League	W-L	G	IP	H	BB	SO
1893	Montgomery	(Southern)	10–19	31	193.0	212	99	76
1894	Kansas City	(Western Lg.)	8–10	20	124.0	157	54	31
1898	Peoria	(Western Assn.)	10–3	16	104.0	107	59	69
1909	Newark	(Eastern)	29–16	55	422.0	297	78	195
1910	Newark	(Eastern)	30–19	61	408.0	325	71	132
1911	Newark	(Eastern)	12–19	43	278.0	269	53	77
1912	Newark	(International)	16–10	37	261.0	293	43	62
1913	Tacoma	(Northwestern)	22–19	68	436.0	418	66	154
1914	Tacoma	(Northwestern)	20–21	49	326.0	295	73	105
1914	Venice	(Pacific Coast)	1–4	8	37.0	42	5	7
1915	Tacoma	(Northwestern)	21–15	45	355.0	291	39	58
1916	Butte	(Northwestern)	20–13	43	291.0	340	63	95
1917	Butte	(Northwestern)	4–4	13	92.0	90	23	22
1917	Great Falls	(Northwestern)	3–0	3	27.0	29	2	6
1918	Vancouver	(PC Intl.)	2–6	9	na	47	14	31
1922	Danville	(Three-I)	1–6	16	79.0	117	12	12
1922	Dubuque	(Miss.Valley)	5–8	19	91.0	94	19	19
1923	Dubuque	(Miss.Valley)	15–12	42	206.0	268	44	41
1923	Des Moines	(Western)	0–1	1	2.0	13	0	3
1925	Dubuque	(Miss.Valley)	6–6	15	85.0	119	18	22
1925	Springfield	(Three-I)	0–1	1	4.1	6	3	0
Totals			235–212	595	3821.0	3829	838	1217

Appendix B. Records Held

Major League Records

Hit batsmen, season—41 (1900)
Batters faced, season—1814 (1903)
Average wins per season, career—24.6

National League Records

Innings pitched, season—434 (1903)
Games started, season—48 (1903)
Decisions, season—51 (1903)

American League Records

Hits allowed, season—412 (1901)

Chapter Notes

Prologue

1. Hugh A. Jennings, "McGinnity Greatest Fielding Pitcher in Game, Says Jennings," *Philadelphia Evening Bulletin*, 18 December 1925.
2. William Henigan, "M'Ginnity Hardest Worker on Mound M'Graw Ever Had," *New York World*, 15 November 1929.
3. Connie Mack, *My 66 Years in the Big Leagues* (Philadelphia: Winston, 1950).
4. *Ibid.*
5. John J. Toohill, "McGinnity Used To Hurl Eight Games a Week While Playing Here," *Illinois State Register*, 15 November 1929.
6. "How M'Ginnity Tabbed His Batters." *Butte* (Montana) *Miner*, 15 May 1916.

Chapter 1

1. Records of Peoria Diocese of Catholic church.
2. Charles W. Brown Jr., *The History of the Denning Family in America*. Unpublished.
3. *Ibid.*
4. *Ibid.*
5. *Ibid.*
6. *Ibid.*
7. Voters and Taxpayers of Cornwall Township 1877, p. 228.
8. Henry L. Kiner, *History of Henry County, Illinois*, (Chicago: Pioneer Publishing, 1919), p. 601.
9. Brown, *The History of the Denning Family in America*.
10. *Ibid.*
11. *Ibid.*
12. Earl Obenshain, "Iron Man" McGinnity Got First Start Here," *Decatur* (Illinois) *Herald*, 27 October 1929.
13. *Decatur City Directory 1884*.
14. *Decatur City Directory 1889*.

Chapter 2

1. Wilton Floberg, *Sporting Life*, August 1923.
2. *jaha.org/FloodMuseum/history.html*.
3. Dayle Cochran Irwin and Karen Anderson, *Decatur Entertainment: A Pictorial History* (St. Louis: G. Bradley Publishing), p. 107.
4. Earl Obenshain, "Iron Man" McGinnity Got First Start Here," *Decatur* (Illinois) *Herald*, 27 October 1929.
5. "Diamond Dust," *Decatur* (Illinois) *Herald*, 29 July 1888.
6. Howard V. Millard, "Joe McGinnity, Famous 'Iron Man' of Majors, Began Great Career on Decatur Sand Lots," *Decatur* (Illinois) *Review*, 27 October 1929.
7. "The I-I League," *Decatur* (Illinois) *Review*, 21 May 1889.
8. *Ibid.*
9. *Ibid.*
10. *Ibid.*
11. *Ibid.*
12. "The I-I League," *Decatur* (Illinois) *Review*, 25 May 1889.
13. "Danville and Decatur," *Decatur* (Illinois) *Review*, 28 May 1889.
14. "The Sunday Game," *Decatur* (Illinois) *Herald*, 4 June 1889.
15. "Still in the Soup," *Decatur* (Illinois) *Review*, 5 June 1889.
16. "Diamond Dust," *Decatur* (Illinois) *Herald*, 7 June 1889; item included an excerpt of an article from the Danville Press.
17. "The National Game," *Decatur* (Illinois) *Review*, 13 June 1889.
18. "What a Crowd," *Decatur* (Illinois) *Review*, 14 June 1889.
19. "The National Game," *Decatur* (Illinois) *Review*, 18 June 1889.
20. "Killed in a Coal Mine," *Decatur* (Illinois) *Herald*, 23 June 1889.

Chapter 3

1. Richard Joyce, "Early Days of Coal Mining in Northern Illinois," *kentlaw.edu*.
2. *Encyclopedia of Oklahoma History and Culture*, chapter on coal.
3. Luther B. Hill, *History of the State of Ok-*

lahoma (Chicago: Lewis Publishing, 1908), pp. 267–268.
4. *Ibid.*
5. *Ibid.*
6. See note 2 above.
7. Charles Saulsberry, "Iron Joe Proves His Mettle Early," *Oklahoma City Oklahoman*, 6 February 1940.
8. *Ibid.*
9. *Ibid.*
10. *Ibid.*
11. *Ibid.*
12. *Ibid.*
13. Charles Saulsberry, "Coal Mine to Big League," *Oklahoma City Oklahoman*, 11 February 1940.
14. "Pitches for Season," *McAlester* (Oklahoma) *News-Capital*, 14 November 1929.
15. See note 13 above.
16. Bob Doucette, "Krebs to honors 100 killed in 1892 blast," *Oklahoma City Oklahoman*, 24 May 2002,
17. See note 2 above.
18. Charles Saulsberry, "Mine Blast Kick Joe Into Game," *Oklahoma City Oklahoman*, 8 February 1940.
19. See note 16 above.
20. See note 16 above.
21. "Terrible Mine Explosion," *New York Times*, 9 January 1892.
22. See note 16 above.

Chapter 4

1. "Daguerreotypes," *Sporting News*, 20 April 1939.
2. Lee Allen and Tom Meany, *Kings of the Diamond* (New York: G.P. Putnam's Sons, 1965), p. 40.
3. "Hoss and Hoss," *Van Buren* (Arkansas) *Argus*, 25 May 1892.
4. Charles Saulsberry, "McGinnity's Miracle," *Oklahoma City Oklahoman*, 7, February 1940.
5. *Van Buren* (Arkansas) *Argus*, 20 April 1892.
6. *Van Buren* (Arkansas) *Argus*, 4 May 1892.
7. "Diamond Chat," *Van Buren* (Arkansas) *Argus*, 25 May 1892.
8. See note 3 above.
9. "Diamond Chat," *Van Buren* (Arkansas) *Argus*, 1 June 1892.
10. "Arkansas vs. Kansas," *Van Buren* (Arkansas) *Argus*, 22 June 1892.
11. *Van Buren* (Arkansas) *Argus*, 6 July, 1892.
12. *Van Buren* (Arkansas) *Argus*, 13 July 1892.
13. "Van Buren-Ft. Smith," *Van Buren* (Arkansas) *Argus*, 27 July 1892.

14. "McCloskey's great team," *Sporting News*, 22 April 1893.
15. Philip J. Lowry, *Green Cathedrals* (Cooperstown, N.Y.: Society for American Baseball Research, 1986), p. 129.
16. See note 14 above.
17. *Sporting News*, 20 May 1893.
18. See note 14 above.
19. *Sporting News*, 29 April 1893,
20. *Montgomery* (Alabama) *Advertiser*, 21 April, 1893
21. Ernest J. Lanigan, *Oneonta* (New York) *Star*, 23 March 1948.
22. See note 19 above.
23. *Sporting News*, 20 May 1893.
24. *Sporting News*, 15, July 1893.
25. See note 23 above.
26. *Sporting News*, 27 May 1893.
27. *Ibid.*
28. *Sporting News*, 1 July 1893.
29. *Sporting News*, 20 June 1893.
30. "The Montgomery's plans," *Sporting News*, 20 June 1893.
31. "New York Taking Them in Big Lots," *Sporting News*, 15 July 1893.
32. "Montgomery Mention," *Sporting News*, 22 July 1893.
33. *Ibid.*
34. *Sporting News*, 22 July 1893.
35. *Sporting News*, 8 July 1893.
36. *Sporting News*, 5 August 1893.
37. "Collapse expected at any time," *Sporting News*, 5 August 1893.
38. *Sporting News*, 19 August 1893
39. "Southern League Meeting," *Sporting News*, 18, August 1893.
40. "Southern League Brevities," *Sporting News*, 12 August 1893.
41. Marriage records, Choctaw Nation, Indian Territory.

Chapter 5

1. Lee Allen, *The American League Story* (New York: Hill & Wang, 1962).
2. *Kansas City Star*, 16 March 1894.
3. "Pitcher Joe M'Ginnity," *Kansas City Journal*, 21 March 1894.
4. *Ibid.*
5. *Kansas City Star*, 20 March 1894.
6. *Kansas City Star*, 29 March 1894.
7. "A Picnic For the Blues," *Kansas City Journal*, 1 April 1894.
8. *Kansas City Star*, 2 April 1894.
9. *Kansas City Star*, 3 April 1894.
10. "The Blues Play Hard Ball," *Kansas City Star*, 4 April, 1894.
11. *Kansas City Star*, 11 April 1894.

12. *Kansas City Star*, 17 April 1894.
13. "Blue For the Brewers," *Kansas City Times*, 26 April 1894.
14. "M'Ginnity on the Coaching Lines," *Kansas City Journal*, 26 April 1894.
15. *Kansas City Times*, 29 April 1894.
16. *Ibid.*
17. "Mr. M'Ginity Went Wrong," *Kansas City Times*, 1 May 1894.
18. *Ibid.*
19. "Made it Three Straight," *Kansas City Journal*, 1 May 1894.
20. "Down Went M'Gintty," *Kansas City Star*, 14 May 1894.
21. "The Blues at Home Again," *Kansas City Star*, 17 May, 1894.
22. "Blues Made Bad Breaks," *Kansas City Times*, 20 May 1894.
23. "Toledo Took the Second," *Kansas City Journal*, 20 May 1894.
24. "McGinnity Was Hit Hard," *Kansas City Star*, 13 June 1894.
25. *Kansas City Star*, 18 June 1894.
26. *Ibid.*
27. *Kansas City Times*, 21 June, 1894.
28. "McGinnity Will Not Do," *Kansas City Star*, 21 June 1894.
29. "Must Have New Pitchers," *Kansas City Journal*, 24 June 1894.
30. John J. Toohill, "McGinnity Used To Hurl Eight Games a Week While Playing Here," *Illinois State Register*, 15 November 1929.
31. "Knocked Hill Out of the Box," *Kansas City Star*, 27 June 1894.
32. *Kansas City Star*, 29 June 1894.

Chapter 6

1. Christina Romer, "Spurious Volatility in Historical Unemployment Data," *Journal of Political Economy*, 1986.
2. "Mines and Miners," *South McAlester* (Oklahoma) *Capital*, 26 April 1894.
3. "A Shameful Story," *Kansas City Journal*, 21 June 1894.
4. *Decatur City Directory 1895.*
5. "Local Baseball," *Decatur* (Illinois) *Review*, 10 July 1894.
6. "McGinnity Hero of Staley Game Today," *Decatur* (Illinois) *Review*, 18 May 1919.
7. "Beaten Three Straight," *Decatur* (Illinois) *Republican*, 29 August 1894.
8. "Toledo 15—Decatur 4," *Decatur* (Illinois) *Review*, 3 September 1894.
9. "Base Ball News," *Decatur* (Illinois) *Review*, 11 September 1894.
10. "Played Horse With 'Em," *Decatur* (Illinois) *Review*, 27 September 1894.
11. *Illinois State Journal*, 3 September 1894.
12. "A Pitchers' Battle," *Illinois State Journal*, 10, September 1894.
13. *Ibid.*
14. John J. Toohill, "McGinnity Used To Hurl Eight Games a Week While Playing Here," *Illinois State Register*, 15 November 1929.
15. "Joe M'Ginnity, Ball Player," *Illinois State Register*, 15 November 1929.
16. *Ibid.*
17. *Ibid.*
18. State of Illinois birth record for Marguerite McGinnity. (Date of birth is listed as June 5, 1895, although the 1930 U.S. census listed her as being 28. She also sometimes went by the name Margaret, signing many letters that way later in her life.)
19. "Gone to Springfield," *Decatur* (Illinois) *Republican*, 2 August 1895.
20. See note 14 above.
21. *Boston Globe*, 27 June 1907.
22. Benton Stark, *The Year They Called Off the World Series* (Garden City Park, N.Y.: Avery Publishing Group, 1991), p. 83.
23. "McGinnity Hero of Staley Game Today," *Decatur* (Illinois) *Review*, 18 May 1919.
24. Walter Trumbull, "M'Graw Picks A's to Win Next Year," *Philadelphia Evening Bulletin*, 16 November 1929.
25. Kevin Kerrane, *The Hurlers* (New Berlin, Wisc.: Redefinition, 1989), p. 100.
26. "'Iron Man' Joe McGinnity," *Dubuque* (Iowa) *Telegraph Herald*, 23 July 1922.
27. See note 24 above.
28. Hugh A. Jennings, "McGinnity Greatest Fielding Pitcher in Game, Says Jennings," *Philadelphia Evening Bulletin*, 18 December 1925.
29. Charles Saulsberry, "McGinnity's Miracle," *Oklahoma City Oklahoman*, 7 February 1940.
30. *Peoria* (Illinois) *Herald*, 19 March 1898.
31. "There May Be No Base Ball," *Peoria* (Illinois) *Herald*, 16 April 1898.
32. "Diamond Dust," *Peoria* (Illinois) *Herald*, 2 May 1898.
33. *Peoria* (Illinois) *Herald*, 19 June 1898.
34. "Diamond Dust," *Peoria* (Illinois) *Herald*, 20 June 1898.
35. *Peoria* (Illinois) *Herald*, 18 June 1898.
36. See note 34 above.
37. "Was a Battle Royal," *Peoria* (Illinois) *Herald*, 27 June 1898.
38. "Diamond Dust," *Peoria* (Illinois) *Herald*, 27 June 1898.
39. See note 37 above.
40. "Base Ball at an End," *Peoria* (Illinois) *Herald*, 29 June 1898.
41. *Ibid.*
42. *Ibid.*

43. *Ibid.*
44. *Illinois State Journal*, 10 July 1898.

Chapter 7

1. "Daguerreotypes," *Sporting News*, 20 April 1939.
2. "'Iron Man' Joe McGinnity," *Dubuque (Iowa) Telegraph Herald*, 23 July 1922.
3. Robert W. Creamer, "Old Orioles played it close but tore the game wide open," *Smithsonian Magazine*, October 1979.
4. Jack Kavanagh and Norman Macht, *Uncle Robbie* (Cleveland: Society for American Baseball Research, 1999), p. 23.
5. Ed Burkholder, "McGinnity was a man of iron," *Sport Magazine*, April 1954.
6. Kavanagh and Macht, *Uncle Robbie*, pp. 33–34.
7. William Hennigan, "M'Ginnity Hardest Worker on Mound M'Graw Ever Had," *New York World*, 15 November 1929.
8. See note 5 above.
9. See note 5 above.
10. See note 3 above.
11. Frank Deford, *The Old Ball Game* (New York: Grove Press, 2005), pp. 28–29.
12. "New York Loses Again," *New York Tribune*, 19 April 1899.
13. Lowry, *Green Cathedrals*, p. 35.
14. Kavanagh and Macht, *Uncle Robbie*, p. 39.
15. *Baltimore American*, 19 July 1899.
16. "Split Even With the Orioles," *Chicago Tribune*, 19 August, 1899.
17. *Ibid.*
18. *Ibid.*
19. "What About the 'Brush Rule?'" *Chicago Tribune*, 20 August, 1899.
20. See note 14 above.
21. *New York Times*, 15 October 1899.
22. *Ibid.*

Chapter 8

1. Clyde Wooldridge, "A landmark worth saving: The 'Iron Man's' abode," *McAlester (Oklahoma) News-Capital*, 24 June, 2006.
2. "'Iron Man' Joe McGinnity," *Dubuque (Iowa) Telegraph Herald*, 23 July 1922.
3. Charles Alexander, *John McGraw*, Reprint (Lincoln: University of Nebraska Press, 1988), p. 69.
4. Frank Graham, *McGraw of the Giants* (New York: G.P. Putnam's Sons, 1944), pp. 16–17.
5. Kavanagh and Macht, *Uncle Robbie*, p. 41.

6. Lowry, *Green Cathedrals*, p. 40.
7. Lawrence Ritter, *The Glory of Their Times* (New York: Macmillan, 1966), p. 91.
8. Ritter, *The Glory of Their Times*, p. 87.
9. See note 5 above.
10. *Staley's Fellowship Journal*, May 1957.
11. "McGinnity Hero of Staley Game Today," *Decatur* (Illinois) *Review*, 18 May 1919.
12. *Ibid.*
13. *Chicago Daily News*, 15 October 1900.
14. *Ibid.*
15. *Ibid.*
16. "Post-season Series of Leaders," *Chicago Tribune*, 16 October 1900.
17. *Chicago Daily News*, 16 October 1900.
18. *Chicago Daily News*, 17 October 1900.
19. *Pittsburgh Chronicle Telegraph*, 17 October 1900.
20. "Brooklyn Clinches the Series," *Chicago Tribune*, 19 October 1900.
21. "Give Cup to McGinnity," *Chicago Tribune*, 19 October 1900.
22. *Staley's Fellowship Journal*, May 1957.
23. *Ibid.*

Chapter 9

1. Graham, *McGraw of the Giants*, p. 17.
2. "Notes of the Diamond," *Mansfield* (Ohio) *News*, 29 May 1903.
3. Ed Burkholder, "McGinnity was a man of iron," *Sport Magazine*, April 1954.
4. Heywood Broun, *New York World Telegram*, 1923.
5. "'Iron Man' Joe McGinnity," *Dubuque (Iowa) Telegraph Herald*, 23 July 1922.
6. thebaseballpage.com, Roger Bresnahan biography.
7. David Marasco, "The Giants and the Color Barrier," thediamondangle.com.
8. Clyde Duncan, "Jim Watson and His Cronies," *Kiamichi Magazine*, 29 June 1969.
9. Alexander, *John McGraw*, p. 78.
10. *Ibid.*
11. *Washington Post*, 1 June 1901.
12. Alexander, *John McGraw*, p. 79.
13. Alexander, *John McGraw*, p. 80.
14. Alexander, *John McGraw*, p. 79.
15. *Ibid.*
16. *Ibid.*
17. *Ibid.*
18. See note 13 above.

Chapter 10

1. Rob Neyer, "Back when baseball was really messed up," *ESPN.com*, 16 July 2006.

2. Deford, *The Old Ball Game*, p. 53.
3. Deford, *The Old Ball Game*, pp. 53–54.
4. Graham, *McGraw of the Giants*, pp. 19–20.
5. *Ibid.*
6. Graham, *McGraw of the Giants*, p. 21.
7. baseballlibrary.com, John McGraw chronology.
8. *Ibid.*
9. Joe McGinnity contract, dated 16 July 1902.
10. Joseph Durso, *The Days of Mr. McGraw* (Englewood Cliffs, N.J.: Prentice-Hall, 1969), p. 51.
11. Deford, *The Old Ball Game*, p. 56.
12. Graham, *McGraw of the Giants*, p. 22.
13. Durso, *The Days of Mr. McGraw*, p. 46.
14. Ray Robinson, *Matty: An American Hero* (New York: Oxford University Press, 1993), p. 43.
15. Mark Alvarez, *The Old Ball Game* (New Berlin, Wisc.: Redefinition, 1990), p. 12.
16. Robinson, *Matty: An American Hero*, p. 218.
17. Robinson, *Matty: An American Hero*, pp. 64–65.
18. Roger Kahn, *The Head Game* (San Diego: Harcourt, 2000), p. 107.
19. *Ibid.*
20. Harry Grayson, "M'Ginnity in Service Long," *Newspaper Enterprise Association*, 19 April 1943.
21. Ed Burkholder, "McGinnity was a man of iron," *Sport Magazine*, April 1954.
22. John J. Toohill, "McGinnity Used To Hurl Eight Games a Week While Playing Here," *Illinois State Register*, 15 November 1929.
23. "Yesterday's Baseball Games," *New York Times*, 30 August 1902.
24. *Ibid.*

Chapter 11

1. Lowry, *Green Cathedrals*, p. 64.
2. "National League," *New York Times*, 8 May 1903.
3. Dennis DeValeria and Jeanne Burke DeValeria, *Honus Wagner: A Biography* (New York: Henry Holt, 1995), p. 114.
4. baseballlibrary.com, Christy Mathewson chronology.
5. DeValeria and DeValeria, *Honus Wagner: A Biography*, p. 117.
6. *New York Times*, 28 June 1903
7. "Giants Take Double Header," *Chicago Tribune*, 2 August 1903.
8. James J. Corbett, "Ol' Joe McGinnity, 50, Still Pitching Victories — Corbett," *Philadelphia North American*, 30 July 1922.

9. *New York Times*, 2 August 1903, National League.
10. *New York Times*, 9 August 1903, National League.
11. "'Iron Man' Joe McGinnity," *Dubuque* (Iowa) *Telegraph Herald*, 23 July 1922.
12. See note 10 above.
13. *Ibid.*
14. *Ibid.*
15. "National League," *New York Times*, 1 September 1903.

Chapter 12

1. Kerrane, *The Hurlers*, p. 104.
2. Sean Lahman, "Dummy Taylor," *The Baseball Biography Project (bioproj.sabr.org)*.
3. Kerrane, *The Hurlers*, p. 100.
4. Gabriel Schechter, "Hooks Wiltse," *The Baseball Biography Project (bioproj.sabr.org)*.
5. Martin Quigley, *The Crooked Pitch* (Chapel Hill, N.C.: Algonquin Books, 1988), p. 95.
6. "New York 5, Birmingham 3," *New York Times*, 24 March 1904.
7. baseballlibrary.com, Day-by-day account of 1904 Giants.
8. M.J. Sullivan, "The Men on Whom the Championships Depend," *Pearson's Magazine*, April 1905.
9. "How M'Ginnity Tabbed His Batters," *Butte* (Montana) *Miner*, 15 May 1916.
10. *Ibid.*
11. *Ibid.*
12. Gabriel Schechter, "Joe McGinnity's Enduring Brilliance," baseballhalloffame.org.
13. "Urges McGinnity As a Model," *New York Times*, 25 June 2004,.
14. William Jerome and Jean Schwartz, *Line it out McGinnity* (1905).
15. Stark, *The Year They Called Off the World Series*, pp. 112–113.
16. "National League Umpire Nearly Mobbed at Polo Grounds," *New York Times*, 5 October 1904.
17. baseballlibrary.com, Joe McGinnity chronology.
18. See note 12 above.
19. See note 12 above.
20. Lowell Reidenbaugh, *100 Years of National League Baseball* (St. Louis: Sporting News, 1976), p. 54.
21. Graham, *McGraw of the Giants*, p. 28.
22. "No Post Season Baseball," *New York Times*, 7 October 1904.
23. *Ibid.*
24. Stark, *The Year They Called Off the World Series*, p. 175.

25. Joseph Reichler, *The World Series* (New York: Simon & Schuster, 1979), p. 13.
26. Paul Adomites, *October's Game* (New Berlin, Wisc.: Redefinition, 1990), p. 83.
27. *Ibid.*
28. Stark, *The Year They Called Off the World Series*, p. 188.

Chapter 13

1. Directory for Pittsburg County, Indian Territory 1905.
2. "McGinnity's Business Venture," *Oklahoma City Oklahoman*, 11 February 1906.
3. "Pitcher McGinnity May Quit," *New York Times*, 4 March 1905.
4. Reichler, *The World Series*, pp. 15–16.
5. "Baseball Season Opens in a Blaze of Glory," *New York Times*, 15 April 1905.
6. "M'Ginnity Puzzled Chicago's Batsmen," *New York Times*, 16 May 1905.
7. Robinson, *Matty: An American Hero*, pp. 64–65.
8. *Ibid.*
9. Reidenbaugh, *100 Years of National League Baseball*, p. 54.
10. *Ibid.*
11. *Ibid.*
12. *baseballlibrary.com*, Joe McGinnity chronology.
13. *baseball-reference.com*, article on Moonlight Graham.
14. Robinson, *Matty: An American Hero*, pp. 43–44.
15. *New York Times*, 8 October 1905.
16. *Ibid.*
17. *Ibid.*
18. Frederick G. Lieb, *Connie Mack, Grand Old Man of Baseball* (New York: G.P. Putnam's Sons, 1945), p. 92.
19. *thebaseballpage.com*, Rube Waddell.
20. Durso, *The Days of Mr. McGraw*, p. 64.
21. Lowry, *Green Cathedrals*, p. 70.
22. "Giants Triumph, 3–0, in Interleague Game," *New York Times*, 10 October 1905.
23. See note 20 above.
24. See note 22 above.
25. Charles Dryden, "Giants Start With Victory," *Chicago Tribune*, 10 October 1905.
26. *Ibid.*
27. "Athletics Turn in and Whip the Giants," *New York Times*, 11 October 1905.
28. "Giants Win by 9 to 0; Athletics' Play Ragged," *New York Times*, 13 October 1905.
29. Charles Dryden, "Giants Capture Third Victory," *Chicago Tribune*, 14 October 1905.
30. *Ibid.*
31. "Giants Win Another; Need Only One More," *New York Times*, 14 October 1905.
32. "Giants Champions, The Score, 2–0," *New York Times*, 15 October 1905.
33. *Ibid.*
34. Reichler, *The World Series*, p. 17.

Chapter 14

1. Alexander, *John McGraw*, p. 119.
2. Michael Betzold, "Mike Donlin," *The Baseball Biography Project (bioproj.sabr.org)*.
3. Durso, *The Days of Mr. McGraw*, p. 71.
4. Marc Okkonen, "Baseball Uniforms of the 20th Century," *baseball-almanac.com*.
5. *New York Times*, 12 April 1906.
6. *baseballlibrary.com*, Mike Donlin chronology.
7. "20,000 Cheer Giants at the Polo Grounds," *New York Times*, 21 April 1906.
8. *New York Sun*, 8 June 1906.
9. "Chance's Men Get Awful Revenge," *Chicago Tribune*, 8 June 1906.
10. *baseballlibrary.com*, Joe McGinnity chronology.
11. "'Iron Man' Arrested By Order of Mayor," *New York Times*, 25 July 1906.
12. *baseballlibrary.com*, Biography of Heinie Peitz.
13. See note 11 above.
14. "The Mayor Apologized," *New York Times*, 26 July 1906.
15. Reidenbaugh, *100 Years of National League Baseball*, p. 56.
16. Alexander, *John McGraw*, pp. 121–122.
17. See note 15 above.

Chapter 15

1. "McGraw Stops Runaway," *New York Times*, 11 January 1907.
2. "He Has a Great Record in the Box," *Police Gazette*, 21 September 1905.
3. John Klima, *Pitched Battle: 35 of Baseball's Greatest Duels from the Mound* (Jefferson, N.C.: McFarland, 2002), p. 8.
4. Klima, *Pitched Battle: 35 of Baseball's Greatest Duels from the Mound*, p. 11.
5. Robinson, *Matty: An American Hero*, p. 78.
6. Christy Mathewson, *Pitching in a Pinch*, Reprint (Lincoln: University of Nebraska Press, 1994), p. 276.
7. Mathewson, *Pitching in a Pinch*, p. 84.
8. Mathewson, *Pitching in a Pinch*, p. 92.
9. "McGinnity Ready to Play," *New York Times*, 5 February 1907.
10. *Ibid.*
11. Durso, *The Days of Mr. McGraw*, p. 72.
12. *Ibid.*

13. baseballlibrary.com, John McGraw chronology.
14. "Who Threw Water on Umpire Klem?," *New York Times*, 24 September 1907.
15. "Baseball Crowd Causes Forfeit," *New York Times*, 12 April, 1907.
16. *Ibid.*
17. *Ibid.*
18. baseballlibrary.com, Fred Clarke chronology.
19. "Snappy Summaries of Sport," *Lake County* (Indiana) *Times*, 24 May 1907.
20. *Racine* (Wisconsin) *Daily Journal*, 25 May 1907, Sporting
21. See note 14 above.
22. *Ibid.*
23. *Ibid.*

Chapter 16

1. Graham, *McGraw of the Giants*, pp. 41–42.
2. Mathewson, *Pitching in a Pinch*, p. 213.
3. "Rain Upsets Giants' Plans in the South," *New York Times*, 31 March 1908.
4. "Giants at 'Iron Man's' Home," *New York Times*, 5 April 1908.
5. Interview with Ed Rothberg (McGinnity's nephew), 1988.
6. Cait Murphy, *Crazy '08* (New York: HarperCollins, 2007), p. 114.
7. W.W. Aulick, "Iron Man 'All In,' Shuts Out St. Louis," *New York Times*, 9 June 1908.
8. Franklin P. Adams, "Baseball's Sad Lexicon," *New York Globe*, 10 July 1908.
9. Murphy, *Crazy '08*, p. 118.
10. Alexander, *John McGraw*, p. 131.
11. baseballlibrary.com, Joe McGinnity chronology.
12. Ritter, *The Glory of Their Times*, pp. 98–99.
13. Tim Burnell, "I Call My Cane 'Merkle,'" netshrine.com.
14. Vic Ziegel, "Merkle miscue still costly," *New York Daily News*, 14 February 1993.
15. "Daguerreotypes," *Sporting News*, 20 April 1939.
16. Charles Dryden, "Game Ends in Tie May Go to Cubs," *Chicago Tribune*, 24 September 1908.
17. Murphy, *Crazy '08*, p. 192.
18. John McGraw, "My Thirty Years in Baseball," *Oklahoma City Oklahoman*, 15 February 1923.
19. "The Merkle Play," *Sporting Life*, 19 October 1914.
20. Henry O'Day, letter to NL president Harry Pulliam, 23 September 1908.
21. "From the Magazine," *Time Magazine*, 13 May 1929.
22. *New York Globe*, 24 September 1908.
23. G.H. Fleming, "The Merkle Blunder: A Kaleidoscopic View," *The National Pastime*, Fall 1982.
24. Ritter, *The Glory of Their Times*, pp. 99–100.
25. See note 19 above.
26. Lee Allen, *Cooperstown Corner* (Cleveland: Society for American Baseball Research, 1990), p. 36.
27. *Chicago Tribune*, 25 September 1908.
28. "Pulliam's Tie Game Decision Upheld," *New York Times*, 7 October 1908.
29. Harvey T. Woodruff, *Chicago Tribune*, 8 October 1908.
30. "Giants and Cubs in Final Battle," *New York Times*, 8 October 1908.
31. "The Cubs Wins the Pennant," *New York Times*, 9 October 1908.
32. "Tries to See Game; Is Killed," *Chicago Tribune*, 9 October 1908.
33. "Notes of the Game," *Chicago Tribune*, 9 October 1908.
34. *Ibid.*
35. See note 31 above.
36. Alexander, *John McGraw*, p. 136.
37. Mathewson, *Pitching in a Pinch*, p. 200
38. See note 15 above.
39. Alexander, *John McGraw*, p. 137.
40. Alexander, *John McGraw*, p. 139.
41. Robinson, *Matty: An American Hero*, p. 109.
42. Alexander, *John McGraw*, p. 138.
43. Murphy, *Crazy '08*, p. 295.
44. Geoffrey C. Ward and Ken Burns, *Baseball: An Illustrated History* (New York: Knopf, 1994), p. 95.

Chapter 17

1. "'Iron Man' Joe McGinnity," *Dubuque* (Iowa) *Telegraph Herald,* 23 July 1922.
2. "McGinnity Gets Release," *New York Times*, 28 February 1909.
3. Joe Murphy, "The Sunset Years of Joe McGinnity," *The National Pastime 2001.*
4. "Newark Club Sold," *New York Times*, 2 March 1909.
5. Charlie Bevis, "Tim Donahue," *The Baseball Biography Project (bioproj.sabr.org).*
6. "Harry Wolverton Killed," *New York Times*, 5 February 1937.
7. "McGinnity Baits Umpire," *New York Times*, 13 April 1909.
8. *New York Times*, 15 August 1909.
9. Joe Murphy, "The Sunset Years of Joe McGinnity," *The National Pastime 2001.*

10. Doc Jekyll, "Sports Here and There," *Syracuse* (New York) *Herald*, 12 February 1910.
11. Alan H. Levy, *Rube Waddell: The Zany, Brilliant Life of a Strikeout Artist* (Jefferson, N.C.: McFarland, 2000), p. 269.
12. Dan O'Brien, "Rube Waddell," *The Baseball Biography Project (bioproj.sabr.org)*.
13. *Newark (New Jersey) Star*, 13 August 1910.
14. "Sutton 'Discovers' McGinnity," *Newark* (New Jersey) *News*, 21 July 1920.
15. William Dowell, "Hick Cady," *The Baseball Biography Project (bioproj.sabr.org)*.
16. "X-ray Shows Fracture in M'Ginnity's Wrist," *Newark* (New Jersey) *News*, 24 March 1911.
17. "Upholds McGinnity's Act," *New York Times*, 23 April 1911.
18. "Satisfactory Progress in Deal for the Stars," *Syracuse* (New York) *Herald*, 7 November 1911.
19. "Newark 'Iron Man' on Eve of Dismissal as Tiger Manager," *Syracuse* (New York) *Herald*, 3 November 1911.
20. "Montreal Club is Not For Sale," *Syracuse* (New York) *Herald*, 10 November 1911.
21. *Spalding's Official Base Ball Guide 1912* (New York: American Sports Publishing, 1912), p. 159.
22. "M'Ginnity's Auto is Stolen, Then Wrecked," *Newark* (New Jersey) *News*, 12 August 1912.
23. "Ebbets Now in Control of the Indians," *Newark* (New Jersey) *News*, 4 October 1912.
24. *Ibid.*
25. *Ibid.*

Chapter 18

1. "'Iron Man' To Visit Tacoma," *Newark* (New Jersey) *News*, 20 November 1912.
2. "Jennings After the 'Iron Man,'" *Newark* (New Jersey) *News*, 30 October 1912.
3. "M'Ginnity Will Secure Tacoma," *Newark* (New Jersey) *News*, 2 December 1912.
4. *Newark* (New Jersey) *News*, 26 December 1912.
5. *Tacoma* (Washington) *Daily News*, 23 January 1913.
6. *Newark* (New Jersey) *News*, 26 December 1912.
7. "Joe M'Ginnity Bids Farewell to Newark," *Newark* (New Jersey) *News*, 9 January 1913.
8. "Joe McGinnity Buys Athletic Park," *Tacoma* (Washington) *Daily News*, 23 January 1913.
9. See note 7 above.
10. Howard W. Rosenberg, *Cap Anson 4* (Arlington, Va.: Tile Books, 2006), p. 380.
11. *Sporting News*, 29 May 1913.
12. *Sporting News*, 22 May 1913.
13. "Reasons to Boast," *Sporting News*, 24 April 1913.
14. Leigh Montville, *The Big Bam: The Life and Times of Babe Ruth* (New York: Broadway Books, 2006), pp. 116–117.
15. *Sporting News*, 19 June 1913.
16. *Sporting News*, 17 July 1913.
17. "Yes, Tacoma Has Had a Few Players, Basil," *Tacoma* (Washington) *Times*, 1 October 1913.
18. *Tacoma* (Washington) *Times*, 24 March 1914.
19. *Tacoma* (Washington) *Times*, 15 April 1914.
20. "Bengals Bang Bee Boxmen By Bingling Basehits by Barrelsful," *Tacoma* (Washington) *Times*, 27 April 1914.
21. "But Redondo Beach Al Wins a Pitcher's Combat From Veteran in Ninth," *Tacoma* (Washington) *Times*, 16 May 1914.
22. "Umpire Shuster Has Real Riotous Time; Tigers Lose Out, As Usual," *Tacoma* (Washington) *Times*, 21 May 1914.
23. *Ibid.*
24. *Tacoma* (Washington) *Times*, 22 May 1914.
25. *Tacoma* (Washington) *Times*, 29 June 1914.
26. "Tigers Win First Game of Session With Nick's Colts," *Tacoma* (Washington) *Times*, 14 July 1914.
27. "Tige Walks Right Over Those Pesky Giants and Win Eighth," *Tacoma* (Washington) *Times*, 23 July 1914.
28. "Hooray for Tiger Boys! A Carnival of Baseball," *Tacoma* (Washington) Times, 21 July 1914.
29. *Tacoma* (Washington) *Times*, 26 September 1914.
30. "Apathetic Season is Over, Tacoma Fans Discouraged," *Tacoma* (Washington) *Times*, 14 September 1914.
31. *Sporting News*, 1915.
32. *Ibid.*
33. *Sporting News*, 13 May 1915.
34. *Sporting News*, 29 April 1915.
35. *Sporting News*, 29 July 1915.
36. *Sporting News*, 5 August 1915.
37. Joe Murphy, "The Sunset Years of Joe McGinnity," *The National Pastime 2001*.
38. "Iron Man Sells Out; Team Over the Mountains," *Tacoma* (Washington) *Times*, 6 September 1915.
39. *Ibid.*
40. *Ibid.*
41. *Sporting News*, 30 September 1915.
42. "Old Joe Drops His Wad as Club Owner," *New York Herald*, 19 January 1915.
43. "Let's All Help Russ Hall to Make

Good!," *Tacoma* (Washington) *Times*, 21 February 1916.
44. *Ibid.*
45. "Peter's Piffle," *Tacoma* (Washington) *Times*, 21 February 1916.

Chapter 19

1. Robert L. Finch, L.H. Addington and Ben M. Morgan, *The Story of Minor League Baseball* (Columbus, Ohio: Stoneman Press, 1953), p. 22.
2. *Ibid.*
3. "M'Ginnity and Redpath Leave For Coal Region," *Butte* (Montana) *Miner*, 13 September 1916.
4. George Everett, "Butte's Street-Straddling Elk of 1916," *butteamerica.com*.
5. "Butte's New Baseball Park is Rapidly Taking Form and Will Be a Dandy," *Butte* (Montana) *Miner*, 16 April 1916.
6. "Signs Contract," *Butte* (Montana) *Miner*, 5 April 1916.
7. "New Butte Ball Park Will Be Creditable," *Butte* (Montana) *Miner*, 6 April 1916.
8. "All is Ready at Butte Camp on Coast," *Butte* (Montana) *Miner*, 9 April 1916.
9. "Young Hovey is Butte's Big Surprise," *Butte* (Montana) *Miner*, 17 April 1916.
10. "Bad Weather is Worrying M'Ginnity," *Butte* (Montana) *Miner*, 20 April 1916.
11. "Infield and Pitching Staff is Bothering Joe M'Ginnity," *Butte* (Montana) *Miner*, 22 April 1916.
12. "How Managers View Their Teams," *Butte* (Montana) *Miner*, 27 April 1916.
13. "Butte Loses But No Excuses Made," *Butte* (Montana) *Miner*, 28 April 1916.
14. "Enormous Crowd Turns Out For Opening Game in Butte," *Butte* (Montana) *Miner*, 17 May 1916.
15. *Ibid.*
16. *Butte* (Montana) *Miner*, 31 May 1916.
17. "Brace of Games is Lost by Locals," *Butte* (Montana) *Miner*, 5 June 1916.
18. "M'Ginnity Gets Notice of Layoff," *Butte* (Montana) *Miner*, 8 June 1916.
19. "How Blewett is Taking the Mixup," *Butte* (Montana) *Miner*, 8 June 1916.
20. "Umpire Bush is Punished by Directors," *Butte* (Montana) *Miner*, 16 June 1916.
21. "M'Ginnity Has Old Mr. Trouble on His Trail," *Seattle Times*, 23 August 1916.
22. "Roberts Canned," *Butte* (Montana) *Miner*, 20 August 1916.
23. See note 21 above.
24. See note 21 above.
25. "Vancouver Wins Easy Contest 13 to 10," *Butte* (Montana) *Miner*, 23 August 1916.
26. "Joe M'Ginnity is in Bad Now With Butte Fans," *Seattle Times*, 29 August 1916.
27. "Resume of the Season Shows Comparatively Good Results," *Butte* (Montana) *Miner*, 6 September 1916.
28. "League Season Better Than Expected," *Butte* (Montana) *Miner*, 9 September 1916.
29. See note 27 above.
30. "Joe M'Ginnity Reelected to Manage Butte," *Seattle Times*, 7 September 1916.
31. "Butte Gets All Big Holiday Datings," *Butte* (Montana) *Miner*, 7 March 1917.
32. "Beans Spilled by Defection of M'Carl," *Butte* (Montana) *Miner*, 19 April 1917.
33. "Cussing Umpires Will Bring Fines," *Butte* (Montana) *Miner*, 11 May 1917.
34. "M'Ginnity Getting Ready to Shape Team For the Opener," *Butte* (Montana) *Miner*, 17 April 1917.
35. "Ironman Signs Entire New Infield," *Butte* (Montana) *Miner*, 4 May 1917.
36. "Pepper Hasn't Gone Up, and the Butte Ball Club Needs it," *Butte* (Montana) *Miner*, 9 May 1917.
37. *Ibid.*
38. "M'Ginnity Says He's After Help," *Butte* (Montana) *Miner*, 28 April 1917.
39. *Butte* (Montana) *Miner*, 12 May 1916.
40. *Butte* (Montana) *Miner*, 21 May 1916.
41. "'Iron Man' McGinnity, at 45, Wins Another Double Header." *Brooklyn Eagle*, 23 May 1917.
42. "M'Ginnity Says Decision is Unfair," *Butte* (Montana) *Miner*, 23 May 1917.
43. *Butte* (Montana) *Miner*, 27 May 1917.
44. "Joke Game Goes to Tigers, 31–12," *Butte* (Montana) *Miner*, 8 June 1917.
45. "Ironman Leaves Baseball in Butte," *Butte* (Montana) *Miner*, 9 June 1917.
46. *Ibid.*
47. "Disaster at No. Butte, Many Lost," *Butte* (Montana) *Miner*, 9 June 1917.
48. "Baseball Clubs Are Heavy Losers," *Butte* (Montana) *Miner*, 15 June 1917.
49. "Montana Clubs Are Outvoted," *Butte* (Montana) *Miner*, 10 July 1917.
50. "Vancouver Won't Feel Effects of War," *Butte* (Montana) *Miner*, 14 May 1917.
51. "New League is Due Tomorrow," *Butte* (Montana) *Miner*, 16 July 1917.
52. "New League is Again 'Busted,'" *Butte* (Montana) *Miner*, 17 July 1917.

Chapter 20

1. Carlos Bauer, "The Year the PCL Threw in the Towel," *minorleagueresearcher.blogspot.com*, 3 January 2006; 1918.
2. *Ibid.*

3. "Crowder Order Not a Hit With Anybody," *Sporting News*, 30 May 1918.
4. "Herrmann Sends Baseball's Plan to Draft Head," *Seattle Times*, 22 June 1918.
5. *Sporting News*, 23 May 1918.
6. *Seattle Times*, 17 June 1918.
7. *Sporting News*, 6 June 1918.
8. "Vancouver Proves Town Worth While," *Sporting News*, 27 June 1918.
9. *Seattle Times*, 1 June 1918.
10. "Brown Declares He Will Run Dugdale Out of Baseball," *Seattle Times*, 2 June 1918.
11. *Sporting News*, 27 June 1918.
12. "Baseball Ends in Northwest For This Year," *Seattle Times*, 24 June 1918.
13. "P.C.I.L. Tries New City With Hope of Living," *Seattle Times*, 25 June 1918.
14. *Seattle Times*, 27 June 1918.
15. "M'Credie and Dugdale Give Brown the Rush," *Sporting News*, 4 July 1918.
16. "Baseball Season Here Ends Today," *Seattle Times*, 7 July 1918.

Chapter 21

1. George Halas, *Halas by Halas* (New York: McGraw-Hill, 1979), p. 56.
2. Halas, *Halas by Halas*, p. 57
3. Dan Forrestal, *The Kernel and the Bean* (New York: Simon & Schuster, 1982), p. 38.
4. R.A. Drysdale, "The 'Iron Man' Passes," *Illinois State Journal*, 15 November 1929.
5. "'Iron Man' M'Ginnity Signs With Staleys," *Decatur* (Illinois) *Review*, 10 May 1919.
6. "Grand Stand is Enlarged," *Decatur* (Illinois) *Herald*, 12 May 1919.
7. "M'Ginnity Day at Staley Park," *Decatur* (Illinois) *Herald*, 18 May 1919.
8. "McGinnity Hero of Staley Game Today," *Decatur* (Illinois) *Review*, 18 May 1919.
9. *Ibid*.
10. "Staley's Capture Another, 6 to 3," *Decatur* (Illinois) *Review*, 19 May 1919.
11. "Mt. Olive Team Defeats Staleys," *Decatur* (Illinois) *Review*, 26 May 1919.
12. *Staley Fellowship Journal*, April 1921, P. 12.
13. "White Sox to Line Up Against Staley's Today," *Decatur* (Illinois) *Herald*, 29 May 1919.
14. "Staley's Hold White Sox Down to Score 7-4," *Decatur* (Illinois) *Herald*, 30 May 1919.
15. *Ibid*.
16. George Vass, *George Halas and the Chicago Bears* (Chicago: Henry Regnery, 1971), p. 22.
17. Vass, *George Halas and the Chicago Bears*, p. 26.
18. Vass, *George Halas and the Chicago Bears*, p. 32.
19. Howard V. Millard, "Joe McGinnity, Famous 'Iron Man' of Majors, Began Great Career on Decatur Sand Lots," *Decatur* (Illinois) *Review*, 27 October 1929.
20. *Staley Fellowship Journal*, January 1921, p. 14.
21. *Staley Fellowship Journal*, April 1921, p. 10.
22. Howard V. Millard, "Babe May Wallop One Out of Staley Park," *Decatur* (Illinois) *Review*, 25 May 1921.
23. Halas, *Halas by Halas*, p. 68.
24. *Staley Fellowship Journal*, April 1921, p. 13.
25. See note 22 above.
26. See note 22 above.
27. Bill Penhallegon, "Staleys Easily Win From House of David in One-sided Battle," *Decatur* (Illinois) *Herald*, 27 May 1921.
28. "M'Ginnity-Brown to Clash Today," *Decatur* (Illinois) *Herald*, 12 June 1921.
29. Halas, *Halas by Halas*, p. 67.
30. "Salary Staley Plant Head Cut Nearly in Half," *Decatur* (Illinois) *Herald*, 23 June 1921.
31. *Ibid*.
32. Forrestal, *The Kernel and the Bean*, p. 49.
33. Forrestal, *The Kernel and the Bean*, p. 51.
34. *Staley Fellowship Journal*, March 1922, p. 15.
35. *Ibid*.
36. *Ibid*.
37. *Ibid*.

Chapter 22

1. *Danville* (Illinois) *Commercial News*, 5 April 1922.
2. "Manager O'Day Given Release," *Danville* (Illinois) *Commercial News*, 10 April 1922.
3. "M'Ginnity Now Looking 'em Over," *Danville* (Illinois) *Commercial News*, 12 April, 1922.
4. *Ibid*.
5. "McGinnity is Much Pleased," *Danville* (Illinois) *Commercial News*, 2 May 1922.
6. "Tractors Play Veterans Lads Opening Match," *Danville* (Illinois) *Commercial News*, 2 May 1922.
7. *Ibid*.
8. "Chicago Visitors Pans Local Fans," *Danville* (Illinois) *Commercial News*, 10 May 1922.
9. "Blank Veterans Saturday," *Danville* (Illinois) *Commercial News*, 29 May 1922.
10. *Staley Fellowship Journal*, June 1922, p. 16.
11. *Ibid*.
12. *Ibid*.

13. *Danville* (Illinois) *Commercial News*, 29 May 1922.
14. "Disgusting Game Lost by Locals," *Danville* (Illinois) *Commercial News*, 14 June 1922.
15. "Bloomington Paper Has Own Version," *Danville* (Illinois) *Commercial News*, 17 June 1922.
16. Curley Anderson, *Moline* (Illinois) *Dispatch*, 1922.
17. *Bloomington* (Illinois) *Bulletin*, 1922.
18. "M'Ginnity Will Resign, is Rumor," *Danville* (Illinois) *Commercial News*, 26 June 1922.
19. *Danville* (Illinois) *Commercial News*, 27 June, 1922.
20. "Trouble on Team is With Players," *Danville* (Illinois) *Commercial News*, 28 June 1922.
21. *Ibid*.
22. *Ibid*.
23. "M'Ginnity Makes Sporting Offer," *Danville* (Illinois) *Commercial News*, 7 July 1922.
24. "Joe M'Ginnity Given Release," *Danville* (Illinois) *Commercial News*, 13 July 1922.
25. *Ibid*.

Chapter 23

1. "'Iron Man' Joe McGinnity," *Dubuque* (Iowa) *Telegraph Herald*, 23 July 1922.
2. *Dubuque* (Iowa) *Telegraph Herald*, 14 November 1929.
3. *Ibid*.
4. *Ibid*.
5. *Ibid*.
6. Bert McGrane, "Johnny Armstrong," *Des Moines* (Iowa) *Register*, 6 May 1951.
7. *Dubuque (Iowa) Telegraph Herald*, 14 November 1929.
8. "'Iron Man' Holds Ansons to 3 Hits," *Dubuque* (Iowa) *Telegraph Herald*, 24 May 1923.
9. *Moline* (Illinois) *Dispatch*, 16 June 1923.
10. Wally Koenig, "M.V. Record For Time of Game is Set By M'Ginnity," *Davenport* (Iowa) *Times*, 16 June 1923.
11. Wilton Floberg, "On the Upper Side of Fifty," *Sporting Life*, August 1923.
12. Paul R. Mallon, "Old Athletes Still Have a Kick Left," *Fayetteville* (Arkansas) *Daily Democrat*, 7 July 1923.
13. Frank J. Price, "M'Ginnity at 52 Still Pitching Ball," *New York Herald*, 29 July 1923.
14. *Ibid*.
15. *Ibid*.
16. *Ibid*.
17. *Ibid*.

18. See note 11 above.
19. "Ironmen, 'Sippi Champions, Again," *Dubuque* (Iowa) *Telegraph Herald*, 4 September 1923.
20. "Dubuque Clouts the Apple in Burlesque," *Davenport* (Iowa) *Times*, 5 September 1923.
21. "M'Ginnity's Dubuque Valley Champions Challenge Decatur," *Decatur* (Illinois) *Herald*, 7 September 1923.
22. "Commodores Will Not Play Dubuque," *Decatur* (Illinois) *Herald*, 7 September 1923.
23. *Dubuque* (Iowa) *Telegraph Herald*, 14 November 1929.
24. Sec Taylor, "Saints Pound M'Ginnity and Take Contest," *Des Moines* (Iowa) *Register*, 17 September 1923.
25. *Ibid*.
26. "Armstrong to Pilot Dubuque," *Des Moines* (Iowa) *Register*, 23 January 1923.
27. "Joe M'Ginnity, 53, Pitched Team to a Flag, Now Retires," *Philadelphia North American*, 30 December 1923.
28. *Ibid*.
29. Dan Daniel, "M'Ginnity and Bresnahan With Giants Outfit," *New York Herald*, 7 February 1924.
30. *Ibid*.
31. "M'Ginnity Spurns Offer From McGraw," *Des Moines* (Iowa) *Register*, 24 February 1924.
32. Macon County (Illinois) deeds, Book 519, p. 245.
33. "'Iron Man' Will Act as Manager," *Dubuque* (Iowa) *Telegraph Herald*, 6 February 1925.
34. "Iron Man McGinnity, at 54, Planning to Pitch 35 Games," *New York Times*, 19 February 1925.
35. See note 33 above.
36. *Dubuque* (Iowa) *Telegraph Herald*, 13 March 1925.
37. "Behind the Screen, by Scoop," *Dubuque* (Iowa) *Telegraph Herald*, 6 May 1925.
38. "Will Pay Honor to Veteran Player," *Dubuque* (Iowa) *Telegraph Herald*, 17 May 1925.
39. *Ibid*.
40. *Dubuque* (Iowa) *Telegraph Herald*, 18 May, 1925.
41. "Good-bye, Good Luck Ironman McGinnity," *Dubuque* (Iowa) *Telegraph Herald*, 8 July 1925.
42. *Ibid*.
43. "Oldtimers Win in Hippodrome Baseball Game," *Illinois State Register*, 29 July 1925.
44. "Bloomers Fall Upon Iron Man Joe M'Ginnity to Sweep Three Games of Series With Solons," *Illinois State Register*, 29 July 1925.
45. "Old Joe McGinnity Helps Brooks

Win," *Newark* (New Jersey) *News*, September 1925.

Chapter 24

1. "Pins Get Wobbly, but Old Wing Is Still There, Says McGinnity," *Newark* (New Jersey) *News*, 20 May 1925.
2. "Uncle Robby Finds 'Em Side-stepping," *Sporting News*, 17 December 1925.
3. Deford, *The Old Ball Game*, p. 191.
4. Kavanagh and Macht, *Uncle Robbie*, p. 185.
5. *Ibid.*
6. Kavanagh and Macht, *Uncle Robbie*, pp. 73–74.
7. "John Redpath is Dead After Sunday Stroke," *McAlester* (Oklahoma) *News-Capital*, 25 March 1926.
8. "Mrs. M'Ginnity to be Laid to Rest on Friday," *McAlester* (Oklahoma) *News-Capital*, 24 June 1926.
9. *Sporting News*, 1 July 1926.
10. Tom Meany, *Baseball Greatest Pitchers* (New York: A.S. Barnes, 1951).
11. "McGinnity's Novel Theory on Durability of Pitchers' Arms," United Press, 5 May 1926.
12. "Only One Iron Man," *Sporting News*, 17 October 1912.
13. See note 10 above.
14. Associated Press, 15 December 1925.
15. *Decatur city directory 1926*.
16. Macon County (Illinois) deeds, Book 598, p. 424.
17. Macon County (Illinois) deeds, Book 585, p. 223.
18. *Decatur* (Illinois) *Review*, 11 July 1927, legal notices.
19. "M'Ginnity, Iron Man of Baseball, Dies," *New York Times*, 15 November 1929.
20. "Iron Man M'Ginnity Goes Under Knife," *New York Times*, 28 August 1929.
21. See note 19 above.
22. William O. Trapp, "'Iron Man' McGinnity, Great Ball Player, Once Quit Diamond as Certain Failure," *New York World*, 28 October 1929.
23. Interview with Ed Rothberg, 1988.
24. "Joe McGinnity's Condition Critical After Operation," Associated Press, 27 August 1929.
25. "Iron Man Losing Death Battle," Associated Press, 22 October 1929.
26. Howard V. Millard, "Joe McGinnity, Famous "Iron Man" of Majors, Began Great Career on Decatur Sandlot," *Decatur* (Illinois) *Review*, 27 October 1929.
27. "McGinnity Near Death," United Press, 28 October 1929.
28. *Dubuque* (Iowa) *Telegraph Herald*, 14 November 1929.
29. *Rock Island* (Illinois) *Argus*, 14 November 1929.
30. Joe Murphy, "The Sunset Years of Joe McGinnity," *The National Pastime 2001*.
31. "The Iron Man," *Newark* (Ohio) *Advocate*, 23 November 1929.
32. "Iron Man Passes," *Montana Standard*, 18 November 1929.
33. Howard V. Millard, "Joe McGinnity To Rest Beside Wife In Oklahoma," *Decatur* (Illinois) *Review*, 15 November 1929.
34. William Hennigan, "M'Ginnity Hardest Worker on Mound M'Graw Ever Had," *New York World*, 15 November 1929.
35. Earl Obenshain, "Iron Man" McGinnity Got First Start Here," *Decatur* (Illinois) *Herald*, 27 October 1929.
36. H.V. Millard, "Bait for Bugs," *Decatur* (Illinois) *Review*, 14 November 1929.
37. "Hold Last Rites For Joe McGinnity," *Decatur* (Illinois) *Review*, 16 November 1929.
38. "Decatur Friends Honor M'Ginnity," *Decatur* (Illinois) *Herald*, 18 November 1929.
39. "Baseball Players With Team of McGinnity Will Be Bearers," *McAlester* (Oklahoma) *News-Capital*, 17 November 1929.
40. Record of funeral, Cheney Funeral Home, McAlester, Oklahoma.

Chapter 25

1. *baseballhalloffame.org*, Joe McGinnity page.
2. Clyde Wooldridge, "A landmark worth saving: The 'Iron Man's' abode," *McAlester* (Oklahoma) *News-Capital*, 24 June, 2006.

Bibliography

Books

Adomites, Paul. *October's Game*. New Berlin, Wisc.: Redefinition, 1990.

Alexander, Charles. *John McGraw*. Reprint. Lincoln: University of Nebraska Press, 1988.

Allen, Lee. *The American League Story*. New York: Hill & Wang, 1962.

Allen, Lee. *Cooperstown Corner*. Cleveland: Society for American Baseball Research, 1990.

Allen, Lee, and Tom Meany. *Kings of the Diamond*. New York: G.P. Putnam's Sons, 1965.

Alvarez, Mark. *The Old Ball Game*. New Berlin, Wisc.: Redefinition, 1990.

Brown, Charles W., Jr. *The History of the Denning Family in America*. Unpublished.

Deford, Frank. *The Old Ball Game*. New York: Grove Press, 2005.

DeValeria, Dennis, and Jeanne Burke DeValeria. *Honus Wagner: A Biography*. New York: Henry Holt, 1995.

Durso, Joseph. *The Days of Mr. McGraw*. Englewood Cliffs, New Jersey: Prentice-Hall, 1969.

Finch, Robert L., L.H. Addington, and Ben M. Morgan. *The Story of Minor League Baseball*. Columbus, Ohio: Stoneman Press, 1953.

Forrestal, Dan. *The Kernel and the Bean*. New York: Simon & Schuster, 1982.

Graham, Frank. *McGraw of the Giants*. New York: G.P. Putnam's Sons, 1944.

Halas, George. *Halas by Halas*. New York: McGraw-Hill, 1979.

Hill, Luther B. *History of the State of Oklahoma*. Chicago: Lewis Publishing, 1908.

Irwin, Dayle Cochran, and Karen Anderson. *Decatur Entertainment: A Pictorial History*. St. Louis: G. Bradley Publishing, 1998.

Kahn, Roger. *The Head Game*. San Diego: Harcourt Inc., 2000.

Kavanagh, Jack, and Norman L. Macht. *Uncle Robbie*. Cleveland: Society for American Baseball Research, 1999.

Kerrane, Kevin. *The Hurlers*. New Berlin, Wisc.: Redefinition, 1989.

Kiner, Henry L. *History of Henry County, Illinois*. Chicago: Pioneer Publishing, 1919.

Klima, John. *Pitched Battle: 35 of Baseball's Greatest Duels from the Mound*. Jefferson, N.C.: McFarland, 2002.

Levy, Alan H. *Rube Waddell: The Zany, Brilliant Life of a Strikeout Artist*. Jefferson, N.C.: McFarland, 2000.

Lieb, Frederick G. *Connie Mack, Grand Old Man of Baseball*. New York: G.P. Putnam's Sons, 1945.

Lowry, Philip J. *Green Cathedrals*. Cooperstown, N.Y.: Society for American Baseball Research, 1986.

Mack, Connie. *My 66 Years in the Big Leagues*. Philadelphia: Winston, 1950.

Mathewson, Christy. *Pitching in a Pinch*. Reprint. Lincoln: University of Nebraska Press, 1994.

Meany, Tom. *Baseball Greatest Pitchers*. New York: A.S. Barnes, 1951.

Montville, Leigh. *The Big Bam: The Life and Times of Babe Ruth*. New York: Broadway Books, 2006.

Murphy, Cait. *Crazy '08*. New York: HarperCollins, 2007.

Quigley, Martin. *The Crooked Pitch*. Chapel Hill, N.C.: Algonquin Books, 1988.

Reichler, Joseph. *The World Series.* New York: Simon & Schuster, 1979.
Reidenbaugh, Lowell. *100 Years of National League Baseball.* St. Louis: Sporting News, 1976.
Ritter, Lawrence. *The Glory of Their Times.* New York: Macmillan, 1966.
Robinson, Ray. *Matty: An American Hero.* New York: Oxford University Press, 1993.
Rosenberg, Howard W. *Cap Anson 4.* Arlington, Va.: Tile Books, 2006.
Spalding's Official Base Ball Guide. New York: American Sports Publishing, 1912.
Stark, Benton. *The Year They Called Off the World Series.* Garden City Park, N.Y.: Avery Publishing Group, 1991.
Vass, George. *George Halas and the Chicago Bears.* Chicago: Henry Regnery, 1971.
Ward, Geoffrey C., and Burns, Ken. *Baseball: An Illustrated History.* New York: Knopf, 1994.

Newspapers

Baltimore American
Bloomington (Illinois) *Bulletin*
Bloomington (Illinois) *Pantagraph*
Boston Globe
Brooklyn (New York) *Eagle*
Butte (Montana) *Miner*
Butte (Montana) *Montana Standard*
Chicago Daily News
Chicago Tribune
Cincinnati Post
Danville (Illinois) *Commercial-News*
Davenport (Iowa) *Quad-City Times*
Decatur (Illinois) *Herald*
Decatur (Illinois) *Republican*
Decatur (Illinois) *Review*
Des Moines (Iowa) *Register*
Dubuque (Iowa) *Telegraph-Herald*
Fayetteville (Arkansas) *Daily Democrat*
Kansas City Journal
Kansas City Star
Kansas City Times
Lake County (Indiana) *Times*
Mansfield (Ohio) *News*
McAlester (Oklahoma) *News-Capital*
Moline (Illinois) *Dispatch*
Montgomery (Alabama) *Advertiser*
Newark (New Jersey) *News*
Newark (New Jersey) *Star*
New York Daily News
New York Globe
New York Herald
New York Sun
New York Times
New York Tribune
New York World
New York World Telegram
Oklahoma City Oklahoman
Oneonta (New York) *Star*
Peoria (Illinois) *Herald*
Philadelphia Bulletin
Philadelphia North American
Pittsburgh Chronicle Telegraph
Racine (Wisconsin) *Daily Journal*
Rockford (Illinois) *Register-Gazette*
Rockford (Illinois) *Republic*
Rockford (Illinois) *Star*
Rock Island (Illinois) *Argus*
Seattle Times
South McAlester (Oklahoma) *Capital*
Springfield (Illinois) *State Journal*
Springfield (Illinois) *State Register*
Syracuse (New York) *Herald*
Tacoma (Washington) *Daily News*
Tacoma (Washington) *Times*
Van Buren (Arkansas) *Argus*
Washington Post

Other Periodicals

Journal of Political Economy
Kiamachi Magazine
Pearson's Magazine
Police Gazette
Smithsonian Magazine
Sport Magazine
Sporting Life
Sporting News
Staley's Fellowship Journal
The National Pastime
Time Magazine

Wire Services

Associated Press
Newspaper Enterprise Association
United Press

Internet Sources

baseball-almanac.com
Baseball Biography Project. bioproj.sabr. org
baseballhalloffame.org
baseballlibrary.com
baseball-reference.com
butteamerica.com
Chicago-Kent College of Law. kentlaw. edu
Encyclopedia of Oklahoma History and Culture. digital.library.okstate.edu/encyclopedia
ESPN.com
Johnstown Flood history. jaha.org/Flood Museum/history.html
minorleagueresearcher.blogspot.com
netshrine.com
thebaseballpage.com
thediamondangle.com

Index

Abbaticchio, Ed 100
Abbott, Fred 84
Abbott, Ody 125
Aberdeen, Washington 129–130, 133, 147–150
Adams, Franklin P. 103, 110
Aetna Hotel, Danville 162
Akron, Ohio 156
Albert, Carl 186
Alderson, Oklahoma 15, 32
Allegheny, Pennsylvania 93
Allith-Prouty Co. 161
Alma, Michigan 154
American Association 25, 27, 28, 111, 155
American League 25, 50, 57–58, 60, 63, 67, 68, 69, 79, 81, 88, 121, 154, 157
Ames, Leon "Red" 75, 79, 83, 89, 90, 92, 100, 102, 104, 108
Anderson, Curley 164
Anson, Adrian "Cap" 122
Arkansas 18–20
Arlington, Hotel, Marlin 101
Armour and Co. 154
Armstrong, Johnny 166–167, 169, 171; athletic ability of 167; as partner in Dubuque 172–174
Armstrong, Red 20
Association of Professional Baseball Players of America 126
Athletic Park, Tacoma 121
Atkinson, Illinois 5
Atlanta, Georgia 28
Atlantic League 40
Atwood, Illinois 154
Augusta, Georgia 20, 22, 23, 44
Aulick, W.W. 102–103

Baker, Newton 147
Baker, Norman 21
Ballard Colts 128, 133

Baltimore, Maryland 44–48, 58–62, 64, 68, 116
Baltimore Orioles 34, 42–45, 50, 57–58, 68, 70, 79, 111, 115; 1899 season 46–48; 1901 season 59–62; 1902 season 63–65; tactics of 44–46, 47–48
Barnes, William 11
Barrow, Ed 116–117
Baseball Hall of Fame 2, 4, 18, 56, 66, 77, 99, 185, 187, 188
Beardstown, Illinois 34
Beckley, Jake 78
Belleville, Illinois 33, 34
Beloit, Wisconsin 154
Bender, Chief 86, 88–90
Benton Harbor, Michigan 158
Billings, Montana 146
Bingham, Theodore 97
Birmingham, Alabama 23, 75, 82
Blackburn, Blacky 174
Blewett, Robert 137, 141, 143–144, 149
Bloomington, Illinois 10, 11, 12, 33, 154, 164, 172, 175
Bloomington Bloomers 163
Boice, George 121
Boston Braves (aka Beaneaters) 26, 52, 70, 83, 92, 103, 104, 108, 112, 117, 171
Boston Red Sox (aka Americans, Pilgrims) 59, 63, 73, 79, 81, 115, 161
Bowerman, Frank 70, 100, 178
Bowers, Earl F. 162
Box Elder, Montana 133, 140, 144
Breen, Dr. John M. 180
Breitenstein, Ted 27, 93
Bresnahan, Roger 36, 58, 64, 70, 72, 78, 84, 88, 90,

91, 97–98, 100, 109, 111, 171, 178, 181, 183, 185; becomes catcher 58; invents shinguards 98
Bridwell, Al 105
Brilley, Pete 163, 183
Brinkley, Arkansas 20
Briscoe Motors 154
Brodie, Steve 47
Brooklyn, New York 49–56, 111, 175, 176–182, 183
Brooklyn Cup 55–56, 101
Brooklyn Dodgers (aka Superbas, Robins) 42, 44, 46, 48, 57, 59, 68, 69, 71, 72, 75, 76, 85, 91, 102, 112, 115, 117, 121, 147, 153, 161, 172; 1900 season 49–56; 1926 season 177–179
Broun, Heywood 58
Brown, Bob 145–146, 148–150
Brown, Charles W. 1, 187
Brown, Clarence 161
Brown, Mordecai "Three Finger" 75, 94, 96; in 1908 playoff game 109–110; with Havolines 158–159
Brush, John T. 64, 79–84, 94, 102, 109
Brush Rules 82–83
Bucknell College 52, 65, 66, 177
Buffalo Bisons 111, 113, 114
Burke, Jimmy 40
Burkholder, Ed 43, 44
Burkville 69
Burlington, Iowa 40, 173
Busby, William 82
Bush, Garnet 135, 137, 143
Bushwicks 175
Butte, Montana 76, 133–139, 142, 144, 147, 148, 182
Butte Baseball and Athletic Association 134
Butte Electric Railway 142
Butte Ironmen (aka Miners):

207

208 INDEX

1916 season 133, 135–140; 1917 season 140–146

Cadigan, Bill 175
Cady, Forrest "Hick" 115
Calhoun, Frank 130
California State League 126
Callahan, Nixey 55
cancer 181
Canton, Ohio 155
Canton Bulldogs 155
Carnival of Baseball 126
Carr, O.E. 172
Carrick, Bill 46
Carruthers, Bob 42
Cassell's Hill 8, 9
Cedar Rapids, Iowa 38, 40, 168, 169
Cedar Rapids Bunnies 174
Central Industrial Baseball Association 153, 156
Central League 120
Centropolis Hotel 28
Cerro Gordo, Illinois 10
Chalmers, John 169
Chamberlain, George E. 151, 155, 159, 163
Chamberlain, Guy 155
Champaign, Illinois 10, 11, 154
Chance, Frank 76, 92, 94, 103, 107, 109, 110, 185
Chapman, Ray 122
Charleston, South Carolina 22, 23, 24
Chatham, Illinois 34
Chattanooga, Tennessee 23
Chesbro, Jack 53, 185
Chicago, Illinois 111, 154, 155, 159, 163, 164, 186, 187
Chicago American Giants 124
Chicago Bears 160, 167
Chicago, Burlington and Quincy Railroad 155
Chicago Cardinals 156
Chicago Cubs (aka White Stockings, Orphans) 28, 34, 52, 55, 76, 78, 83, 84, 92, 94, 100, 103, 122, 129, 158, 173; in Merkle game 104–107; in 1908 playoff game 108–110
Chicago White Sox 60, 61, 94, 101, 128, 154, 156, 161
Choctaw Coal Company 16
Choctaw tribe 13
Church of Our Lady of Refuge, Brooklyn 183

Cicotte, Eddie 154
Cincinnati, Ohio 25, 28, 97, 107
Cincinnati Reds 35, 47, 52, 64, 76, 78, 79, 85, 93, 98, 100, 101, 102, 104, 117, 135, 137, 154
Clark, Potsy 152
Clarke, Fred 22, 53, 54, 55, 70, 98, 178
Clay County, Indiana 6
Clearwater, Florida 176
Cleveland Indians (aka Spiders) 42, 50, 122
Clinton, Illinois 41
Coakley, Andy 87, 89, 107
Coal mining 7, 12, 13, 16–17, 32
Coalgate, Oklahoma 15
Cobb, Ty 185
Cohan, George M. 88
Colclough, Tom 22
Cole, Archie 40
Collins, Bill 15, 184
Collins, Eddie 154
Columbia College 166
Columbia Gardens, Butte 142
Columbia Park, Philadelphia 88
Columbia-Willamette Shipbuilders League 150
competitiveness 34, 168
Coney Island 107
Connolly, Tommy 61, 63
Connors, Jerry 40
Continental Hotel, Newark 112
Cooperstown, New York 185
Corbett, "Gentleman" Jim 88, 90
Corcoran, Tommy 47
Cornwall Township, Illinois 5
County Antrim, Ireland 28
Coveleski, Stanley 96
Cowden, Illinois 154
Crandall, Otis "Doc" 102, 103, 104
Creamer, Dr. Joseph 109
Cregar, Dr. P.B. 91
Crittendon, Dick 123
Cronin, Jack 64
Cross, Lave 88, 89
Cross, Monte 89
Crowder, Enoch 147
Cushman Indians 124
Cvengros, Joe 165

Dahlen, Bill 78
Dallas, Texas 17, 96, 101
Daniels, Pete "Lucky" 27–29
Danville, Illinois 10, 11, 161–163, 165, 166, 172, 174
Danville Veterans 1922 season 161–166
Darby, George "Deacon" 27, 28, 29
Davenport, Iowa 28, 168
Davenport Hotel, Spokane 140
Davis, George 52
Davis, Harry 59
Decatur, Illinois 7–12, 32–34, 36, 53, 151–154, 156–159, 161, 163, 165, 170, 171, 172, 178, 180, 183; boyhood home of McGinnity 7–13
Decatur Baseball Association 9
Decatur Coal Company 7, 9
Decatur Commodores 163, 170
Decatur Fans Association 163, 170
Decatur Shamrocks 10–12
Deegan, Dummy 74
Degman, James 82
Demmitt, Ray 156–157, 158, 159
Denison, Texas 15
Denning, Jane 6
Denning, John 5, 6, 7, 133, 186
Denning, Kris 187–188
Denning (Little), Rebecca 5, 6, 186
Denning Coal Company 6
Des Moines, Iowa 170–171
Detroit, Michigan 25, 30, 60
Detroit Tigers 60, 61, 63, 110, 120, 128
Devlin, Art 100
DeWitt Clinton High School 77
Dexter Park, Brooklyn 175
Diamond Café 43
Diehl, William 54
disputes with umpires 60–61, 68, 69–70, 125, 135, 137, 143
Doheny, Ed 52, 70
Donahue, Tim 26, 28, 55, 111; death of 31; fight with

Brodie 47; sabotage of McGinnity 31, 35, 36
Donlin, Mike 59–61, 64, 88, 91, 106, 109
Donohue, Tommy 15
Douglas Park, Rock Island 168
Doyle, Jack 69
Doyle, Larry 102, 104, 107, 112
Dressen, Charlie 153, 155, 156
Dreyfuss, Barney 52, 81, 84
Dryden, Charles 88, 89, 106
Dublin, Ireland 5
Dubuque, Iowa 3, 167–170, 172–175
Dubuque Boosters Association 174
Dubuque Ironmen (aka Climbers, Dubs, Mullenites): hiring of McGinnity 166; 1923 season 166–170; 1925 season 172–174
Dugdale, Daniel 121, 122, 134, 145, 146, 149
Dunn, Jack 52, 61, 111, 115, 162

Earling Park, Great Falls 146
East Enders 10
Eastern League 41, 111, 112, 117
Eastman Hotel 59
Ebbets, Charles 42, 117, 118
Eckman, Edward 143
Elberfield, Kid 61
Elk House Hotel, McAlester 17
Ely, Bones 54
Emslie, Bob 93, 98; in Merkle game 105–107
Equality Point, Illinois 7
Evers, Johnny 76, 92, 103, 178, 185; in Merkle game 105–107
Exposition Park, Kansas City 28, 30
Exposition Park, Pittsburgh 54, 79

Fairbanks Morse Fairies 154, 157
Fall River, Massachusetts 27
Farrell, Frank 111–112
Faulkner, Louise 162
Federal League 133
Feeney, Fatty 34
Felsch, Happy 154–155

Ferguson, George 92
Ferrell, Brown (aka Bruno Ferrero) 6, 13, 133
Ferrell (Denning), Elizabeth 6, 13, 133
Ferrero, Bruno see Ferrell, Brown
fielding ability 3–4, 37, 96
Fields, Happy 184
Figueira, Joe 34
Fine, Henry 161
Fisher, Tom 15
Fitzsimmons, Tom 142
Fleischmann, Julius 64
Fleischmann, Max 64
Fleurys 10
Floberg, Wilton 169, 171
Fogel, Horace 65, 66
Foley, John 121
Forbes, Dr. Jesse F. 77
Ford, Gabe 33, 175
Fort Smith, Arkansas 15, 18–20, 32, 52
Foster, Rube 124
Foundation Ship Building Corporation 149
Fox, Art 180
France, Joseph 64
Freedman, Andrew 63–65
Freeman, Al 154
Fresno, California 126, 141
Frill, John 112–113

Gaffney, John 52
Galesburg, Illinois 20
Gallatin County, Illinois 7, 8
Gandil, Chick 154
Ganzel, John 113
Garvey, A.P. 148
Gehrig, Lou 178
George, Billy 20, 21, 22
George W. Jones team 32
German, Les 22
Gettman, Jake 112, 114
Gibson, Sam 33, 175
Giddings, Bun 141
Gilbert, Billy 69, 72, 78, 89
Gillenwater, Roy 165
Gipe, Alva 125, 126, 147
Girot, Jerry 124
Gogerty, J.C. 10
Goldman, Harry 61
Gordon, Joseph 80
Gorin, O.B. 9
Graham, Archibald "Moonlight" 85
Graham, Frank 80

Grand Rapids, Michigan 25, 30, 35
Granite Mountain 144
Grant, Charley 59
Great Falls, Montana 133, 136–137, 139, 144–148
Great Lakes Naval Air Station 155
Great Northern Railroad 134
Grover, Roy 135, 147
Guigni, Frank 138–140
Guigni-Williams dispute 138–139

Halas, George 155–156, 157, 158, 159; and Chicago Bears 160; hired by Staley 155
Hall, Bert 145
Hall, Russ 126–128, 130–132, 145, 148, 165
Hall of Fame 185
Hamilton, Ontario 162
Hanlon, Ned 34, 42, 44, 46, 48, 50, 52, 57–59, 71
Harkins, Pat 164
Harris, Skin 125
Hart, Burt 60
Hart, Charles 23
Hartsel, Topsy 89
Hartshorne, Oklahoma 16, 19, 32
Haskell, John 60
Hassamaer, Bill 20
Havre, Montana 145
Hawley, Emerson "Pink" 19, 27, 52
Hay, Ralph 155, 160
Haynes, Ned "Spike" 135, 137, 139–143
Hebgen Park, Butte 134, 138, 143
Hemingway, Eddie 157
Hennigan, William 183
Henry County, Illinois 5–8, 115
Hernon, Tommy 28
Herrmann, August 147
Herzog, Buck 109
Hester, Herb 145, 147
Heydler, John 183
Hill, "Still" Bill 31
Hillsboro, Illinois 33
Hillsdale Colored Giants 175
Hillyard, Dave 141
Hite, Mabel 91
hitting ability 22, 46, 72, 77, 123, 136, 143, 145, 173
Hoffman, Dan 90

Index

Hoffman, Dutch 141, 143
Hofman, Artie 105–106
Hogan, Hap 128
Hokey, Harry 14, 15, 184
Holmes, Ducky 60
Hornsby, Rogers 178
Hot Springs, Arkansas 59
House of David 158
Houston, Texas 19, 21
Howell, Harry 52, 55, 59, 60
Howley, John 183
Hoy, Dummy 74
Hunt, Ben 143
Hunt, John 48
Hurst, Tim 72
Hydorn, Rex 136

Illinois-Indiana League 10
Illinois Power and Light Co. 183
Indianapolis, Indiana 25, 30, 64
Indian Refining Company Havolines 153, 158–159
Indian Territory 13–17
injury 116
International League 117
Interstate League 10
Irwin, Arthur 68
Ivanhoe 21

Jackson, Bill 175
Jackson, Michigan 154
Jackson, "Shoeless Joe" 154
Jacksonville, Illinois 34
Jamestown, New York 28
Janesville, Wisconsin 154
J.D. Moore's Dental Parlor 33
Jeffries, Jim 83
Jennings, Hughie 3, 37, 46, 51, 110, 120
Jerome, William 77
Jersey City Skeeters 113
J.L. Hudsons team 19
John Hopkins University 46
Johnson, Ban 25, 63–65, 69, 162; disputes with McGraw 59–60, 63, 79–81; founds American League 57; suspends McGinnity
Johnson, Eddie 135, 139, 141
Johnson, Herbert 118
Johnson, Judy 175
Johnson, Walter 185
Johnstone, James 70, 78, 94, 109
Johnstown Flood 9, 11

Joliet, Illinois 34, 154
Jones, Fielder 121, 122, 125, 126
Jones, Oscar 72
Jordan, Dutch 72

Kafora, Frank 143
Kansas City, Missouri 1, 25–32, 35, 37, 55, 59, 96, 111
Kansas City Blues 1894 season 25–31
Kansas City Cowboys 25
Kansas City Reds 26
Kaufman, Dick "Izzy" 124
Keeler, "Wee" Willie 45, 46, 51
Keister, Billy 47, 50, 59, 61
Kelley, Joe 46, 54, 55, 63, 64, 112, 176, 180
Kennedy, Brickyard 52
Kenosha, Wisconsin 154
Kieran, John 177
Kilpatrick, Charles 11
Kinsella, Dick 182
Kippert, Ed 135
Kirschler, Charles F. 93
Kitson, Kitty 52, 55
Klem, Bill 83, 97, 109; in opening-day forfeit 98; and water incident 100
Klima, John 95
Kling, Johnny 106
Klusman, Bill 27, 28, 30
Knisely, Pete 161, 165
Knowles, Fred 96
Koehler, Bob 155
Kotzelneck, "Happy Jack" 157, 159
Kraft, Dave 124
Krebs, Oklahoma 13, 18, 25, 31, 32, 144, 183; baseball teams 14–16, 19; coal mining disaster 16–17
Kroh, Floyd 106
Kroman, Harry 115
Kurfess, Harry "Kid" 121–124

Lafayette, Indiana 10
Lafayette County, Missouri 6
Lake View Park, Peoria 38, 39, 42
Lamb, Dave 175
Lambrecht, Jim 154, 156
Lane, Charles 136–137
Lappen, Alloy V. 180
Lappen, James 183
Lardner, Ring 65

Latham, Arlie 43
Law, Ruth 177
Lawrenceville, Illinois 154, 158
Leach, Tommy 53, 70
Leever, Sam 53, 55
Lehigh, Oklahoma 15
Lehigh Valley Railroad 121
Leitner, Dummy 74
Levin, Joe 142
Lewisburg, Pennsylvania 177
Lewistown, Montana 146
Lincoln, Illinois 157
Linn and Scruggs Dry Goods and Carpet Company 32
Lister, Ernest 125
Liverpool, England 5
Logansport, Indiana 11
Lohman, Pete 38
Los Angeles, California 95, 96, 101, 159
Lotshaw, Andy "Windy" 157
Louden, Baldy 112
Louisville, Kentucky 50, 53
Louisville Slugger 49
Lowdermilk, Grover 154

Mace, W.L. 19
Mack, Connie 4, 86, 87, 115
Macon, Georgia 24
Magoon, George 46
Mahon, John 55
Mallon, Paul 168
Mannassau, Al 47
Manning, Jimmie 59; as manager in Kansas City 25–31
Maquoketa Independents 172
Marlin, Texas 101
Maroa, Illinois 154
Marquard, Rube 111, 176, 178
Marshall, Doc 78
Marshalltown, Iowa 168, 169
Mathewson, Christy 3, 65, 66, 68–70, 73–75, 78, 80, 84, 91–93, 95, 96, 101–104, 106–107, 109, 171, 181, 183, 185; death of 177; illnesses of 91, 177; major league debut 52; personality of 65–66, 85–86, 95; pitching ability of 65, 74, 85–86, 96; World Series heroics of 88–90
Mathewson, Jane (Stoughton) 65, 66, 91, 95
Mauck, Hal 31
Mays, Carl 122

Index

McAlester, Berry 184
McAlester, Bunn 184
McAlester, James J. 13, 184
McAlester, Oklahoma 1, 13, 14, 16, 17, 24, 32, 49, 57, 82, 83, 96, 101, 102, 151, 172, 177, 178, 183, 186–187
McAlester Foundry and Machine Shop 14
McBride, Henry 108
McCarl, Clifford 140, 141, 144
McCarthy, Charles 174
McCarty, Lew 115
McCloskey, John 18, 20–22, 60
McCormick, Moose 79, 105
McCredie, Alice 147
McCredie, Walter 125, 147
McCredie, William Wallace 147, 149
McCully, Jack 15
McEntire, Reba 186
McGann, Dan 64, 84, 89, 91, 93
McGinnity, George (brother) 32, 159
McGinnity, Hannah (sister) 7, 159
McGinnity (Denning), Hannah (mother) 5–8, 13; death of 159; married 6; widowed 7
McGinnity, Rev. Joseph 186
McGinnity, John (brother) 32, 159
McGinnity (Redpath), Mary (wife) 14, 24, 25, 32, 34, 49, 82, 101–102, 114, 135, 150, 161, 169, 171, 176, 181, 183; death of 177
McGinnity (Lappen), Marguerite (daughter) 34, 49, 82, 102, 135, 150, 152, 161, 180, 182, 183, 185
McGinnity, Peter (father) 5, 6; died 7
McGinnity, Peter, Jr. (brother) 7
McGinnity, Rebecca (daughter) 32, 178
McGinnity, William (brother) 6, 7
McGinnity's Giants 172
McGlade, Avery 157, 165
McGraw, Blanche 95
McGraw, John 4, 36, 37, 42–48, 51, 52, 55, 57–61, 63–66, 69–72, 74, 75, 78–82, 84, 87, 88, 90, 91, 93, 94, 95, 97, 100–102, 104, 106, 107, 110, 111, 117, 153, 156, 162, 165, 171, 176, 177, 183, 185; feud with Ban Johnson 57, 60, 61, 63, 79–81; hired by Giants 63–65; innovations of 75, 79; jumps to AL 57; personality of 43, 45, 46–48, 58, 84, 94, 97, 176; traded to St. Louis 50
McGraw, Minnie 48
McGuire, Barney 15
McGuire, Jim 15
McGuire, Johnny 15, 19, 184
McGuire, Pat 15
McKeever, Edward 118
McKeever, Stephen 118
McKinsey, Beverlee 186
McManus, William J. 117
McMullin, Fred 124, 128, 154, 156
Meadowbrooks 175
Meany, Tom 178
Meikle, Sash 143
Meinert, Walter 156
Memphis, Tennessee 24, 101
Merkle, Fred 104–110, 178
Merkle boner 104–107
Mertes, Sammy 69, 72, 76, 88, 89
Meyers, Chief 167, 176
Millard, Howard V. 157, 158, 182, 183
Miller, Otto 176
Millikin University 9, 156
Million, Ten 125
Milwaukee, Wisconsin 25, 26, 28, 29, 30
Milwaukee Brewers 61
Minersville, Ohio 14
Minneapolis, Minnesota 25, 27, 29, 30, 31
Minnehan, Danny 20, 21, 22
Minnesota Twins 25
Mississippi Valley League 3, 166, 169, 170, 172
Missouri-Kansas-Texas Railroad (Katy) 15, 17
Missouri Valley White Sox 157
Mobile, Alabama 21, 24, 28
Moline, Illinois 164, 168
Moline Plowboys 165
Montgomery, Alabama 18, 20–24, 25, 53; 1893 season 20–24
Montreal Royals 113, 115, 116
Moran, Augie 70
Mount Olive, Illinois 153, 154
Mueller, Arthur 112
Mullen, Larry 166
Mullen, Scarface 15
Murphy, Charles 108
Murphy, Rev. M.B. 24
Murphysboro, Illinois 34
Muskogee, Oklahoma 15

Nashville, Tennessee 20, 21, 23, 24
National Association of Minor Leagues 168
National Association of Professional Baseball Leagues 133
National Baseball Commission 147
National Football League 160
National League 3, 19, 22, 25, 28, 33, 37, 45, 46, 48, 49, 50, 53, 57, 60, 63, 64, 67–69, 74, 76, 78–81, 92, 107–108, 112, 114, 137, 153, 167, 176, 178
Nattress, William 116
Navin, Frank 120
Nee, Johnny 115
Negro Leagues 124, 175
Neighbors, Cy 125
New England League 28
New Orleans, Louisiana 24, 97
New York City 77, 82, 85, 91, 102, 105, 108–109, 178
New York Giants 22, 23, 25, 46, 52, 59, 63–66, 68–79, 81–98, 100–105, 107–112, 122, 153, 159, 167, 169, 171, 177, 178, 182; hire John McGraw 64; in 1905 World Series 86–90; refuse to play 1904 World Series 79–81; rivalry with Cubs 92–93, 94, 103–110; rivalry with Pirates 70, 84, 93
New York Yankees (aka Highlanders) 65, 79–81, 112, 155, 158, 178
Newark, New Jersey 111–119, 121, 122, 134, 138, 175, 179
Newark Indians: 1909 season 112–114; 1910 season 114–115; 1911 season 115–117; 1912 season 117–118; pur-

chased by McGinnity 111; sold by McGinnity 118–119
Nichol, Sam 27, 28
Nichols, Kid 26
Nickel rocket 36
Nicklin, J.B. 23
nickname 5, 49
Niles, Billy 28
Nops, Jerry 59
Norfolk, Virginia 40, 52
North Butte Mining Company 144
North Carolina League 144
Northern Hotel, Peoria 38
Northern League 144
Northwestern League 120, 121, 122, 124, 130, 132, 133, 140, 141, 147, 182; rules on foul language 141; terminates 1917 season 145–146

Oak Hill Cemetery 32, 178, 186
Oakland, California 112, 114
Obenshain, Earl 9, 183
Oberofskie, Charles 12
O'Day, Charles 161–162, 165
O'Day, Hank 75, 93, 94; in Merkle game 105–107
Oklahoma City, Oklahoma 14, 187
Old Sal 35–37, 44, 76, 122
Oriole Park, Baltimore 59
Osage Coal Company 13, 14, 16
Ottumwa, Iowa 3, 38, 169
Ottumwa Cardinals 173

Pacific Coast International League 147–149
Pacific Coast League 114, 126, 128, 147
Pacific Northwestern League 40
Pahlman, Otto "Lefty" 157, 164
Panic of 1893, 23, 25, 32, 40
Patterson Field 20
Patterson Mercantile 16
Peitz, Heinie 93–94
Penhallegon, Bill 158
Penn Station 108
Pensacola, Florida 23, 24
Peoria, Illinois 34, 37–41, 42, 122, 154, 172, 175; in 1898 season 37–41
Peoria Tractors 162
Petty, Charlie 22
Pfiester, Jack 106, 109–110

Philadelphia, Pennsylvania 65, 112
Philadelphia Athletics 59, 62, 115, 135; in 1905 World Series 86–90; in 1907 preseason series 97
Philadelphia Phillies 66, 72, 75, 77, 84, 94, 97–98, 104, 111
Phillippe, Deacon 53
Pillette, Herman 142
Pinckney, George 42
pitching philosophy 76–77, 171, 178–179
pitching tactics 35–37, 51, 76–77
Pittinger, Togie 71
Pittsburgh Pirates 22, 28, 59, 68, 70, 73, 76, 78, 79, 81, 84, 85, 92–94, 102, 104, 107–108, 115, 125; in 1900 postseason series 52–55
Plainfield, New Jersey 91, 181
Plank, Eddie 86, 89, 185
Polo Grounds 52, 63, 69, 70, 71, 76, 78, 83, 88, 89, 90, 92, 93, 94, 97–98, 104, 107, 108, 112, 178
Pomeroy, Ohio 14
Pony, Montana 133
Portland, Oregon 122, 125, 128, 133, 147–150
Powers, Bill 15, 184
Powers, Johnny 15
Price, Frank J. 168
Primitive Methodist Church 6
Promontory, Utah 14
Providence, Rhode Island 87, 117, 118
Puget Sound Ministers 141
Pulliam, Harry 78, 84, 94, 98, 100, 107, 108
Pullman railroad company 32
Puyallup, Washington 134, 136, 140, 141
Pyle, Tom 161

Quad-City Sports Hall of Fame 1, 186
Quincy, Illinois 38
Quinn, Tom 40

Rail Lights 158
Raymond, Harry 20
Raymond, Tealey 143
Red-Bird 21, 22, 23

Red Hook, Brooklyn 51
Redpath, Ed 16
Redpath, Frank 37, 82, 117, 140, 186; and Guigni-Williams dispute 138–139; as partner in Butte 133–134; as partner in Tacoma 121, 129, 131–132
Redpath, John 49, 82, 177; death of 186; early life of 13–14
Redpath, John, Jr. 82
Redpath, Lula May 102, 181
Redpath (Potts), Margaret 14
Redpath, Mary see McGinnity, Mary
Redpath, Thomas 82
Redpath, William 82
Republic Trucks 154
Rhines, Billy "Bunker" 35
Roach, "Old Man" 38
Roberts, Skipper 138
Robinson, Wilbert 42–47, 50–52, 57–58, 60–61, 65, 172, 185; and grapefruit incident 177; handling of pitchers 58; as manager of Brooklyn 176–179; relationship with McGraw 43–44, 176
Rochester Hustlers 113–118
Rock Island, Illinois 5, 168, 173
Rock Island Independents 156, 167
Rockford, Illinois 164, 180–181
Rothberg, Ed 181
Rothfuss, Charley 121
Rothstein, Arnold 156
Rowne About 21
Ruether, Dutch 136
Rush, Harry 156
Rusie, Amos 22
Ruth, Babe 116, 158, 178, 185

St. Joseph, Missouri 39–40, 170
St. Joseph's Cemetery 17
St. Louis, Missouri 19, 27, 57, 58, 183
St. Louis Browns 19, 20, 27, 34, 115, 137, 156, 157, 158
St. Louis Cardinals 27, 42, 50, 76, 78, 94, 96, 98, 100, 102, 104, 115, 156, 157, 178
St. Louis Standards 10
St. Paul, Minnesota 155
St. Petersburg, Florida 171

Index

Samson Tractors 154
Sangamo Electric 152, 154
Sangamon, Illinois 10
Saranac, New York 177
Saulsberry, Charles 14
Savanna, Oklahoma 16
Savannah, Georgia 22, 23, 25, 28, 31, 82
Schaffer, Charles 157, 162
Schalk, Ray 154
Schechter, Gabriel 77
Schmidt, Henry "Tex" 72
Schwartz, Jean 77
Scruggs, Minnie 32
Scruggs, William 32
Seattle, Washington 40, 121, 123, 125–126, 128–130, 134–140, 145, 148–150
Seib, Clyde 157, 159
Seisler, Davy 39
Sexton, Michael H. 168
Seybold, Ralph "Socks" 89
Seymour, Cy 59, 64, 109, 110, 117
Sharp, Peck 27, 30
Sharpe, Bud 112
Shawneetown, Illinois 7
Sheckard, Jimmy 46, 48, 69
Sheely, Earl 136
Sheridan, Jack 60
Sherman, Texas 15
Sherman Hotel, Chicago 156
Shibe, Ben 90
Shibe, John 97
Shreeder, George 120, 129
Shugart, Frank 60
Simmons Bed Co. 154
Sioux City, Iowa 26, 29, 31
Smith, Aleck 48
Smith, George "Heinie" 65, 66
Smith, H. Clay, as partner in Newark 111, 117–119; as part owner in Danville 161
Smith, Harry 117, 118
Smith, Harry F. 10
Smith, Robert 36
Snodgrass, Amzie Beal "Chappie" 59
Snodgrass, Fred 104
Solomon, George L. 118
Southern Illinois Amateur League 34
Southern League 18, 20, 22–25, 28, 31, 121
Spade, Bob 100, 114
Spahn, Warren 16
Spanish American War 37, 38, 40, 133

Spitz, Ben 28
Spokane, Washington 123, 125–126, 129–131, 136–142, 145, 148–149
Sportsmans Park, Springfield 33, 34
Springfield, Illinois 1, 7, 33–35, 37, 40, 41, 102, 111, 135, 152, 172, 175, 182; baseball teams 33–35
Springfield Coal Company 7
Springfield Senators 175
Stafford, Jimmie 20
Stafford Hotel, Baltimore 64
Staley, A.E. "Gene" 151–152, 155, 159–160
Staley Manufacturing Company 56, 161, 162, 163, 164, 165, 171, 172, 180, 183; baseball team 151–159; football team 155–156, 159–160; termination of sports programs 160; wage cuts 159
Stanley, Lou 125
Stark, Walter 15
Steinfeldt, Harry 106
Stengel, Casey 177
Stewart, Samuel 136
Stokke, Gil 136, 140
Strang, Sammy 72, 94
Streator, Illinois 6
Street, Gabby 177
Sullivan, Charles 149
Sullivan, Illinois 33
Sullivan, Ted 23
Summers, Ray 157
Sutton, Larry 115
Syracuse, New York 41, 117

Tacoma, Washington 40, 120–132, 134–136, 143, 148, 154, 165, 172, 174
Tacoma Railway and Power Company 121
Tacoma Tigers 136, 138, 140, 142–143, 145, 148–149; 1913 season 122–124; 1914 season 124–128; 1915 season 128–131; purchased by McGinnity 120–121; sold by McGinnity 132
Tannehill, Jess 53, 55
Taunton, Massachusetts 28
Taylor, John 81
Taylor, Luther "Dummy" 83, 88, 100, 102, 104, 114; use of sign language 74–75
Taylor, Sec 171

Taylorville, Illinois 41
Tearney, A.R. 144, 164
Tenney, Fred 102, 104, 109
Terre Haute, Indiana 6, 10, 11
Terre Haute Terre-irs 120
Texas League 20
Thomson, Bobby 153
Three-I League 10, 102, 144, 161, 167, 170, 175, 180
Tinker, Joe 92, 103, 106, 110, 185
Toledo, Ohio 26, 27, 28, 30, 33
Toledo Mudhens 111, 171
Toohill, John J. 31
Tooley, Bert 117
Topeka Jayhawks 120
Toronto, Ontario 112, 118
Trapp, William O. 181
Troy, New York 91
Truby, Harry 39, 40
Twineham, Art 20, 27

Ulrich, George 27, 28
umpires, disputes with 60–61, 68, 69–70, 125, 135, 137, 143
Union Association 25
Union Iron Works 14, 82, 83, 151
Union Pacific Railroad 14
Union Park, Baltimore 46
University of Dubuque 166, 167, 169
University of Illinois 152, 155

Van Buren, Arkansas 15, 18–20, 27
Vancouver, British Columbia 122, 124–126, 128, 130, 138–140, 142–143, 145, 148–150
Vancouver, Washington 149
Veach, Walter 156, 157
Venice, California 128
Vickers, Rube 115
Victoria, British Columbia 123, 130, 133
Virginia City, Montana 6, 133
Virginia League 144
Visner, Joe 30
Von Der Horst, Harry 42, 44

Waco, Texas 101
Waddell, Rube 54, 86–88,

114–115, 185; in 1900 post-season series 53–55; signs with Newark 114–115
Wagner, Honus 53, 70, 76, 185
Walsh, Christy 106
Walsh, Watty 34
Warner, John 69, 76
Warren, Joseph 31, 35
Washington Monument 177
Washington Nationals 50
Washington Park, Brooklyn 51, 52
Washington Senators 20, 25, 33, 59, 125, 177
Watch Factory 34, 135
Waterloo, Iowa 167
Watkins, Edd 120
Watkins, George 157
Weaver, Buck 154
Weequahic Park, Newark 118
Weidenmayer Park, Newark 112–113
Weir City, Kansas 19
Weisher, Abe 121

Welch, John 3, 173
West, Frank 124
Western Association 37–38, 40
Western League 25, 27, 28, 33, 35, 40, 57, 122, 170
Western Washington Fairgrounds 135, 141
Wharton, J.R. 142
Wheeling, West Virginia 28
Wicker, Bob 76, 78, 129–130
Wilburton, Oklahoma 187
Williams, Jimmy 55, 59
Williams, Ken 137
Williams, Nick 136, 138–139, 147
Williams College 180
Williamson, Frank 186–187
Wilson, Frank 20, 22
Wilson, Parke 22
Wiltse, Hooks 78, 79, 100, 102, 104, 178; origin of nickname 75

Wolverton, Harry 111, 112, 113, 114
Woodruff, Harvey 108
Woodworth, Buster 157
Work or fight 147
World Series 73, 79, 81, 82, 85, 94, 97, 110, 115, 128, 154, 155, 156, 176, 177; 1905 series 88–90
World War I 141, 147, 177
World War II 186
Wright, Mike 34
Wright, Pat 34, 37, 40, 175
Wylie, Gene 170

Yager, Abe 49, 183
Yager, Freddie 35
Yohe, Bill 125
Young, Ranney 156, 157, 159
Young, Cy 2, 3, 42, 96
YWCA 130

Zimmer, Charlie 97
Zimmerman, Eddie 112, 117

www.ingramcontent.com/pod-product-compliance
Ingram Content Group UK Ltd.
Pitfield, Milton Keynes, MK11 3LW, UK
UKHW041954140426
5217IPUK00015B/802